Manchester United

The Untold Story

Manchester United

The Untold Story

NED KELLY

with ERIC ROWAN

MICHAEL O'MARA BOOKS LIMITED

First published in Great Britain in 2003 by
Michael O'Mara Books Limited
9 Lion Yard, Tremadoc Road
London sw4 7nq

A CIP catalogue record for this book is available
from the British Library

ISBN 1-84317-053-1

3 5 7 9 10 8 6 4 2

Photograph credits:

Author collection: pp. 1, 2 (*both*), 3 (*both*), 8 (*above*), 14 (*above*), 16 (*below*);
PA Photos: pp. 4 (*both*), 5 (*both*), 6 (*below*), 7 (*both*), 10 (*both*), 11 (*both*),
13 (*above*); Rex Features: pp. 6 (*above*), 9 (*below*), 16 (*top*); TopFoto/UPPA:
pp. 8 (*below*), 14 (*below*); News International Syndication: pp. 9 (*above*),
15 (*above*); Atlantic Syndication: p. 15 (*below*)

Designed and typeset by Martin Bristow

Printed and bound in England by Clays Ltd, St Ives plc

Contents

Introduction

MANCHESTER UNITED is, without doubt, the world's most famous football club, as well as one of the richest and the most successful. Supported by millions of fans across the globe, the team that dominated the 1990s under the leadership of its manager, Alex Ferguson, continues to be a force to be reckoned with in the twenty-first century, both domestically and on the international stage.

I had been an avid supporter of the club since childhood, and so it was a dream come true for me when, in March 1990, I was offered a job at Old Trafford, providing security for the club using the skills I had developed during a successful twenty-three-year career in the British Army, latterly in the SAS. I could hardly believe my good fortune.

For almost twelve years I observed the highs and lows experienced in top-flight football, but, most importantly, I witnessed at first hand the growing success of Manchester United under Alex Ferguson, and watched the team win title after title during the most successful decade in its entire history: winner of four FA Cup titles, a European Cup-Winners' Cup title, one League Cup title, seven Premier League titles, and its first momentous Champions' League European Cup title, all of which included two doubles and one historic treble.

Not only did I have a unique opportunity to observe the team's triumphs on the pitch at close quarters, but my association with the Reds also gave me the chance to get to know all the players and the back-room staff who made the club what it was.

Being responsible for the safety of the players, supporters and staff of Manchester United, whether on trips abroad, at away games or on the hallowed ground of Old Trafford, was a pleasure and a privilege for me, and has given me a wealth of memories I will always treasure.

CHAPTER I

Ooh, Aah, Cantona!

O N WEDNESDAY 25 JANUARY 1995, my life changed for ever. For almost five years I had been combining my role as head of security at Manchester United with building up my business, Special Projects Security (SPS). Since leaving the armed services, I had enjoyed considerable success, and at the start of 1995, life looked rosy.

As a former SAS man, I had a natural dislike of publicity, and preferred to remain very much in the background. It had proved impossible to be completely anonymous at Old Trafford, but I was still relatively unknown outside Manchester, and had largely managed to stay off the television screens and out of the newspapers. I felt that it was my work behind the scenes that had made me valuable to United. From that day on, however, I would never be far from the public eye, thanks to my personal and professional association with the man I considered to be the world's finest footballer at that time – Eric Cantona.

On that fateful day, United had a League game against Crystal Palace at Selhurst Park. Usually at away games, after seeing the players and officials safely off the coach and to the dressing-room door, I could relax, and let the home team worry about match security. On this occasion, my security services were not required, but as I desperately wanted to see my team play, I made arrangements to fly down with a friend, businessman and fellow United supporter Ron Wood, and then organized a flight back on the Manchester United chartered plane.

I sat in the stand and watched the first fifty minutes of a hard but mediocre game that eventually ended 1–1, though the result would not be as memorable as the off-the-ball incident that would shock the footballing world.

During the match, Eric Cantona received more than his fair share of rough-house treatment, but, like the trouper he was, Eric was equal to it. He had, after all, had a tough upbringing in Marseilles and in the boondocks of French football. The Crystal Palace players clearly forgot it on that particular day, and Eric's response was muted until one provocation too many. He saw red and retaliated, booting Palace player, Richard Shaw, just a few minutes into the second half. Everybody in the ground saw it, including the referee and, not for the first time in his career, Eric was sent off. Norman Davies, Manchester United's sixty-four-year-old kit man, rushed to escort him to the dressing room along the side of the pitch, while the Palace fans gave the shamed player a barrage of predictable abuse.

From my position in the stands I noticed a Crystal Palace supporter leave his seat and run twenty yards down to the low barrier separating the spectators from the players, before launching into an animated tirade of abuse against the Frenchman. Eric clearly heard what had been said and in response he lost control of his senses. He jumped over the barrier and launched a kung-fu style kick into the chest of the startled supporter, one Matthew Simmons it was later revealed, before adding some more punches for good measure. All hell then broke loose, and there was a mad rush to drag Eric away from the Palace fan and remove him from the crowd before any more violence ensued. While Paul Ince dealt with a couple of interfering spectators, the United players pulled Eric away and tried to lead him to the dressing room, which was a difficult undertaking after Eric had gone off like a Roman candle. No one had ever witnessed anything like this at a football match, and many could scarcely believe what had happened.

There has been so much nonsense published about Eric, especially regarding this unfortunate incident, that I feel it is time the record was set straight. I barged my way down the steps toward the pitch, brushing aside Palace's stewards as if they were cardboard cut-outs, and ran to the dressing room to find Norman and Eric. Norman was visibly shaking and Eric was standing with nostrils flaring, ready to take on the world.

'I'll handle this now, Norman. You get back to the dugout,' I told the relieved-looking kit man.

Norman left. Eric and I were alone. I stared at him and said nothing. Not a word. He remained broodingly silent. And it stayed that way for almost half an hour. Both of us deep in thought, contemplating the repercussions of the incident. I positioned myself at the door to ensure that no one could enter uninvited, and no blazing-mad Frenchman could leave. After what seemed like an eternity, the game was finally over and the teams returned to their respective dressing rooms. The Manchester United guys all went to Eric and offered him words of support and friendly backslaps, while manager Alex Ferguson and some of the club's directors huddled in a corner for an urgent discussion.

By now the dressing-room door was coming off its hinges as the press desperately tried to get a story, a photo or both, but I made sure they were kept at bay. Nobody was gaining access to that room while I was there. Fergie gave me a nod: 'I'll go out and talk to the press, Ned.'

'Right, Boss,' I replied, and led him out to face a sea of reporters and photographers.

The rest of the players began bathing, dressing and preparing to leave, but I held them back while a decision was made about how best to make our exit. The ground was thick with press, TV and radio crews, as well as Palace fans baying for blood. I suggested that we just rushed for the coach and, really, there was little other option. The club secretary, Ken Merrett, remarked, 'It's a bloody good job you were here, Ned.'

The players made for the coach while I hung back with Eric. I'd decided that we would be the last to run the gauntlet. I winked at Eric and he smiled and shrugged back. In seconds we had sprinted to the coach. We made the great escape unscathed, but the chanting Palace fans, who were by now spitting at the bus, held nothing back in their vitriolic rantings against the Manchester United team.

As we sped toward Gatwick to catch our plane, we received telephone calls warning us of a massive press presence at Manchester airport, so I had to think of a plan, quickly. By good fortune, Ron Wood had made arrangements for his car and driver to meet the return flight so I contacted Manchester airport security and told them of our dilemma. To avoid any impromptu press frenzy at the airport, it was agreed that the security people would liaise with Ron's driver and allow him to drive directly on to the tarmac to meet our private jet.

The police and security men and women at Manchester airport were, as always, more than helpful to our cause, and all went according to plan. I got Eric into Ron's car straight from the steps of the jet and we drove to the airport car park, where Eric had left his car, leaving the press wandering about the terminal building searching in vain for the fiery Frenchman. Before he sped off in to the night, I said goodbye to Eric, who was grateful for being looked after so well, but by now, after plenty of time to think about the situation, he knew he had made a terrible mistake, and we both realized that this was only the start of his troubles.

Eric's assault made headlines all over the world. The TV news bulletins led on it, the radio sports shows and phone-ins featured views on nothing else, while the newspapers were full of reports about the events at Crystal Palace. Not for the first time in his career, Eric was attracting attention for all the wrong reasons.

By the next morning a press circus had set up camp outside Eric's house. Reporters and photographers were hiding in hedges, hanging out of trees, or were perched on stepladders and on the roofs of vans. Eric wisely stayed hidden behind closed curtains.

There was undoubtedly an air of panic the following day at Old Trafford as the club faced losing the man Fergie later rightly called 'the talisman'. The situation wasn't helped when Graham Kelly, the FA's chief executive, weighed in with his official view, with a statement that read: 'What happened last night was a stain on our game. If any offence is proved the player concerned is bound to face a severe punishment. We are confident that Manchester United will meet their responsibility, not just to their own club but to the widest interest of the game. The FA believes that last night's incident was unprecedented. It brought shame on those involved, and worst of all, on the game itself.'

Effectively this statement strongly suggested that Eric should expect a stiff penalty for his conduct, perhaps even a lengthy absence from the game. Such a tough response from the FA put severe pressure on United to act. Seeking some respite in the Alderley Edge Hotel in Cheshire, Fergie met with Martin Edwards (Manchester United's chairman and chief executive), Maurice Watkins (the club lawyer), and Professor Sir Roland Smith (chairman of the plc board). I later discovered that they had discussed sacking Eric, but it was decided he deserved a second chance, though everybody knew the club would have to be seen to take strong action against him.

A statement was issued announcing that Eric had been suspended from playing for Manchester United until the end of the season. He had also been fined two weeks' wages – the maximum according to League rules. Furthermore, it was reported that he had been summoned by Croydon police to appear at South Norwood police station on 21 February 1995 for questioning over his impromptu display of kick-boxing. The future looked far from rosy for the Frenchman.

Sensibly, in an effort to escape the prying eyes of the world's press, Eric quickly made arrangements to leave Britain with his pregnant wife Isabelle, and his son Raphael. Even while suspended and on holiday, and supposedly hidden away on the French Caribbean island of Guadeloupe, the media still wouldn't leave him alone. An ITN crew approached them and a reporter got a slap from Eric for invading the privacy that his family deserved.

While United's season carried on, not quite as normal, the wheels of justice turned pretty quickly for once. On the morning of 21 February I collected Eric from his home, and as we headed south I decided, after the normal exchange of pleasantries, to leave him to talk to me. I imagined how low he must have been feeling, so idle chatter from me would probably not have helped.

After an hour or so into the journey we started talking about the weather, current affairs, clothes, food and drink. In fact, anything to take his mind off the day ahead, and he finally began to relax.

As we neared London, talk inevitably turned to the matter in hand.

'It's not a murder inquiry, Eric. It'll blow over,' I said to him, trying to sound light-hearted.

'Fuck him anyway, Ned,' Eric replied, angrily. 'He was just a hooligan. You can insult me all day, but he said terrible things about my mother, wife and children.'

I was surprised. Until that moment I had not asked Eric what this particular individual had done to deserve such special retribution. Having heard his reason, I wasn't sure if this constituted a defence in law, but it was a good enough excuse for Eric's outburst as far as I was concerned.

'You're right, Eric. Fuck him,' I agreed.

I delivered Eric to the police station on time and we met up with Maurice Watkins and George Scanlon, Eric's interpreter, who had travelled south separately. Eric disappeared with Maurice, George and the detectives for his interview, and I was stuck in the canteen with a CID officer who, for the next two hours, proceeded to grill me about all things Manchester United. I barely responded to any of his questions, but he did not take the hint. Eventually, I had to ask him whether *I* was under investigation. He assured me I was not, so I merely glowered, and turned and stared out of the window.

About three hours later, Eric, George and Maurice reappeared and we all got into my car. On leaving the station, I almost ran over a dozen or so paparazzi as they threw themselves at the passing vehicle in an attempt to photograph Eric.

Maurice Watkins declared he had business to attend to in London and asked to be dropped off at East Croydon train station. 'Eric has been charged with common assault on Simmons and has to appear at Croydon Magistrates Court on Thursday 23rd March, Ned,' Maurice informed me. 'You and I will need to meet up in Manchester and work out the arrangements.'

I darted a quick look at Eric, but he was staring into space.

As I dropped off Maurice and George at the station, Eric grunted his goodbyes and we headed back to Manchester. There was little conversation between us on the way home as Eric was clearly considering the ramifications of being charged and facing trial. Though I knew he could cope with the situation, I could tell he was worried about the hassle his family and friends would doubtless receive now the affair had developed into something more serious.

I tried hard to reassure him that he was among friends and 'it was all bollocks', but I suppose it was easy for me to say. I wasn't the one facing a potential jail sentence or staring at a glittering career in tatters. Eric asked if he could use the car phone and proceeded to have a long chat with his wife, who was expecting their second baby in June. He then made a second phone call to his family in Marseilles to break the news, which relaxed him a little, and meant that the last leg of the ride home was more pleasant and jovial.

We arrived back at Eric's house at around 8.00 p.m. and discovered a single female press reporter with a cameraman there. As we left the car, they made a beeline for Eric, but I was too swift for them and positioned myself in front of him. 'Could we have a quick word?' she asked.

'Velocity,' I replied, and brushed Eric past her into his house.

After wishing Eric goodnight, I returned to my car, gave the reporter a cheeky wink and drove off.

The next day I was called in to the office of the ticketing officer, Ken Ramsden, for a meeting with him and the club secretary, Ken Merrett, to give them a detailed account of what had happened at the police station. They asked how Eric was coping, and I got the impression that they wanted to know if Eric had said anything about the case that they should know. He hadn't actually spoken a word about the case, and even if he had I wouldn't have shared his views with either of them, especially as Maurice Watkins would already have given them an account of the proceedings. The only observation that I could honestly make was my concern that Eric and his family were hopelessly exposed in the house that the club had provided for them. It was more of a council-estate abode than the home of a megastar. I suggested they relocate him immediately.

To my surprise they agreed and made arrangements to move Eric and his family into a house rented to Manchester United by Mark Hughes, in the Cheshire village of Prestbury. The residence was very secluded, and it turned out to be an ideal hideaway for the Cantonas.

Eric's next 'court' appearance over the Crystal Palace fracas was up in front of an FA disciplinary commission, to face charges of bringing the game into disrepute. He had asked for a private hearing and the FA had agreed. It was scheduled to be heard at the Sopwell House Hotel in St Albans, Hertfordshire, and Eric and the Manchester United deputation agreed to meet up earlier in the day for a briefing in the Royal Lancaster Hotel, Hyde Park, London, before travelling on to St Albans for the FA hearing.

I was instructed to pick up Fergie, who was flying to Heathrow from Manchester, and who had to be at the Royal Lancaster Hotel for 11.00 a.m. I collected the manager and hammered back towards Central London to find the motorway gridlocked. Undeterred, I drove the last ten miles on the hard shoulder, just making it to the hotel in time for their tactical talks.

I had arranged taxis to ferry everyone to the hearing, and Eric asked me if he could travel in one of them with his agent, a French lawyer named Jean-Jacques Bertrand.

'No fucking way, Eric. Fergie would have my balls,' I replied firmly. 'You're stuck with me, son. Get in the car.'

I had a vision of Eric arriving at the hearing and clouting a reporter on his way in. I could not allow him out of my sight until after his appearance in front of the FA committee. On our arrival at the hotel, the press surrounded our cars and, once again, I had to drag Eric in my wake to the safety of the hotel conference room, to wait with his entourage until his case began.

I had personally always viewed FA officials as a bunch of spineless, grey-suited men, accountable to no one, who pontificated about a game I doubt many of them had even played. In my experience of dealing with them, both on a personal level on their beanos to Old Trafford, and also having been involved in carrying out some of their directives to clubs and players, I believed that their knowledge of the game was sadly lacking, and regarded them as being incapable of feeling the passion the game can evoke in players like Eric. Now these 'suits' would sit in judgement on arguably the most influential player in the game.

Jean-Jacques and I sat around in an ante-room while the hearing went on. After an infernally long two hours, they all trooped out.

The FA had fined Eric a further £10,000 and – which was much worse – had decreed that he could not play again until 30 September, extending the ban that Manchester United had already imposed on him. It would now be more than seven months before Eric could play competitive football again. The United officials were livid as there had been a tacit agreement that the FA would not lengthen the period of suspension.

It transpired that one of the commission had even asked Eric if he was a student of kung fu – though if he had been, Simmons would doubtless have been hospitalized. I thought the whole thing was a farce and I couldn't wait to get the Frenchman and his entourage out of the building.

Eric returned immediately to France with Jean-Jacques, and after dropping Fergie off at Heathrow for his journey back to Manchester, I pointed my car north and went home the hard way.

Before Eric's court appearance on 23 March I attended another briefing with Maurice Watkins to discuss a plan that was really a carbon copy of the police station visit. It was decided that I would collect Eric on the evening of 22 March, under the cover of darkness, drive him down to Croydon, check into the Croydon Park Hotel, and be ready for the court case the next morning. Everyone was happy with that. Except Eric.

He had decided that he would travel down with Paul Ince, who was to appear in the same court ahead of Eric on two charges of assault and using threatening behaviour during the fracas at Crystal Palace. I began to hear the distant sound of alarm bells, and with hindsight I should have acted on them.

I made my way to Croydon alone and duly checked into the hotel. In the morning I met up with Maurice Watkins and a criminal barrister, David Poole, QC, whom Maurice had retained to defend Eric. Paul Ince had apparently made his own arrangements.

Maurice seemed far from happy when I greeted him that morning.

'Where's Eric, Ned?' he asked, with the look of a man who already knew the answer.

I coughed and replied, 'He made his own way down with Paul Ince.'

'He made his own way on to the front page of today's papers too!' Maurice revealed, throwing down a few copies of the tabloids with pictures of Eric and Paul leaving Browns, a London nightclub, at 3.00 a.m.

'That won't help his case,' David Poole added, ominously.

We had tea and toast in comparative silence, and eventually the missing pair trooped into the hotel. Paul had his wife, Claire, with him and also his solicitor. While Paul was smartly dressed in a suit and tie, Eric was clad in a grey T-shirt, blue jacket and black trousers, apparently having put little or no thought into dressing to impress the magistrates, in an effort to prove his innocence in court.

The hotel security staff vainly tried to keep the press at bay, but the place was now under siege. I managed to get Paul, his wife and his lawyer through the sea of reporters, and over to the court. Once I was sure that that they were safely inside, I went back to the hotel to collect Eric, as he was due in court later in the day. Paul pleaded not guilty to the charge and his case was set for May. Two months later, the magistrates would find in his favour and he would walk from court a free man, but Eric Cantona was not destined to have the same success. The British justice system was determined to have its pound of flesh from a wayward Frenchman who had been seen by millions committing common assault.

Maurice Watkins and Eric's barrister were finishing their briefing as I arrived back, but having taken time to digest the size of the press contingent, I worried about delivering Eric to the court in time, or, indeed, getting him there at all. There were press and TV people from every corner of the globe and the noise as they gibbered away in various different languages was deafening.

I gathered the three men together in the lobby and issued my orders: 'Eric, I'll hold your hand. Push through the crowd and you other two keep right behind Eric. Don't stop. Charge straight ahead.'

As we got outside I noticed Eric's expression change at the sight of the herd of press and couldn't decide whether it was to one of anger or fear. Either way, I didn't take any chances.

'Don't push anyone, Eric. I'll do enough pushing for the both of us,' I told him urgently.

He smiled. I think I had read his mind correctly. Heads would have rolled (mine in particular) if Eric had clobbered one or two reporters on the way to court.

As we were about to leave, one of the hotel security guys stopped us and helpfully mentioned that if we cut through the building opposite the hotel, we would exit just by the courthouse door. I gave the command 'Go' and we made a run for it. The noise and camera flashes were terrifying but I managed to get them across the street in one piece and we made our way through the building across from the hotel. We emerged from the back entrance only to run across the garden area right into a brick wall at the end of a cul-de-sac . . .

So much for SAS-jungle-trained tracker Ned! We all burst into fits of laughter, which helped ease the tension that had built up during our frantic attempt to flee the press. I eventually found the right way and we crossed the street to the courthouse. Here the scene was a hundred times worse than at the hotel, as it seemed the whole world and its camera was there. I pulled the guys through the crowd, we entered the court and were shown to a room where we had to remain until the case was announced. As usual, Eric was inundated with people asking for his autograph – even the police, court officials and others awaiting trial. As always, Eric agreed to every single request.

When we were called into court, the officials agreed I could stay close to Eric during the hearing, and the case commenced. There was an interpreter on hand to translate the court proceedings to Eric. It had been his decision to plead guilty, and he duly did so, but it would prove to be a costly error of judgement.

The court first heard a fair outline of the events from prosecutor

Jeffrey McCann. He said that one Manchester United fan reported hearing another supporter say to Eric as he walked along the touchline: 'You are a fucking animal, Cantona. You are a fucking French bastard. Fuck off back to France. You don't deserve to be on a football pitch.' Another supporter said he heard the words: 'Fuck off back to France, you French motherfucker.'

According to McCann, Eric had alleged that Simmons had made obscene gestures and shouted racial and abusive remarks. Eric's police statement, which was read to the court, recalled the words used by Mr Simmons as: 'You fucking, cheating French cunt. Fuck off back to France, you motherfucker.' McCann asserted that Simmons had denied using those words, though he was due to face two public-order charges arising from his involvement in the incident.

In his plea in mitigation, David Poole highlighted the provocation that Eric had suffered. Apart from the swearing, he pointed out that Simmons had clenched his hand in a 'gesticulation connotating sexual self-abuse'. Poole then added that Simmons had questioned Eric's relationship with his mother, suggesting it had been unnatural, which was no less than what Eric had hinted to me in the car almost two months earlier.

The defence submission ended with a final flourish of character references and testimonials, and a suggestion that the proper penalty would be a conditional discharge. Poole also pointed out that Eric had already been heavily punished by the club, the FA and even his home country – by then, the French FA had stripped him of his captaincy of the national side.

The three magistrates, led by Jean Pearch, left to consider their sentence. Mrs Pearch had been a music teacher before becoming a magistrate. As chairman of the bench she was obviously immensely qualified, but I wondered whether she had ever experienced such a case as this before, involving the most intense media coverage. After a short time she returned to the bench and began some discussion with the Clerk of the Court. She called forward the French interpreter so that there would be no misunderstanding. She then told Eric, 'You are a high-profile public figure with undoubted gifts, and as such you are looked up to by many young people. For this reason, the only sentence that is appropriate for this offence is two weeks' imprisonment forthwith.'

There were gasps and moans all around the court. Nobody could believe it. We all thought we had heard her incorrectly.

'Could you kindly repeat that?' a startled Mr Poole asked.

She did: 'Fourteen days' imprisonment. Take him down.'

Eric gave a sort of enigmatic smile. The rest of us just sat there stunned. The notion of our biggest star going to jail had never even entered the equation.

Members of the press who had piled in to the court beforehand were now stuck in a jam trying to leave it. As Eric was about to be taken down to the cells, Mr Poole was on his feet requesting bail for Eric while an appeal was prepared. Mrs Pearch said the court was unable to grant bail, which meant that Poole and Maurice Watkins would have to go next door to the Crown Court to make a second application for bail.

I followed Her Majesty's latest convict downstairs where I was allowed to accompany him into the cell. Within minutes Maurice and Mr Poole came down to say that they had started the appeal process, but needed a judge to sign the interim liberation papers that would free Eric immediately, pending his appeal. They left, still looking shocked, and Eric borrowed my mobile phone to tell his wife about his present circumstances. In the meantime I quizzed the police and court officials about which prison Eric was most likely to be taken to.

To my knowledge it has never been reported that Eric was quite so resigned to going to jail. He was entirely philosophical about the events – too much so, for my liking.

'I think I'll just do the time, Ned. Get it over with,' he declared, calmly.

My jaw dropped; I couldn't believe what he was suggesting. Here was the greatest footballer in England quite prepared to spend two weeks in prison for an assault for which most members of the public, especially first-time offenders, would have received a small fine. I pleaded with him to put up more of a fight.

'No. Don't be daft, Eric. Wait until the appeal, mate. You could be out of here in an hour or two,' I urged him.

A prison officer entered the cell and asked Eric for his autograph. Though he had just locked the man up, he now wanted a favour from him. I couldn't believe the cheek of the guy, but Eric, ever willing, gladly obliged, which says a great deal about his nerve at that time, and the type of generous person he really is. Eric's friendly gesture was not without reward, as the officer mentioned he could bring us some food, and because he described the normal courthouse fare as 'shite', he suggested the local McDonald's was the safest option. We agreed enthusiastically, and twenty minutes later were presented with two Big Macs and fries. Eric and I both burst out laughing at the unlikely situation in which we found ourselves: Eric Cantona, one of the world's highest-profile football stars, and me, Ned Kelly, ex-soldier, sitting in a grimy cell in Croydon, wolfing down a meal from McDonald's. It was all so surreal.

Maurice and Mr Poole later returned, jubilantly confirming Eric's successful appeal, waving the official document like Neville Chamberlain on acid, and they told us it was time to leave. Eric was free for now, and bailed to reappear at the court on Friday 31 March.

The police kindly offered to drop Eric off at the hotel and I parked my car near a side door to spirit him back to Manchester. The plan worked well, as only a couple of snappers got pictures of any worth.

Manchester United had no matches until 2 April, when we were scheduled to play Leeds United at Old Trafford, but in the meantime the club was busy trying to conduct a damage-limitation exercise on the Eric affair, without much success.

On the drive back home to Manchester, Eric made a few calls to his wife and family in Marseilles on my car phone, and was visibly happier and more relaxed. We got through the London traffic fairly quickly, and I let out a sigh of relief when I saw the sign for the M40 North. It was good to have London in the rear-view mirror. We chatted away about everything and anything, and at one point I casually alluded to the preferred dress code for court appearances in Britain, and gently suggested a shirt and tie would have done him no harm. Eric laughed. Joking apart, I hoped he would bear this in mind on his appeal date.

Nearing Manchester I asked Eric if he would like to join me for a beer at Mulligans, a favourite haunt of the Manchester jet set.

'Yeah, that sounds good, Ned. Let's do it.' He really seemed in much better spirits and we had a couple of beers, before I drove him back to the safety of his home.

The following Wednesday, I had a meeting with Ken Merrett and Ken Ramsden to discuss getting Eric to Croydon Crown Court for his appeal two days later, and we all agreed that nightclubs were definitely out of the question this time. On Thursday evening I drove to Eric's house and we slipped down to London, arriving at the Croydon Park Hotel for 10.30 p.m. We went straight to our rooms, as Eric had a big day ahead of him, and he'd know in the morning if he still faced a spell behind bars.

The next day I was relieved to see that Eric had obviously heeded my advice, and was resplendent in a suit, shirt and tie.

Eric entered the dock and the proceedings got under way. Judge Ian Davies, QC, agreed with David Poole that Eric did not deserve imprisonment on the charge he had faced. He did not regard Eric to be a bad man, and considered him no danger to the public. For good measure, the wise judge also added that Simmons's behaviour would have 'provoked the most stoic', which was a view that proved prophetic, because when, several months later, Simmons appeared in the same court for his case, he promptly attacked the prosecutor from Eric's trial, Jeffrey McCann. Thus the only person to spend a night in jail following the regrettable episode at Crystal Palace was Simmons, who was locked up for contempt of court.

As Eric stood to attention, Judge Davies decreed that he was setting aside the sentence of imprisonment, and replacing it with 120 hours of community service, which he would allow Eric to serve in the Manchester area. We were delighted and, not surprisingly, it was a much happier Eric whom I accompanied back to the hotel. But as with so much in Eric's life, nothing was that simple.

As Eric left the court, a group of photographers ran backwards to get the best shot of him, with the result that one ended up flat on his back, camera still clicking. I managed to skirt around him, but Eric could only see the back of my head, and consequently ran right over the top of the floored cameraman, who was bravely still flashing away, no doubt taking some great shots of Eric's tan boots.

Back at the hotel, we had coffee and made plans for the dash north, but again everyone was congratulating Eric and asking for an autograph, and he made sure that no one was disappointed. I telephoned Old Trafford and told Ken Merrett the good news and he wished me a safe journey home. He also warned me of a heavy press presence along the route, which filled me with little delight. Maurice Watkins was to hold a press conference in the hotel so I tried to hurry Eric along, but he was deep in conversation with his agent, Jean-Jacques Bertrand. I feigned impatience in an effort to move them along, and it seemed to work, but as Jean-Jacques arose from his chair he asked me: 'Ned, what do you call a fishing boat in England?'

I thought this was a strange question from a French football agent, but I replied, 'A trawler.' He turned to Eric and they continued their discussions in French. Then Jean-Jacques asked me another question: 'What do you call the small fish in the sea?'

I was intrigued now, but thought carefully for a moment and said, 'Sardines.'

Again they carried on chatting in excitable French, but at that moment I put the questions out of my head because one of the hotel staff came in and told me that Maurice Watkins was ready to start the press conference and Eric's presence was urgently required.

Maurice told the world's press that Eric and Manchester United were delighted with the day's outcome and everyone at Old Trafford wanted to put the episode behind them and get on with the game of football. Eric was asked for a quote and it was then that my earlier questioning from Jean-Jacques began to make sense: 'When the seagulls follow the trawler it is because they think sardines will be thrown into the sea. Thank you.'

He then got up and walked out leaving a puzzled press pack scratching their heads. Some of them still don't know what he meant and never will, but I still felt proud that I was the man who had contributed to the translation for perhaps the most famous footballing quote since the BBC's Ken Wolstenholme said 'They think it's all over . . . it is now' at the end of the 1966 World Cup final.

The famously enigmatic remark by Eric would even help to get him a record deal, as it was reported the following year that he had signed up with the pop impresario, Pete Waterman, the man who gave the world Kylie Minogue.

'He can sing, though I wouldn't say he's Frank Sinatra,' Waterman apparently said. 'The record will focus more on his poetry and ideology. Any man who can talk about sardines following a trawler is a genius in my book.'

We were able to speed away from the press pack surrounding the hotel without encountering any difficulties, until I noticed that a motorbike had joined our convoy. I told Eric that we had a press bike trailing us, and he duly phoned Jean-Jacques who was following in the car behind to let him know we were being tailed. As we stopped at traffic lights, I couldn't contain myself any longer. Charging out of my car, I stormed past the puzzled looking Frenchman and had a few harsh words with the motorcyclist.

'Why don't you just fuck off?' I blasted.

He lifted his visor and shook his head: 'Only doing my job, mate.'

'Then I'll do mine and wrap that fucking bike around your neck. Give Cantona a bit of peace, you've had your press conference,' I exploded.

Our discussion was brought to a premature end as a traffic jam of horn blowers had piled up behind us, so I jumped back into the car and sped off. I suggested to Eric that he call Jean-Jacques to make arrangements for us to stop off and grab some food, which would give them a chance to talk.

The intrepid biker sat outside for two hours watching us have a meal. I didn't know what sort of scoop he was hoping for, but I imagined that the headline, 'Eric Cantona Eats' would hardly sell any more newspapers. During the meal the French contingent enjoyed a very animated conversation and, being a true gentleman, Eric turned to me every couple of minutes and translated their discussion. I nearly fell off my chair as Eric told me Jean-Jacques was suggesting that he should try and play football in Europe while he served his ban in England. 'Typical bloody agent,' I thought to myself, but smiled, hoping I could witness the scene when one of them suggested it to Fergie!

At the end of the meal, Eric and I said our goodbyes to Jean-Jacques, who was driving to Gatwick for a flight back to Paris, and we headed north for Manchester. The biker followed us for about another ten miles, but it would seem he was eventually overcome with boredom and turned back towards London.

This particular incident in Eric Cantona's eventful life was now more or less over. His remarkable good grace in accepting his fate was applauded by many, and he never once complained about the terms of his sentence; indeed he kept on coaching youngsters even after he had completed his 120 hours of community service.

During my time at Old Trafford, I never met anybody like Eric Cantona. I spent a long time in his company in the year or so after the incident at Selhurst Park, and I can honestly say it was a privilege to be with him. When difficulties arose and things got tough, I made sure he could always rely on me for support. Though he was far from perfect, he lived under the most incredible pressure. For instance, just four months after he had returned to professional football in February 1996, rumours abounded about the police being warned of a bizarre plot to beat Eric up.

Apparently a group of thugs from Bolton had generated a '£10,000 pot' which was payable to anyone brave enough to have a go at Eric. United were due to play at Bolton Wanderers at the end of February, and local police Inspector Graham Robertson, who handled security at the match, was most concerned by the threat. He told the press: 'We have heard there is a whip-round available for the man who attacks Cantona. This has come to us from police on the beat.'

Armed with this worrying information, I was well prepared for any hint of violence heading Eric's way, and was even more concerned for his well-being than usual. But it didn't happen; the match was trouble-free. Whether it was due to the police warning beforehand, I don't know, but Eric always knew that anyone who wanted to attack him would have to deal with me first.

CHAPTER 2

The Road to Old Trafford

As a young child growing up in Kilrush, in County Clare, Ireland, and on the streets of south-east London, my unwavering support of Manchester United Football Club had been one of the few constants during a difficult childhood.

At the age of fifteen, my mother gave birth to me in Guy's Hospital, London, having fled her devout Irish Catholic home, but after living with a variety of relatives in London, she and I ended up returning to Ireland. From that day, my grandmother took responsibility for my upbringing. Indeed, it was she who originally inspired my enthusiasm for United, telling me many wonderful stories of the great players, for the club had always been much loved in Ireland.

After a childhood spent being shunted back and forth between London and Ireland, I drifted through secondary school and, to be honest, my only qualification achieved there was the record for truancy. I only really excelled at sport, especially swimming and football. I would always imagine in my school kickabouts that I was starring for my beloved Manchester United, even though it was an unusual choice of club to support for a kid in London in those days.

I left school at fifteen and went straight into a job labouring on a building site. It was hard work, with good wages, but I decided I wanted something more from life, and when I saw an Army recruitment poster promising 'real-man' adventures in places I could scarcely pronounce, it seemed like the perfect opportunity to escape my mundane existence. So in 1965, aged seventeen years and two months, I duly enhanced the swelling ranks of Her Majesty's armed forces and joined the famous Green Jackets Brigade, which later became the Royal Green Jackets Regiment, at Winchester Barracks.

Army life seemed to agree with me and the friendships and bonds that were made during my initial training, and then cemented on active service, in some way made up for my lack of real family life in my formative years.

After ten years' Army experience on postings to places such as Malaya, Borneo, Germany and Northern Ireland, I was selected to attend a counter-terrorism course at Bradbury Lines (later renamed Stirling Lines), in Hereford, the home and training base of the Special Air Service Regiment. Even in those days, before some of the more high-profile feats of derring-do by the SAS, I knew what a real honour I had been given, but also what an almighty challenge lay ahead. The course showed me the highest level of soldiering and the briefings illustrated to me the potential of man's inhumanity to man. On my return to the UK after a posting to Gibraltar, I received notice that I had been accepted into the SAS Training and Selection course proper, and following an intense period of hell-on-earth training, I was badged as a full member of the 22 Special Air Service Regiment in June 1977, one of only 5 who made the grade from an intake of 128 hopefuls.

'Many are called. Few are chosen.' The motto of the SAS training ground was no joke.

I spent eleven great years with the SAS and was involved in many dangerous situations, all with my comrades standing shoulder-to-shoulder, but we had our diversions and sport featured highly in the off-duty pursuits of these super-fit guys. When not participating in various sporting activities we would watch football coverage on television avidly. I was fortunate to be in good company as the base had more than its fair share of Manchester United fans, so we rarely missed a televised match.

In August 1984, during a break from the relentless training that comes with the badge, I ventured over to the Special Projects (counter-terrorism) team hangar to scrounge some coffee and, as my mate Rusty was filling my tin mug, he asked me whether I fancied the job of managing the football team.

I laughed. I knew the team were regularly thrashed seven or eight goals to nil, so most guys in the camp would rather storm an embassy than admit to coaching the football team.

'You're joking, Rusty. Me? I'd end up strangling half of them,' I replied.

'Just for three weeks then, Ned. Could you?' Rusty persisted.

'We've got to register team listings and the manager's name by 1.00 p.m. or we're out of the league.'

I glanced at the clock showing 11.30 a.m. and broke the golden rule of soldiering – I volunteered. 'Just for three weeks, Rusty. That's it.'

By 12.30 p.m. the Army Hereford Football Club had a new manager, but I didn't just stay for three weeks, I stayed for five years, and managed to turn round the fortunes of the team with immediate effect. Under my management we won the Hereford Amateur Premier League (twice), the Amateur Premier Cup, and the Sunday Cup, all with virtually the same players, who had obviously been under inspired before I took over. So chuffed was I after our rapid improvement in 1985 that I wrote, rather cheekily, to Bobby Charlton explaining my lifelong love for Manchester United and the present fortunes of the 'SAS Eleven', and inviting him to come down to Hereford to present the team with their hard-earned medals after winning the Hereford-shire Sunday League Premier Cup.

It was an audacious request, really, and I never honestly expected that one of my heroes and such a living legend would give of his valuable time, but to my delight and amazement Bobby Charlton agreed, and made the journey down with Freddie Pye, his friend and the then vice-chairman of Manchester City. It was a truly memorable occasion for all the lads and their families, and a great boost to the team's morale. I was almost speechless, but it was the first and certainly not the last occasion that Bobby was to display great kindness to me.

I had never imagined that my association with an army football club would lead to my first encounter with one of Manchester United's footballing greats, nor that it would stand me in good stead for my future post-Army career. At the time I was simply another star-struck fan and just pleased to be in the same company as the legendary player.

A couple of seasons later, taking the view that, once again, I had nothing to lose, I invited Manchester United's chairman, Martin Edwards, to Hereford to present the medals at the end of the season. Few of my players believed that I would be so fortunate this time round, and even I began to doubt my chances. Though it is more than common for players and ex-players to visit army bases, hospitals, and schools, I wondered whether this attempt to arrange a visit from Manchester United's chairman to present amateur prizes was perhaps, even for me, a bridge too far. My worries were unfounded, however, as

Bobby Charlton had encouraged Martin to attend, having told him of the great time he had on his visit, and so my team of sceptics were proved wrong.

Accompanied by Freddie Pye, Martin carried out the prize-giving with absolute charm and made a great speech, and once again the players and their families and friends had an unforgettable day.

My last season in charge of the football team coincided with my last year in the Army. After more than two decades in the armed forces, I thought it would be fitting to have my farewell dinner coincide with the last prize-giving for the football team under my management, and was able to secure the guest appearance of Manchester United's relatively new manager Alex Ferguson, and Bobby Charlton, along with Freddie Pye and club chairman Martin Edwards.

The event was a tremendous success. The SAS lads loved having these stars in their midst, while I was chuffed to bits at this turnout for my send-off.

The only sour note during an otherwise perfect day occurred when Martin Edwards was spotted following a soldier's wife into the ladies' lavatory. The soldier concerned, Andy, was all for tearing Edwards's head off and pissing in the hole in his neck, but to keep the peace I managed to quieten down the fracas and spun the blame on to drink. I suggested that it was just a mistake, which was the first excuse to spring to mind, but I was to learn much later that far from being a one-off, Edwards's 'problem' was his party piece!

The next day I took Alex Ferguson and Bobby Charlton out on to the firing ranges and let them fire real guns with live ammunition. Alex wasn't a bad shot to be honest, but Bobby was woeful. He couldn't have hit a barn door with an Exocet.

'Christ,' moaned Eddie Stone, a proud Jock and a brave soldier. 'I wish he'd shot like that when he played against Scotland.'

It was a joke that Bobby well appreciated, as he knew the heartache he'd caused the Scottish fans on many an occasion at Wembley and Hampden Park.

The visit was cut short as Alex Ferguson had to go and check out the new scoring sensation of the day, David Kelly of Walsall, so it was with great sadness but heartfelt appreciation that I said goodbye to the United contingent, little knowing that it would not be very long before I was to see them again.

After leaving army life in 1988, I took advantage of the SAS old-boy network and, from September, worked in Bahrain as Superintendent of Security Operations at a petroleum company. For fifteen months I enjoyed a fantastic life in the Middle East, but eventually I decided that the time was right to return to Britain to realize my ambition of establishing and building my own security business. Before putting my plan into action, however, I took the opportunity both to earn some extra cash and to add to my existing security experience by accepting work as a bodyguard on Michael Jackson's eleven-date UK tour in summer 1988.

All of Michael Jackson's gigs were complete sell-outs, with 80,000 near-hysterical fans packing Wembley every night; the experience would prove to be an eye-opening initiation into the security problems caused by large crowds of screaming fans, and the occasions spent guarding the world's biggest pop star as he moved from stage to dressing room to hotel, gave me a valuable insight into how to protect important individuals in situations when they were at their most vulnerable.

I think it is fair to say that this gig changed my life. It suddenly dawned on me that if the authorities would allow private security firms effectively to police rock concerts on such a massive scale, taking into account the heights of hysteria that fans can and often do reach, surely there must be a case for private security on a similar scale at football stadia?

I wrestled with this idea for a couple of weeks, drifting between bouts of euphoria at my estimation of the plan's potential to 'it'll-never-work' pessimism as self-doubt crept in, believing that football clubs would always prefer to have the police control their crowds. Despite my reservations, however, I decided to test the water.

I wrote to six football clubs – Manchester City, Liverpool, Tottenham Hotspur, Arsenal, Everton and, of course, my beloved Manchester United. I received only one reply – from Manchester United. I assumed that my earlier encounters with Charlton, Edwards and Fergie at Hereford would have carried considerable weight, and I felt that they probably took my security proposal seriously because of my reputable SAS background.

Anyway, I had at least done enough to secure myself an interview, and so it was that I found myself on my way to Old Trafford, the most famous ground in Manchester, and a mecca for the legions of Reds fans around the world.

As a fan I'd visited the Old Trafford ground countless times, and had always been impressed by the sheer scale of the place. On match days, in the midst of a throng of hurrying supporters, it feels exhilarating to be part of such a vibrant mass, but when I arrived at a virtually deserted Old Trafford on a cold Tuesday morning in March 1990 for an appointment with the Manchester United hierarchy, it was a sobering experience.

After unloading my projector and presentation paraphernalia, and approaching the office reception, I was shown into an empty room with fine wood-panelling and a vast boardroom table. A secretary brought me coffee and told me that the management meeting would be finishing shortly, after which Alex Ferguson, Martin Edwards and company would join me for my interview. As I sat there, drumming my fingers, swallowing hard, I heard a commotion in the corridor outside. Three loud bangs on the door later, it flew open and the board and manager of Manchester United burst into the room wearing balaclavas! Their unexpected SAS-style entry gave me the fright of my life, but it certainly broke the ice prior to my presentation, and we all had a great laugh.

So anxious was I to make a good impression on the assembled committee that I was full of nerves as I set up the projector and laid out the paperwork I had cobbled together, outlining my master plan for the future security of Manchester United. Looking around the table, I couldn't help but feel overawed by the number of interviewers I faced: as well as Alex Ferguson and Martin Edwards, there was Nigel Burrows, club director, Maurice Watkins, club director and company lawyer, Mike Edelson, another director, and Ken Merrett, the company secretary, not to mention the catering manager, Mike Whetton, plus Danny McGregor, the commercial manager, and even the ticketing officer, Ken Ramsden. It struck me that the cleaners must have been busy or they would probably have been there too. With the motto 'Who Dares Wins' at the forefront of my mind, along with the six 'Ps' I had learned in the Army – Prior Planning and Preparation Prevents Piss-poor Performance – I set up my stall and got started.

My unique selling point was that in engaging security staff for a match, football clubs could save approximately £14 per man per hour. I could supply men or women at £10 per hour compared to the £24 per hour charged by the local police authority for a constable, and more for a senior officer. The police authority would only contract to a minimum of six hours and I offered to do it for a minimum of three hours. I thought it unusual that the board did not have many questions for me, and I took this as a bad sign. I finished my presentation and was rewarded with a small ripple of applause from my bemused audience.

My fears over the board's silence proved to be unfounded because, as we left the room, Ken Ramsden asked me when I would be able to start work.

I was reeling with shock. I had never imagined that my ambition to work for Manchester United would be fulfilled so quickly. However, I recovered sufficiently to reply as enthusiastically as possible. 'Yesterday,' I lied, knowing full well that I was holding my entire security empire under my arm in a cardboard box.

'How many men can you supply, Ned?' asked Ken.

'As many as you need,' I lied again.

'OK. We'll give you a four-match trial with eight men,' he suggested. 'Do you think you can handle that?'

'Of course, Ken, of course.' I was sweating heavily now.

'Good. That's settled then. You can start on Saturday week at the Liverpool game. But not on the terraces. I want you to secure the main reception areas, the restaurants and executive suites. If it goes well, we will look at the stadium security too.'

Fortunately for me, Ken Merrett intervened, suggesting that I might need a little more time to organize myself. Instead they decided that my first day of work would be at the Coventry City game on 31 March.

'Come to my office on the twenty-eighth, Ned, and I'll brief you on what's what at the ground,' smiled Ramsden, shaking my hand.

'Not a problem,' I smiled back, but of course there was a problem – there was only me! At the time of my appointment I was a one-man band so I had to put a rapid expansion plan into operation. By the time I had loaded my presentation kit back into the boot of my car, I knew exactly where I would find my eight men for the job – Hereford.

CHAPTER 3

Part of the Family

I COULDN'T TAKE THE SMILE OFF MY FACE as I drove home after my extraordinarily successful interview at Old Trafford. I had my first big break and I was determined to make it work. I contacted my Army mates, both in and out of the service, and in no time I had the eight men 'good and true' who would be my team for my big debut at the end of March.

As agreed, I attended the meeting at Ken Ramsden's office on 28 March for my first pre-match briefing, where Ken explained the problems with ground security on match days. He was keen to stem the flow of gatecrashers, ex-players, their families, hangers-on and football groupies, who all saw Old Trafford as their own private club.

'If they don't have the right ticket or pass, just turn them away,' said Ken. 'It's hard for us because we usually know half of them. It'll be easier for you.'

'They won't get past me or the lads,' I assured him, as Martin Edwards joined us in the office and corroborated what Ken had said: 'Ex-players, Ned, they're the worst. Alex Stepney, Paddy Crerand and Co. They drink the place dry.'

I gulped hard at this, inwardly dreading having to turn away guys who had always been heroes of mine. I soon realized that the job would not be as straightforward as I had imagined, but I vowed to do everything I could to impress my new employers and make a success of my fledgeling career in security at Manchester United.

My big day dawned and I stood for the first time as security manager at Old Trafford and positioned two men at the main reception, two on the door of the Trafford Suite, two on the door of the Stretford Suite, one man on the door of the Europa Club and one on the Red Grill Room door. I was stationed by the entrance to the executive seating area, the main target for the freeloaders, confident that we had covered the principal executive hospitality areas where largesse was dished out by the club and its associates. Manchester United was a big club with deep pockets, but some people had taken advantage for too long, and it was costing United a small fortune, especially in drink.

At the main reception area my men blocked the oldest trick in the freeloaders' book: jockeying two people in on one pass. My man, Joe, pulled up the first contender of the day who was trying to march his girlfriend in on his solo pass.

'But I always bring my girl in on this pass,' he moaned. 'Don't I?' looking pleadingly at the now shrugging commissionaire.

'Well, Sir, you can't now. New rules, sorry,' replied Joe.

'We'll see about that,' he fumed as he and his dyed-blonde partner marched back out, red-faced.

In my first report to the board I explained that people had been breezing past the receptionist, and the commissionaires, whose job it had been to man the doors of the executive areas and to keep an eye on security. Nobody had been checking tickets and, as a result, the situation had developed into a free-for-all. I suggested that, in future, an up-to-date list of all directors, players and box-ticket holders be made available to my staff, which would make it far easier to stop the flow of hangers-on and undesirables using these points of entry to the executive complex.

At the Trafford Suite door it was open season for the freeloaders and chancers, as a wink to the commissionaire seemed to be all that was required to gain access. The other old favourites were the excuses 'I've got to meet so-and so at the bar,' or 'Director so-and-so invited me for lunch.' All lies, of course, but in the absence of a list it was, to be fair, impossible for the commissionaires to separate the wheat from the chaff, and they were most concerned not to upset a bona-fide guest of a board member or other VIP. The same circumstances applied to the other facilities we were guarding within the ground, and I don't think even the board realized the volume of their gatecrashing visitors. Quite apart from the loss in revenue, it obviously raised serious security and safety implications, so the board agreed to my proposals and we set about stepping up resistance against the freeloaders. The introduction of two-way radios certainly improved communications and removed the need for the poor old commissionaires having to traipse up and down the stairs to find a board member or player every time someone asked for them.

Originally I was quite puzzled by the instructions from Martin Edwards and Ken Ramsden regarding ex-players and their families. I could understand the reasons for cracking down on the freeloading corporate crew, but I naively thought such benefits as free drink were among the perks associated with being a Manchester United celebrity, faded or otherwise. But I also realized that if every ex-player was to turn up at the executive suites, all with families and friends in tow, there would be chaos. At the end of my first shift in charge of security operations at Old Trafford, I was satisfied it had been a success, and so the 3-0 victory against Coventry City was the perfect end to a triumphant day.

'You got it right, Ned,' an obviously happy and relieved Martin Edwards assured me, as we had the first of our post-match meetings. 'Good job, well done.' Though some people in football talk about the chairman's vote of confidence being the kiss of death, for me it was the complete opposite. Things seemed to go from strength to strength from that day forward.

I was relieved that the first match had passed off without any real incident, because I harboured the fear that one or two of the ex-players and other celebrities would complain about their treatment at our hands. But if they were refused entry to the executive suites, it seemed they were invited into the wealthy fans' hospitality boxes instead, where they were plied with free booze by box-holders who would boast about entertaining various famous names.

After my team of men started turning former Manchester United stars away from the executive areas, sponsors at Old Trafford began to start paying ex-players to act as 'greeters', which, in my view, was a good result all round.

Bobby Charlton then invited me to join his company, Bobby Charlton Enterprises Ltd, part of Conrad Continental plc, and become Head of Security at £30,000 per annum plus bonuses and a car. A handsome offer indeed and one that I gladly accepted, scarcely believing my good fortune that, so soon after starting out on my own, I was now receiving a regular income, as well as being in business with such distinguished gentlemen.

In the first few weeks and months of my employment, I was

concentrating on finding my feet, and events on the pitch passed me by in something of a blur. Manchester United's performance in league football that season had been a disappointment and eventually we would finish a lowly thirteenth in the Barclay's League Division One, but on the upside, the Reds were thriving in the FA Cup.

Earlier in the season, Alex Ferguson's future at Old Trafford had hung in the balance, the team having failed to win a single trophy in four years. Banners had been displayed around the stadium proclaiming 'Fergie Must Go', but United's FA Cup run proved to be his salvation, with players such as England hero and 'captain courageous' Bryan Robson, Welsh firebrand Mark 'Sparky' Hughes, the brainy Scotsman Brian 'Choccy' McClair, Steve Bruce and Gary Pallister producing particularly good performances. It is widely believed that if United had not beaten Nottingham Forest in the FA Cup third round, in January 1990, Fergie would have been sacked.

Having drawn 3–3 against Oldham Athletic in the semi-final, it took goals from Brian McClair and Mark Robins in the replay to secure a cup-final place for the fired-up Reds.

On the day of the FA Cup final, on 12 May 1990, I travelled to Wembley with Martin Edwards and the board for the match against Crystal Palace, an event that Fergie would later say had been the most emotional experience of his career to date. The noise, the emotion, the whole atmosphere of the occasion had Fergie choking back the tears as the great twin towers of Wembley came into view. As the crowds sang the traditional football anthem 'Abide with Me', and then the national anthem, the whole place seemed to turn into a sea of United supporters, all of them cheering the team on to success. As a United fan I found myself caught up in the tide of emotion as well, but I had a job to do and I never lost sight of my duty to ensure the complete safety of everyone in the official party.

The final was a hard-fought contest that went agonizingly into extra time. An equalizer from Palace substitute Ian Wright late in normal time made the score 2–2, and the extra thirty minutes that followed almost proved disastrous as Wright scored again to put Palace in front. Fortunately, a Mark Hughes goal eight minutes from time produced a 3–3 final score. Goalkeeper Jim Leighton came in for much criticism for a nervous performance which almost allowed Palace's forwards to snatch victory.

Alex Ferguson and the entire team were bitterly disappointed with the result, as was every United fan in the stadium. The sense of frustration around the ground was tangible; even most neutrals agreed that Manchester United had done enough in normal time to win the match and take the honours.

On leaving Wembley, I accompanied Martin Edwards and the board members back to the Royal Lancaster Hotel in London's West End, and set about securing the function room to allow the board, Alex and the players to dine in peace. There was the usual assortment of 'players' best pals' whom the players didn't even know, as well as uninvited press and D-list celebrities trying to make the Sunday newspapers for me to contend with, but I simply turned them all on their heels. My new mantra had become 'No pass, no glass.'

Two days later, back in Manchester, the replay tickets for Thursday 17 May went on sale, and along with two of my men I patrolled the ticket-office queues, removing the odd tout pretending to look like a genuine United fan in need of extra tickets.

On Tuesday evening Martin Edwards decided to have a stroll along the line of queuing fans, so I accompanied him on this patrol. Though he had convinced himself that the fans saw him as the saviour of the club, he was, in fact, completely deluded as he did not seem to me to be even popular with the fans. More than one member of staff had already hinted to me that Martin didn't live in the real world.

Not surprisingly he was in a jovial mood that night, as the replay was further boosting the big money an FA Cup final earns for any club.

'Tickets are selling well, Ned. Especially for a Thursday evening match,' he smiled.

While we chatted he revealed that following Jim Leighton's less than convincing performance in the first match, the goalkeeper was due to be replaced by Les Sealey for the replay. I was surprised, and wondered how the fans would react to losing their star goalie. However, the final went our way this time, with the only goal, scored by Lee Martin, ensuring that the cup was bound for Manchester. While celebrating the club's victory, the United fans did not forget their former hero, Steve Coppell, by then manager of Crystal Palace, and a chorus of appreciation for him brought tears to the eyes of the former Old Trafford legend.

While Steve Coppell wept tears of gratitude, Jim Leighton wept tears of despair in the United dressing room after the match. Having witnessed Les Sealey's crucial clean sheet performance, and fearing that his career was in jeopardy, he was virtually inconsolable and, despite the best efforts of his team mates, bordered on the hysterical. Most people in the dressing room could sense that Jim's days at Old Trafford were numbered, but it was far from pleasant to witness his suffering as that realization sunk in.

The ever generous Les tried very hard to comfort the man he had just replaced, and even tried to give him his FA Cup winners' medal in an act of unparalleled kindness. The proud Scot, however, refused to accept it. He soon relinquished his hold on the number-one goalkeeping position at Old Trafford, as Sealey took over, but the arrival of the incomparable 'Great Dane', Peter Schmeichel, in August 1991 ensured that Sealey's reign would be short-lived. Later in his career, Les had another spell at Manchester United as second-choice goalkeeper. He was a real character, the fans' favourite before Schmeichel's arrival. Sadly, in August 2001, Les had a heart attack and died at the tragically early age of forty-three, but the Old Trafford faithful will never forget his role in that first trophy success for Alex Ferguson, the achievement that heralded the start of Manchester United's footballing domination throughout the 1990s.

After the victory at Wembley, we returned to Manchester by train on Thursday night, a palpable feeling of relief and excitement very much in evidence throughout the journey. We were bringing back the FA Cup and I was proud to have the responsibility of keeping it safely by my side on the train all the way home. It was a great feeling and happily only the first of many great football trophies I guarded over the next few years. It was later said that you could always tell when I was around by the smell of Brasso in the air!

Towards the end of my first year with Conrad Continental, I approached Martin Edwards and Maurice Watkins to discuss returning to my original plan of building up my own independent security company, and I enquired about the opportunities that would be available to me at Manchester United if I were to leave Conrad.

'It would be great to bring you on board, Ned,' Martin Edwards assured me. 'I'm sure that Maurice Watkins will agree and guide us through the legal niceties.'

In the meantime, Conrad Continental had been so impressed with my work as Head of Security that they informed me that they wished to offer me an improved package. I had no choice but to stall them, telling them I needed more time to consider their proposition. I contacted Martin Edwards again to explain how I was beginning to run out of excuses to Bobby Charlton as to why I hadn't yet confirmed my intention to remain an employee of his company. Fortunately, it was not too long before Martin gave me the good news: I could have a year-to-year contract supplying security personnel to Manchester United.

I could scarcely contain my excitement as I walked out of Old Trafford that evening. I was walking on air. And over the years, when the stresses and strains of the various situations and escapades I encountered in the football world had me tearing my hair out, I had only to remember the moment when Special Projects Security (SPS) was born.

Initially, I was a little concerned that Bobby Charlton and his associates might regard my actions as disloyal at worst, and ungrateful at best, but I had to put aside such worries if I was to realize my long-held ambitions and finally put all my energies into running my own company.

Curiously enough, the very next morning my exhilaration was temporarily put on hold when Bobby Charlton approached me. His expression spoke volumes. 'I've just heard about your new deal, Ned. So you're leaving us?'

'Yes, Bobby,' I replied. 'I just want to do the same as you. Run my own business. I'll never forget the kindness you've shown me, and without your help I'd never have had this opportunity.'

Bobby just shrugged. 'Good luck then, Ned,' he said, and walked off.

I felt really low and hoped he didn't view my ambition as betrayal. However, before my deal was tied up with Manchester United, there were further discussions among the other directors about my future. Charlton's fellow Conrad Continental director, Mike Edelson, telephoned Ken Merrett, and told him that I was breaking away from Conrad Continental to form my own security company. For some reason Edelson had formed the impression that I was going into business with the Manchester United and England captain Bryan Robson, and his close friend, Mike Profitt, owner of the Amblehurst Hotel near Manchester, which was complete nonsense.

I was duly summoned to Ken Merrett's office and he asked me outright, 'Ned, we all trust you here. What's all this about you and Robson?'

I had to ask him to explain, before setting him straight: 'No, Ken. It's all bollocks.'

Fortunately, the misunderstanding was soon resolved, and Ken made the agreement official. Shaking me firmly by the hand, he informed me, 'The business is yours, Ned. Good luck, son.'

I thanked him for his support and trust, and, while eating a celebratory meal of fish and chips in my car in the Old Trafford car park, I considered my good fortune and looked forward to making a great success of my new business venture.

CHAPTER 4

Back in Europe

IN THE SUMMER OF 1990, UEFA announced that English football clubs were to be readmitted to European competitions after a five-year ban resulting from the Heysel stadium disaster in Belgium, when fighting broke out before the 1985 European Cup final between Juventus and Liverpool fans. A wall collapsed under the weight of fleeing supporters, and the incident left hundreds of people injured and thirty-nine dead.

Though Liverpool still remained banned from Europe, UEFA's decision meant that United, as FA Cup winners, would enter the 1990–1 Cup-Winners' Cup, the second most prestigious of the three European tournaments at that time. With this news there was an extra buzz around Old Trafford over the summer as the new season approached. The Reds would learn who would be their first-round opponents by mid-August, and there was much excitement at the club's return to the European stage.

At the pre-season tactical meeting at Old Trafford, which I attended to discuss security issues, I was delighted that the board had decided to increase my security team from eight to twenty men. I also learned that a former senior policeman, Arthur Roberts, was to join Manchester United as the club's first ever safety officer. As I would now be responsible for some stadium security, we had a productive meeting with the Manchester police chief superintendent, Ivor Jolly, who was in charge of Old Trafford on match days. It was clear to me that he knew everything there was to know about stadium security and crowd control, and his help and advice were instrumental in improving my knowledge of the mechanics involved in making sure every individual entered and left the football ground safely. If any fan attempted to jeopardize the safety of others, Ivor knew exactly how to eject him or her with the minimum of disruption. Another development was the appointment of a firefighting crew from the local station, a tremendous idea in the light of the Heysel and Hillsborough tragedies, and it illustrated to me just how forward-thinking Manchester United had become in their approach to safety.

A 'minder for the manager' had been Ken Ramsden's idea, and I sat open-mouthed as he explained why it was necessary to keep a close eye on Fergie on match days: 'There are many fans who want him out, Ned, and they can get quite excitable, especially if we lose. I want someone guarding him at all times he is exposed.'

It was around this time, prior to the start of the 1990–1 season, that Alex Ferguson crossed swords in dramatic fashion with Bryan Robson. Rumours had been circulating that Bryan was waiting in the wings to take over as manager of United, and it was at a meeting between the two men in Fergie's office at the Cliff training ground that the Boss fired questions at Bryan to discover whether there was any truth in the gossip. The club captain stood his ground and, putting his face close to Ferguson's, told him in no uncertain terms that he had never gone behind his back, and that if he had anything to say about Fergie or his ability to manage, he would tell him directly.

With such intense conflict between the Boss and the skipper, whose professional relationship should have been strongest of all, it was easy to understand how the fans at that time might be reacting to the sense of unrest that was palpable throughout Old Trafford. So I agreed with Ken about a guard for Fergie, especially having witnessed at first hand the fans' vitriolic reaction to him if the result on the pitch was unfavourable. At the time, however, it struck me as bizarre to be bodyguarding the manager from our own fans. Looking back it is difficult to imagine that at one time in his United career, Sir Alex Ferguson needed such protection, having experienced unparalleled success ever since, and gone on to join Old Trafford legends such as Sir Matt Busby in the Manchester United Hall of Fame.

In the second week of August, UEFA held the draw for the European Cup-Winners' Cup and Manchester drew Pécsi Munkas from Hungary. It was a memorable weekend for us all at the club: on the Friday we were back in Europe and, on the Sunday, we played Liverpool in the FA Charity Shield, in a hard-fought match that ended in a 1–1 draw.

The new season kicked off with a 2–1 win in a home game against Coventry City and, at the pre-match briefing, Ken Ramsden asked for more of the same standard of stewarding in the executive suites and restaurant areas, but advised me to be guided by the police on the subject of ground security.

During this game I met up again with Paddy Crerand. I was still acutely embarrassed about having to turn him away from the executive club the previous season, but mercifully, Paddy clearly bore me no grudge; he just winked, flashed the correct pass and went inside. I was so relieved as I didn't relish another season of confrontations with my heroes. Years later Paddy told me that he understood my position and appreciated that I was only being paid to enforce someone else's rules.

Preparations for the security arrangements at the forthcoming games in Europe soon became paramount. After Heysel, UEFA were going to be watching English teams and their fans especially closely, and everyone at Manchester United was committed to ensuring that we would set an example to the world.

As we had been the first English club to get into Europe under Sir Matt Busby, any European game is of special significance at Old Trafford, but this game against Pécsi Munkas, after the five-year exclusion ban, sent a tingle down my spine. We won 2–0 with goals from Clayton Blackmore – our first goal in Europe since March 1985 – and Neil Webb, and it was always good to get through the first leg without conceding goals.

Known around the club as 'Sunbed' because of his addiction to ultra-violet fluorescent tubes, Clayton will always be remembered for his great skill and personality during his twelve-year career at Old Trafford, but had events on the infamous 1987 tour of Bermuda gone differently, he would probably just be applying for parole to the Bermudan authorities. In my view people don't realize how close Clayton Blackmore came to spending fifteen years in an island jail, after being arrested and locked up on a charge of rape.

The club's diligent lawyer, Maurice Watkins, who by pure good fortune had connections in Bermuda, was able to spirit Clayton out of Bermuda and back to Britain before he could be vilified by the press, many of whom confused a rape allegation with proof positive of the crime. The allegations were groundless. No attempt was ever made to extradite Clayton to Bermuda, and so he never faced a trial in connection with the alleged crime, which allowed him to further his highly successful career at Old Trafford.

I remember his wife Jackie well. She was blonde, slim and attractive, and once asked me to come out for a drink while the players were away. Players' wives were always a no-go area to me, and despite being flattered by her invitation, I had to turn her down. She later split with Clayton and began seeing one of my security guys. We didn't talk much after that.

At the end of that first European game spirits were running high amongst the players and directors. United were back in Europe, and back with a bang. I was in seventh heaven and could hardly believe my luck: I was a mad Manchester United fan doing a job I loved amongst my heroes. As far as I was concerned it couldn't get any better than this, but I was proved wrong when Martin Edwards tapped me on the shoulder and said: 'Ned, meet Denis Law.'

'Good to meet you,' smiled Denis.

My shock and surprise rendered me speechless. All I could manage was an incomprehensible mumble and I just shook and shook his hand. I was still shaking his hand when he eventually prised it free, and moved on to more adulation. I had just met Denis Law, the King of Old Trafford. I could have happily died that night and gone to the next world with a smile on my face!

The second leg of the European Cup-Winners' Cup was to be played in the Hungarian town of Pécs on 3 October, and it was not until the tickets went on sale that the club could get some idea of the numbers likely to be travelling to the game, and begin the mammoth task of preparing security arrangements for the trip and the match. What was not in doubt was that I would be one of the security personnel. There was no way on earth that I was going to miss Manchester United's first game on the Continent for six years. In fact, I was fully prepared to walk to Hungary with a nail in my shoe for this one.

The club refused to issue tickets to individuals, and all tickets were sold only as part of a 'club tour', to ensure that the travelling support was kept firmly under the control of the club, and denying fans the opportunity to make their own way there, which was potentially dangerous. The system proved to be a success, and we had one plane-load of supporters flying to Hungary, accompanied by my security crew.

Upon arrival in Pécs, Barry Moorhouse, the club's membership manager, and I were taken immediately to meet the police who would be in charge of security at the game. The meeting went well and it was soon apparent that we all had the same aim, simply for the game to be played out in peace with safety assured for both sets of supporters. We moved on to a restaurant for our pre-match meal and to rendezvous with the Manchester United fans to distribute their tickets. Barry volunteered me to tell our fans that drinking was forbidden and anyone smelling of alcohol would not receive their match ticket.

To ensure that I received their undivided attention, I jumped up on to a table and made the unpopular announcement. Surprisingly, it was met with a deathly silence, but if looks could kill, I would have been six feet under at that point.

'No tickets will be issued until we are on the coaches,' I barked. In truth the travelling supporters would have agreed to anything because all they wanted to do was to get to the stadium and watch the game.

It was a great tribute to Manchester United's fans' devotion to the club and the preservation of its good name throughout the world, because not one supporter was refused a ticket on the grounds of alcohol abuse, although I can't deny that there was a strong aroma of peppermint on the coaches!

It was a great night and all the better for Manchester United winning 1–0 through a Brian McClair goal. We were now in the draw for the second round and the fans had behaved impeccably. The police were delighted and escorted our coaches to the airport, from where we headed back to Manchester. We arrived home at 2 o'clock in the morning, tired but elated, not only to be through to the next round, but also for the chance to show UEFA that the majority of English fans were still amongst the best behaved in the world.

Though we had had a good start in Europe, our form in the League was less impressive, and never more so than after losing 1–0 at home to Arsenal – the game better known as 'The Brawl at the Old Trafford Corral'. A seemingly innocuous incident in the second half between Anders Limpar of Arsenal and our own Denis Irwin saw an explosion of violence on the pitch, and almost every player became embroiled in an episode of mayhem for several minutes. Punches and kicks flew, but it was mostly pushing and shoving. Over the years I formed the impression that footballers really do look like they are shadow boxing when the balloon goes up, and it strikes me that it is very much a case of 'hold me back' at these times.

On this particular occasion, however, there were serious consequences – an FA commission was set up to investigate the trouble, and United and Arsenal were docked one and two points respectively, as well as being fined £50,000 each. There was never anything I could do to prevent such battles – once the players were on the pitch during a ninety-minute game their safety was no longer my responsibility, but it was often frustrating for me having to watch occasional bouts of pugilistic playground antics from the dugout or the stands without being able to intervene and rescue the situation.

On top of the FA punishment Arsenal saw fit to fine their 'hard man' Scottish manager George Graham two weeks' wages for the lack of on-field discipline, presumably because the London club had previously had its knuckles rapped and been fined by the FA for a similar incident the previous season. Even after a few months at Old Trafford I had become familiar with the lie of the land within the club, and remember thinking that if Fergie had been fined by United, there would have been a queue of people a mile long hoping to catch a glimpse of the showdown in the boardroom!

Although my security business was building nicely, and I would soon have a regular team of thirty on match days, I still did not have the use of an office at Old Trafford and was continuing to issue fluorescent vests and jackets to my staff from the back of my car in Car Park B. This also doubled as a location point for my security team as I briefed them there and despatched them around the ground. It was not an ideal situation but Eddie Casan, the stadium manager, kindly found me a location in the tunnel area underneath the South Stand. I had to share the premises with the BBC outside-broadcast unit, but it was such a luxury to be able to lock away the radios and jackets until the next game instead of lugging them with me every time I went to a match.

A nice diversion at our next home game in November against Sheffield United, which we won 2–0, was a Bobby Charlton Soccer School final that was played before the game. It was wonderful to see all that young talent being encouraged, and to consider that we might have been watching football superstars of the future.

Part of my duties that day involved hunting down rogue ticket-holders. Ken Ramsden had handed me a list of seat numbers where the corresponding tickets had mysteriously gone missing, and so during the game I walked around the stands to check out the seat numbers in question, only to find they were nearly all occupied. I informed the unlucky punters that they really only had two choices; either I would call the police and they would have to explain why they were in possession of stolen goods, i.e. the tickets, or they could get up and leave the ground and there the matter would rest. Most people selected the latter option.

The next big night was the Bryan Robson testimonial match against Celtic, followed by a large party for all the players and guests at the Disco Royale in Manchester. It was a great occasion, and the stadium was packed to the rafters to pay tribute to this tremendous player and captain who had given ten great years to the club.

When the game ended, Bryan elected to do a lap of honour and as he got himself mobbed by fans, it was down to me to wade in and drag him clear. It would not be the last time I would have to intervene to save a United star from overenthusiastic fans, especially when sometimes the latter were more intent on lynching than lauding the player.

Some of the big games in the early 1990s were truly memorable. In the League Cup against Arsenal, in November 1990, it was widely predicted that the Reds would get hammered away from home against the current League leaders. After the match, which had been massively over-hyped following the trouble a month earlier, the pundits were left red-faced as United triumphed with a 6–2 victory, including a wonderful Lee Sharpe hat-trick.

Lee won the PFA Young Player of the Year award in 1991, but within five years he was gone from United and his career has been in decline ever since. In spite of his undoubted talent on the pitch, the fact that Lee Sharpe never realized his true potential at Old Trafford was probably due more to his maddening off-the-field behaviour. I once had occasion to take him aside in the old centre tunnel at a League game and tell him that the Manchester lads from around the discos and nightclubs had told me that he was being a bit overindulgent, and if Fergie had got to hear about it his kit bag would have been packed that day.

'If you leave this club, there's only one way you'll be going, and that's down,' I said to him in a cautionary manner, hoping that he would heed my well-meaning advice.

On other occasions Fergie also had to speak to Lee about his love of the night life, but the young player didn't listen. Aged just nineteen, earning a fortune and enjoying the celebrity limelight to the full, it is hardly surprisingly he lost his way, but it still saddened me that things went so wrong for the lad who played so well against the mighty Arsenal that night.

Into the New Year, the strain on the players and back-room staff was immense as the club was still involved in four competitions, in both the domestic and European arenas. Reaching the final of the League Cup, then known as the Rumbelow's Cup, was our first target, because victory would secure us a place in the UEFA Cup competition the following season. Even the small taste of European football we had enjoyed until then made us hungry for more.

We got to the final for the first time in the club's history by beating Leeds United in the semi-final and would face Sheffield Wednesday on 21 April. The Wembley crowd had an additional clash of titans to savour as this game was a showdown between Alex Ferguson and the former Manchester United manager, the colourful Ron Atkinson, then in charge at the Sheffield club.

Despite a stirring fightback, in which former United goalkeeper Chris Turner starred for Wednesday, the Reds lost the final 1–0. A terrific game was marred, however, by the serious injury sustained by our courageous goalkeeper, Les Sealey. Despite being in great pain, Les bravely hung on until the final whistle.

The season had not progressed as we had hoped it would, having been the losing side in the League Cup final, knocked out of the FA Cup, and unable to challenge for the League title, but we still had the European Cup-Winners' Cup in our sights, and by April we were in the semi-finals.

In the quarter-final in March we had faced French side Montpellier at Old Trafford. Montpellier took an early lead and looked like coming away with a result, but in the dying seconds of the match, Brian McClair popped up to score. His goal gave us a much-needed draw, albeit against ten men because French player Pascal Baills had been sent off earlier for a foul on Mark Hughes. This incident would give Sparky Hughes and me some heartache in the second leg.

The second leg in Montpellier two weeks later was a real 'Red-letter' day for me as, for the first time, I flew with the team as head of their security, which gave me the opportunity to get to know the lads in the squad on a more sociable level. Until then I had been largely concerned with getting the basics of the security operation right for the fans, but from this moment onwards I would spend much more time working closely with the players on a personal basis, which was an aspect of my job I was more than happy with.

After the sending-off incident in the first leg I had to keep a special eye on Mark Hughes, following a remark made by a Montpellier club official who had said he was not welcome in the town. Such a comment could easily have been misinterpreted by the lunatic fringe, but I had no fears that Sparky would react or inflame the situation as he was known for being single-minded about the game, so much so that he rarely looked right or left at the fans – he came, he played, he mostly conquered.

Some years after Mark had left United for good, I met him by chance in a Manchester nightclub where he was having a late-night drink with his lovely wife, Jill. Whether it was the lateness of the hour, the strength of the alcohol, or something he had read in the memoirs of Alex Ferguson, Sparky wanted to talk only about his former manager.

'Fergie never really rated me as a player, Ned,' he complained. 'I was only brought back from Barcelona to keep the fans happy.'

'That's bollocks,' I remember telling him, but Mark refused to listen. He was more interested in berating Fergie. It was sad that one of Old Trafford's most hard-working players who had given such sterling service to the club had spent all those years believing his manager had thought so little of him.

On the journey to France, I insisted to the airport check-in staff that the players should occupy the front of the plane, while I positioned myself behind them and in front of the press, to give the players a bit of peace from the constant requests they endured for private interviews and comments. I made it my job to make sure that no one from the press or the travelling public got to my 'boys'. It made me unpopular with certain members of the press, but most realized I was just doing my job.

Another important contingent flying with us were a team from the Manchester police who specialized in football hooliganism. Their input liaising with the local police was vital in identifying travelling thugs and pointing them out, before they got a chance to damage our reputation abroad.

On landing at Montpellier airport, I shepherded the players and management on to the coach amid great cheering from the locals, who appeared to be far more sporting than their less than diplomatic club official, and I viewed it as yet another testament to the high esteem in which Manchester United is held by true fans of football around the world. Even in a foreign country they were cheered before they kicked a ball.

We arrived at the team hotel in time for lunch and then most of the players opted for an afternoon nap before the start of that evening's light training, during which the squad enjoyed an hour working out and getting the feel of the playing surface. Once back at the hotel the majority of players took the opportunity to grab an early night after the evening meal with only a few electing to sit around the restaurant chatting and relaxing.

After breakfast the next morning, Fergie took his team to a private training ground. I was responsible for looking after numerous pieces of personal property from the players, which I began concealing about my person. As the players ran on to the pitch, Bryan Robson turned to me and said, 'Here Ned, look after this for me please.'

I held out my hand and Bryan placed a gold watch in my palm. It was quite ordinary-looking, and Bryan noticed that I seemed less than impressed. He simply remarked: 'Read the back, Ned.'

I turned it over and the inscription elevated the watch way above the 'ordinary' category. It read: 'The fastest goal scored in a World Cup – Bryan Robson – Spain 1982'. The watch had been presented to Bryan for scoring *that* goal after just twenty-seven seconds against France in the 1982 World Cup finals.

After their training session, it was back to the hotel for lunch and this time all the lads took an afternoon nap. They polished off a light meal at 4.30 p.m. and then we were off to the stadium. My heart was pounding, fit to burst with pride, when we arrived at the ground amid a sea of red-and-white banners and scarves – the United fans had turned up in massive numbers to support their team.

A hard-fought contest saw us win 2–0 with a goal from Clayton Blackmore and a penalty from Steve Bruce. The fans went wild and the whole Manchester United outfit went crazy with excitement, safe in the knowledge that we had made it through to the semi-finals of the European Cup-Winners' Cup.

The following Friday, I was on duty during a general meeting of the board. When I answered the phone in the office it was Ken Ramsden's secretary Maria on the line, who told me that the draw had been made and we were to face the Polish team Legia Warsaw, with the first leg due to be played in Poland on 10 April. I immediately passed a note through to the members of the board, and mentally began preparing for what I thought might be a difficult trip abroad, as Poland had only recently emerged from the Soviet bloc.

Our flight to Warsaw followed the same pattern as our Montpellier trip, with me acting as a buffer between the players and the press. On arrival in Warsaw we headed off in a convoy of coaches to the Marriott Hotel and I had my first look at Poland. At first glance it appeared a grey and depressing place, and Warsaw seemed to be a city drenched in depression.

We all stayed in the hotel on the second day as Fergie had elected to rest his squad, and I spent the day getting to know the players better, and became especially close to Paul Ince.

Paul was a typical East Ender, a real Londoner who always had something smart to say and loved to show off with his wide-boy act. His bravado always evaporated, however, when Alex Ferguson was on the scene. Alex's put-downs to cocky players was legendary, so 'Incey' had to pick his moments, but I formed a great rapport with him and over the years we would get embroiled in some hilarious high jinks. I always thought that Paul felt obliged to push his chest out a bit as the sporting world knew that he was the cousin of Nigel Benn, one of the most explosive boxing talents Britain has ever produced, a double world champion at a time when the middleweight and super-middleweight divisions contained some mighty talents.

Once again the Reds were victorious and came back from a goal down to thrash Legia Warsaw 3–1 on their own territory, leaving us all very confident that we would reach the final of the competition in Europe. Having maintained an unbeaten away record in the tournament, the whole Manchester United entourage were buzzing all the way home.

The return leg at Old Trafford promised a great night of football. The capacity crowd was rewarded with a nail-biting ninety minutes ending in a 1–1 draw, but it was enough for Manchester United to proceed to the final and was considerable compensation for the defeat by Sheffield Wednesday in the League Cup final three days earlier. Now the club was set for a much more important final in Rotterdam against one of the greatest names in world football, the mighty Barcelona, a team managed by the legendary Dutch footballer Johan Cruyff.

Meanwhile, in the League, our next game was against a team that often inspired the atmosphere and passion of a cup final every time we met – Manchester City. This became a milestone game in one young gun's first-team career – that of the seventeen-year-old Ryan Giggs. It soon became clear that this young man with lightning speed and great dribbling ability was about to set the football world alight. He made his debut in a style entirely his own, scoring the only goal in a 1–0 victory for the Reds. A star was born.

The following Saturday witnessed the debut of another player who also enjoyed a controversial career at Old Trafford. Although the £1 million signing Andrei Kanchelskis promised much for the Reds against Crystal Palace, even his great talent was not enough to prevent our 3–0 revenge drubbing at the hands of the previous season's losing FA Cup finalists.

Three days later, the team departed for Holland. On this occasion I was left behind to organize security personnel to accompany the 113 coaches heading for the European Cup-Winners' Cup final, to be held at Feyenoord's stadium in Rotterdam. There were also nine plane-loads of fans travelling from Manchester and two from Gatwick. It was the biggest movement of English football fans following our readmission to UEFA club competitions, and, as ambassadors for the country, there was considerable pressure on the club to ensure that everything worked like clockwork.

A crowd of 45,000, mostly made up of Manchester United fans, packed into the stadium for what proved to be a tense final. The weather was atrocious and it never stopped pouring with rain through-out the whole game. Our fans had little or no cover but, despite being completely drenched, they never stopped singing their hearts out. They were eventually rewarded for their magnificent support when Mark Hughes touched home a Steve Bruce header after a free kick in the sixty-eighth minute, and, seven minutes later, followed up his first goal with a thunderous shot to give the Reds a 2–0 lead.

With about ten minutes to go, victory was within our reach, until Barcelona's Dutch international midfielder, Ronald Koeman, stepped up to take a free kick in clear sight of the goal. Koeman's accuracy was legendary, and true to form, he did not let his team-mates down. With Barcelona back in the game, creating chance after chance, our one-goal lead looked very fragile, especially after the Spanish side had a goal disallowed, and a Michael Laudrup strike cleared off the line.

Alex Ferguson later called it 'the worst ten minutes of my life'. The Reds held on, however, to win the European Cup-Winners' Cup, the club's first European trophy since the famous European Cup win at Wembley in 1968.

The players rightfully did a lap of honour and Alex Ferguson called me on to the pitch with the team to keep an eye on the trophy. Ken Ramsden and Ken Merrett later challenged me about my appearance on the pitch, seemingly annoyed at my camaraderie with the players, but they were well and truly silenced when I explained that I was there at Alex Ferguson's request.

I left the pitch running ahead of the team to secure their dressing room and I caught up with an ecstatic Alex Ferguson being warmly congratulated by Bobby Charlton. Though he had never struck me as a sentimental person, I was surprised to notice that Alex's eyes were filled with tears. He had kept his emotions in check at the FA Cup final a year earlier, but this victory – his second Cup-Winners' Cup, having already won it with Aberdeen in 1983 – seemed to have opened the emotional floodgates. So moved was I at seeing these two legends enjoying this great night for the club they loved, that my eyes welled up too.

As the champagne began flowing in the dressing room, I guarded the door as the knocking started. Among the folk trying to bluff their way in was a priest and, being a good Catholic boy, I thought it best to check with Alex Ferguson or Martin Edwards if he could come in.

'Ned. We don't want him in here. He's always hanging around the dressing room,' instructed Edwards.

I politely told the good Father that the dressing room was at full capacity and he could not go in. He smiled and went, leaving me chuckling at the thought of Manchester United having groupies from the priesthood.

I guarded the European Cup-Winners' Cup back to the hotel where the celebrations were well under way. Champagne corks were popping in time to the camera flashes as all of the invited guests had their photographs taken with the trophy.

After an unforgettable night of high-spirited revelry, we flew back to Manchester the next day, and boarded an open-topped bus for the drive into the city centre. According to police estimates, 750,000 fans lined the route into Manchester, and at times the bus could scarcely get through the crowds. Each of the players proudly held the Cup aloft, while Alex Ferguson kept reminding me, 'Watch it doesn't go overboard, Ned.'

'Sure, Boss. I'm on the case,' I answered, bobbing and weaving behind the players, making sure it didn't fall, because if that trophy had toppled overboard it would have taken a braver man than me to have jumped into that mêlée to retrieve it. European trophies are hard enough to win, but it would have been harder still to rescue it from the sea of Reds in the city that night.

The following Saturday we played the last game of the season against Spurs at Old Trafford and drew 1–1. Playing on home turf just days after their victory in Europe, the team received a fantastic reception, and, despite the result, it was a memorable end to an extraordinary season.

CHAPTER 5

United Go Public

Prior to the start of the 1991–2 season, I had major tactical meetings with Ivor Jolly, Arthur Roberts and the board at Old Trafford. They had both given my company, SPS, a great recommendation to the board, and had convinced them of my employees' ability to handle the fans firmly but fairly. So much so that our workforce was increased to 200 people on match days.

Along with the extra staff came extra responsibilities, as Martin Edwards was anxious to curb black-market ticket sales, which were losing the club some of its valuable revenue. It was strongly suspected that most of the tickets were finding their way into touts' hands from within the ticket office at Old Trafford; even from the players themselves. It was my understanding that, occasionally, some tickets were not posted to their rightful owners, and instead were sold to touts by ticket-office staff. When irate supporters rang to complain about not receiving their tickets, they were issued with replacements. Consequently, the original tickets that had supposedly been lost in the post could never be traced back to the staff who had sold them to the illegal traders. 'They are taking the piss,' I recall Martin Edwards moaning.

Armed with a list of seat numbers relating to the tickets that had 'gone astray', my colleagues and I were able to check the occupants of specific seats and pinpoint exactly who had bought a ticket from an illegal source. Those who had would be escorted from the ground, and they would sometimes be asked for a description of the tout they had used by a police officer.

I knew that it would be difficult to eliminate the black market in tickets, as the unlawful enterprise had been part of football since the birth of the spectator sport, but eventually we had some success, and it seemed that the 'Buy a ticket from a tout, SPS will throw you out' warning was getting through to the punters.

At the time of the clampdown on ticket touting, my increased security operations received their ultimate accolade: the Manchester United fanzines started slagging me relentlessly, and I loved it. I was blamed for everything by the fans. Losses, draws, the weather, cold Bovril – I was always to blame. My men were christened 'The Suits' and for a while I was 'Kelly – the King of the Suits'. Then I started wearing Drizabone trenchcoats and the fans christened me 'Herr Flick', after the character in the television comedy series *'Allo, 'Allo*. I took it all in good humour, and felt relieved to have people laughing at me rather than fighting with me.

The 1991–2 season was full of uncertainty, mainly due to the fact that the top clubs in England had taken the decision to break away from teams in the lower divisions and form their own Premier League, comprising the top twenty-two clubs. It was felt that the other teams were holding back the progress of the top clubs and so, with the FA's backing, they had given the necessary one year's notice before creating a separate new league. It was a bold move, and no one really knew how it would develop. However, its potential success was bolstered by a large injection of television money – one of the keys to United's later vast riches. A deal with BSkyB brought more than £300 million into the game, of which United got a share, even though Fergie lambasted the idea of satellite television taking over from terrestrial coverage, as it would stop poorer people having free access to televised matches in their homes.

Fergie's socialist leanings also caused him to be quietly critical of the board's decision, earlier in 1991, to float the club on the Stock Exchange. Though the flotation was designed to make the club cash rich, and should have enhanced its ability to buy top-flight players and compete with the richest clubs in the world, it didn't always work in practice. The board of the plc still had a miserly attitude to paying top players the wages they could command elsewhere because, it was claimed, they had a prior responsibility to the shareholders. Looking back, the conversion to Manchester United plc did lose the club much of its family identity, but the compensation was that United became the biggest football 'company' in the world, and developed a massive fanbase across the globe.

From my perspective it just meant that I had a few more men in suits to guard, because not only was there a plc board, but also the directors of the subsidiary company which was set up to run the football side of the club, including Sir Bobby Charlton. On occasions, however, Manchester United plc was anything but 'united', and there existed quite sizeable divisions between Sir Bobby and other members of the board, notably Martin Edwards and Maurice Watkins. One of the more curious arguments between Edwards and Charlton concerned Michael Knighton, the 'nearly man' of a few years earlier. He had 'nearly' bought control of United but it transpired that he had only 'nearly' the money he claimed to have had. Sir Bobby Charlton wouldn't talk to Knighton whenever he was at Old Trafford and neither did most of the directors. I don't think they had got over the embarrassment of the club's dealings with the man who had played 'keepie-uppie' in front of the United crowd when he wrongly thought he was going to get away with buying the club.

On the field, the Reds were determined to win the last ever First Division title, and it would prove to be a very close-run contest. The first game of the season was against the newly promoted Notts County and they proved their First Division mettle as it took United all their skill and effort to record a 2–0 victory over the new boys.

Meanwhile, Alex Ferguson's two new signings had caused quite a stir amongst the fans. Goalkeeper Peter Schmeichel was signed from the Danish team Brøndby for £505,000, which was one of the best bargain buys the manager ever made. Fergie had spotted him when Brøndby and United shared a training ground on a Spanish holiday, and once again his eye for a player did not let him down, as Schmeichel went on to become an Old Trafford legend. Another useful acquisition, at least for a time, was England international full-back Paul Parker, who was signed from Queens Park Rangers for £2 million, but only once Alex Ferguson had satisfied himself that Denis Irwin could play on the left.

I would occasionally have a pint with Denis after matches, and found the Irishman to be great company. I asked him if he had any difficulty switching to left back, and in true footballer fashion he quipped: 'Ned, I'll play anywhere as long as there's a ball involved!'

In my view Denis Irwin was a good guy, and a great team player. Signing for United in June 1990, he was one of the first players to join the club after I began working at Old Trafford. He would go on to play more than 500 games for the club and was a regular in the side throughout the successful 1990s.

He was a good mate of mine, and in all the time I knew and worked beside him, the only occasions when we nearly fell out were when Denis had that one drink too many. He would come and annoy me with the stupid question: 'What's a good County Clare man like you doing in the fucking SAS?'

I always gave him the same answer, and it always shut him up, for a minute or two at least: 'Denis, if I told you, I'd have to kill you!'

Undeterred, a few drinks later, Denis would be back; same question, same answer. I suppose it offended his Irish sensibilities that a fellow Irishman had worked so long for the British Crown. Nevertheless, from 1990 until summer 2002, he was a wonderful servant to Manchester United, a good and true team-mate, and he deserved every medal he won.

My company's increased presence among the crowd meant we were on the front line against the mindless thuggery which, at that time, often blighted our game. A vital home game in August against Leeds, who were widely tipped to be our biggest challengers for the League title that year, was a match that provoked much tension and hatred between the fans. After a Bryan Robson strike, Manchester United tried hard to maintain a 1–0 lead, and a good result was looking promising for us until Schmeichel completely misjudged a cross and it was tucked away by Lee Chapman for the equalizer. All hell then broke loose, and my crews' radios were red hot with calls for assistance in the executive areas. Most fights and scuffles break out among the mass of fans in the stands but, that day, the action took place in an executive box rented by Leeds businessmen, who became over-excited when Leeds scored. The surrounding Manchester United fans in the area went crazy at hearing the enemy in their midst, and a scene of chaos ensued.

I sprinted to the executive area with three of my men and restored some kind of order, but got verbally abused by our own fans for doing our job with shouts of: 'What are those Leeds bastards doing in our section? Get them out!'

There was little point in trying to appease them. So I simply explained that they would all be thrown out of the ground if their antisocial behaviour continued and left two of my biggest guys on the door to discourage any further uprising.

During the 1991–2 season I met and befriended a lovely lady, Sheena Gibson, née Busby, the daughter of 'Mr Manchester United', the great Sir Matt. Sheena accompanied her father to matches at Old Trafford and guarded him with great care. It was my privilege to look after both of them on match days because it was difficult for him to walk more than two inches without being mobbed by the faithful. My new home was close to Sir Matt's house, and he and Sheena used to invite me round most Sunday mornings for tea and bacon sarnies, while I would sit enthralled at the stories this great man would tell.

As he regaled me with tales of the greats from the 1950s onwards, he would often smile and wave his finger knowingly when I questioned him on Alex Ferguson's ability to take Manchester United back to the heights that he had scaled in the 1960s.

'Ned, Alex Ferguson will take us to the top,' Sir Matt would say. 'He doesn't know any other way. He's single-minded for the team. He'll do the business, mark my words.'

At that time I was not so sure, but history would record that Sir Matt was as good at predicting as he was at managing. I'm proud to have known him, and have wonderful memories of my 'Sunday School lessons' with 'The Master'.

My socializing with the players was becoming a regular event now. I loved their company and banter, and they knew that, quite literally, I would take a bullet for them.

Most Sunday evenings I would get a call from Mike Profitt, the amicable owner of the Amblehurst Hotel, and best pal of Bryan Robson, asking me to round up the lads. 'A few of the boys are coming round to the hotel for a drink. Can you pick up Robbo and Viv Anderson, and maybe Neil Webb?' he would say.

I didn't need to be asked twice to go out on the piss with the players, so I would start to phone round. Calling Paul Ince was always tricky, because if his wife Claire answered the phone I would have to bend the truth somewhat, and say that Paul was needed immediately on some urgent business. She would have probably strangled me if she had known it was monkey business, not club business. I usually collected the lads and we'd start the session by having a few in the Amblehurst. A fleet of taxis would then take us into Hale to the Townhouse, the trendy bar of the time. It was normally crowded with queues at the door, even on a Sunday, but not for the players. They would be shown straight in, the owners fully aware of the publicity these stars would generate for the place.

Joining us in our revelry would be Kevin Moran, Norman Whiteside and, occasionally, Paul McGrath. Former United stars who had been hugely popular with the fans, Whiteside and McGrath had been cleared out of Old Trafford when Alex Ferguson decided to put paid to the drinking culture that had been part of the players' scene at the club even before the days of George Best. The lads could all put it away, especially Robbo, big Paul and Norman.

Being out on the town most Sundays with the players was wonderful for me because I still viewed them as celebrities, not guys I worked with. The biggest name among them all at that time was undoubtedly Bryan Robson. The public adored him. He was a real star, and though he could certainly shift the drink, he worked hard on the training pitch, and was never known to be the worse for wear while playing – unlike some of the others. In his later managerial career, I always thought that Bryan Robson ran Middlesbrough FC very well, albeit a little less strictly than the norm. He created a good team spirit, and Paul Gascoigne is said to have enjoyed his time under Bryan's stewardship of the club.

With the new season well under way, among the new faces was assistant manager Brian Kidd. He had replaced Archie Knox, who, at the end of April 1991, had left United to become assistant manager alongside Walter Smith at Rangers, Fergie's old club in his playing days, and a team that was then on the verge of great success in Scotland.

I was surprised that Knox had forsaken Fergie, his friend and mentor, especially just days before the European Cup-Winners' Cup final, but the lure of better pay and the idea of working for a club run by a dynamic businessman, David Murray, rather than a penny-pinching board, was perhaps too good an offer for Knox to turn down. At Old Trafford, the Kidd appointment looked like a marriage made in heaven at that time, but seven years later, it would all end in acrimonious divorce between him and Fergie.

In September 1991 we were preparing for our first defence of the European Cup-Winners' Cup against Athinaikos in Athens. It was prior to the start of this trip that I made my first totally out-of-character mistake as an employee of Manchester United, when, to my utmost shame, I slept in and missed the flight to Greece. A mad dash to London followed, as I rushed to catch the earliest available flight out of the UK. When I caught up with the squad at the hotel, my face redder than our strips, some of the players whom I saw first greeted me with a 'Ooh, you're in trouble, Ned.' They could have been right, but thankfully both Ken Ramsden and Ken Merrett saw the funny side of it, with Ken Merrett joking: 'We knew someone was missing, Ned. We just couldn't think who.'

I felt I had had a narrow escape, however, and I made a mental note to buy an extra alarm clock to avoid any similar nightmare scenarios in the future. It was a blessing that nothing disastrous had happened in my absence, or my career in the football security game might have come to a grinding halt right there and then.

The European fixture produced an uneventful 0–0 draw, which had not been helped by the fact that UEFA, in its wisdom, had decided that clubs could only field four foreign players in European competitions. For Manchester United in particular, this was outrageous, as the term 'foreign' included players from Scotland, Wales and Northern Ireland, so United could only play four from among its overseas stars and members of the large contingent of Scottish, Irish and Welsh players at the club.

In the League Cup we played Cambridge United and cruised to a 3–0 win, but they had a big lad, a striker, who caused us endless problems throughout the match. His name was Dion Dublin, and during the game Fergie pointed him out to me, and remarked, 'He's one to watch, Ned.'

Before the start of the next season, in August 1992, I was on the pitch talking to Keith Kent, the head groundsman, when Alex Ferguson walked out of the tunnel followed by a tall black guy and two club officials. Alex had the look of the cat who had got the cream.

'Here, Ned,' Alex Ferguson beckoned, and as I made my way over to his party he couldn't resist quipping: 'Getting some gardening tips, big man, eh?' knowing perfectly well that I had a flat.

'Only for the window boxes,' I replied.

'Ned, meet Dion Dublin. He's a Red now.'

I shook hands with Dion, welcomed him to Old Trafford, and recognized him as the big striker who had created so much trouble for us when we played Cambridge. Fergie had a filing cabinet of a mind when it came to spotting potential talent that he could use at a later date, and he certainly hadn't forgotten the talents of Dion Dublin in a hurry.

Having disposed of the Greek side 2–0 in the second leg at home, for the next round we were drawn away against Atletico Madrid, in October. This tie would be a real challenge for the team to face, but first we had Arsenal, the League champions, to contend with at Old Trafford, against whom we could only manage a 1–1 draw. During that particular League game, I was going about my usual match-day routine when Ken Merrett pulled me aside, and informed me: 'We don't need you to come to Madrid, Ned. We'll manage.'

I shrugged, in an attempt to seem outwardly indifferent to his surprising decision. Unfortunately, in the absence of lucky Ned Kelly, United went down to a crashing 3–0 defeat in Spain. The return leg at Old Trafford, thirteen days later, produced a 1–1 draw, which confirmed that United were well and truly out of the competition we had won the previous season.

There was still some European business to finish, however. The Super Cup was contested by the winners of the European Cup and the European Cup-Winners' Cup, which meant that we were due to play the Yugoslavian champions Red Star Belgrade. Owing to the unrest in that troubled part of the world, UEFA decreed that it was unsafe for the Super Cup to proceed on the usual two-legged basis, so a one-off final was staged at Old Trafford in November 1991. In front of a disappointingly small crowd of 22,000, United beat Red Star 1–0 thanks to a Brian McClair goal. It was a third European trophy for the club, and the second time Fergie had won the Super Cup, having lifted it at Aberdeen against Hamburg in 1983.

After the Super Cup match, United embarked on a solid run in the League, which was to be the basis of a serious challenge for the title. The team was similarly successful in the League Cup, culminating in another trip to Wembley for the final on 12 April.

Our opponents were Nottingham Forest, managed by a true legend of English football, the inimitable Brian Clough. Victory by a single goal gave United the League Cup for the first time in the club's history, but it was to be small consolation for what would prove to be a disappointing end to our promising League campaign.

Heading into the second half of April, with just five games to go, we were two points clear of Leeds United with a game in hand over them. I couldn't help but believe that the long wait for the League title would shortly be over. But with the Old Trafford pitch in a poor state and the team crippled by injuries, United fell at the final hurdle. The club was not helped by the intransigence of the Football League, which refused to re-schedule their fixture list so that United were required to play five games in eleven days. Even for the mighty Reds, this was a feat of Herculean proportions and was ultimately beyond them.

In the meantime, a 1–1 draw with Luton was followed by the visit of Brian Clough's Nottingham Forest on Easter Monday. I have always been a great admirer of Cloughie, and was looking forward to his visit, even though Forest were intent on taking revenge for the League Cup final defeat.

After the game, which we lost 2–1, the Nottingham Forest coach was ready to leave but the Forest manager was nowhere to be seen. I was asked to go and find him, and I duly discovered him huddled in a corner of the away-team dressing room. He looked appalling, and was clearly very ill. I told him that the team bus was waiting outside, but it was obvious that the level of alcohol consumed that day had taken its toll. I was greatly saddened to see this wreck of a man make his way falteringly to the coach. It was no surprise to me that Clough's drinking eventually destroyed his health, and led to a much-needed liver transplant.

From being well within our reach, the League title slipped agonizingly away from our grasp. Leeds United, inspired by former United hero Gordon Strachan and a team that contained a certain Frenchman by the name of Eric Cantona, clinched the title. At Anfield, following a 2–0 defeat against Liverpool, it was heartbreaking to see the banners on the Kop proclaiming; 'Twenty-five years and you still can't win it'.

After the match, I was enjoying a drink with former Liverpool hero and television pundit Ian St John, who said to me ruefully, 'Ned, if you want to win a League title, you have to win your home games, and you lost the title against Notts Forest.' I was too choked to answer.

It was a long and despairing drive back along the M62 to Manchester. I couldn't believe that we had come so close to winning the championship, only to throw it away in the last few games.

In the VIP suites after the final game of the season, I had a drink with Martin Edwards, who rather unconvincingly suggested that if the League had only thirty-eight matches instead of forty-two, United would have won the title. In a philosophical mood, I replied: 'If your auntie had balls, she'd be your uncle. But anyway, Chairman, remember what Scarlett O'Hara used to say – "Tomorrow is another day".'

After a series of futile attempts to cheer up the chairman at this disappointing time, I finished my drink and went home desolate.

The first taste of success: Accompanying the FA Cup-winning team back to Manchester in May 1990 was an exciting moment for me; for Alex Ferguson it was to be the first of many cup and championship title victories as manager of the Reds.

TO:
ACTING STAFF SERGEANT
MICHAEL THOMAS KELLY
THE SPECIAL AIR SERVICE REGIMENT

On behalf of the Army Board I write to thank you for the contribution you have made to the Army and for all that you have done during your 22 years' loyal service.

You have had to take your share of the arduous duties and difficult challenges which the British Army is so often called upon to undertake and you may justly claim to have played your part in upholding its highest traditions and fostering loyalty and pride in your unit, your Regiment and in the Army as a whole.

In sending you my thanks, I also take this opportunity to wish you good fortune and happiness in the future.

ADJUTANT GENERAL

Who Dares Wins: After receiving my honourable discharge certificate (*left*), I could look back on a proud career in the Army and SAS.

Visits from Bobby Charlton (*pictured below in May 1985*) and other Manchester United dignitaries, who came to present numerous awards to my successful football team, made my time at Hereford even more memorable.

To Ned.

Many thanks for a great day.
Bobby Charlton Man U.F.C.

In June 1988, Alex Ferguson was guest speaker at the annual end-of-season dinner held in the Sergeant's Mess at the SAS barracks in Hereford, which was my last dinner in charge of the football team.

In October 1990, at the Piccadilly Hotel, Manchester, members of the Manchester United team celebrated at a dinner held in honour of their 1990 FA Cup victory. While I hung on to the trophy, those seated were (*from left to right*): Freddie Pye (former vice-chairman of Manchester City), Bryan Robson, Lee Sharpe, Archie Knox and Alex Ferguson.

Eric Cantona – hero

Eric signed for the Reds in November 1992 (*below*) from local rivals Leeds United for £1 million.

Over his four-and-a-half-year career at United, Eric developed into one of Alex Ferguson's most prized assets – competitive, skilful, fiery, he had the ability and determination to change the fortunes of any game to the Reds' advantage (*right*).

Accolades a-plenty: Helping United to four Premier League titles during his career at Old Trafford, Eric raises the championship trophy in May 1996 (*far left*). In the 1994 FA Cup Final, Eric proved his worth, scoring two goals in the 4–0 victory over Chelsea at Wembley (*right*).

Eric Cantona – villain

After a sending-off against Crystal Palace in January 1995, the red mist descended upon Eric in his confrontation with Palace fan Matthew Simmons (*above*).

As a consequence of his pitchside outburst, Eric faced an FA disciplinary hearing at the Sopwell House Hotel in St Albans. After I had driven him there from London, we were greeted by a massive press presence, and met by Fergie, who accompanied him into the meeting.

Although Eric was initially sentenced to two weeks' imprisonment for his kung-fu attack on the Palace fan, on appeal, at Croydon Crown Court, his punishment was reduced to 120 hours of community service. I felt relieved to be able to lead him away from the courthouse a free man.

At the press conference that was held following his successful appeal, Eric baffled journalists with the enigmatic remark: 'When the seagulls follow the trawler it is because they think sardines will be thrown into the sea.'

Living legend: It was one of my greatest honours to be acquainted with and provide security for the legendary Sir Matt Busby, pictured here with me in April 1990.

Divided we stand: During my time with the club, I felt there was a degree of paranoia and mistrust among certain board members, particularly as far as Martin Edwards was concerned. Pictured in March 2000 (*from left to right*) – Professor Sir Roland Smith (chairman of the plc board), David Gill (finance director), Martin Edwards (club chairman) and Peter Kenyon (deputy chief executive).

CHAPTER 6

The Shape of Things to Come

IT IS NOT DIFFICULT TO CONVEY THE MOOD inside Old Trafford at that time. Cups were all very well, but United needed to lay the demons to rest and win the League. We all felt it, from boardroom and manager's office to boot room and turnstile, from corporate suites to the fans at the back of the stands.

The United side of Manchester spent the summer praying that, perhaps, this season we could be victorious in the League. The diehards among us had found some football solace in the performance of the youth team which had won the FA Youth Cup in sensational fashion, and the future looked rosy if only we could win the elusive League title.

There had been an incident at Easter, at a time when a number of crucial League games had to be played and won, when Ryan Giggs and Lee Sharpe found themselves in terrible trouble with Fergie over their attendance at a party, to which a lot of the younger players had been invited. It was a pity for them that the manager arrived on the scene before me because he gave them the full Fergie fury treatment – known as the 'hairdryer' because of the hot blast he could produce – while I would have just packed them off to bed. He gave them a roasting, and while it was a lesson that Giggsy largely learned, Lee Sharpe would decide not to heed the warning. But after that night all the youngsters understood what standards were expected of them and how the manager would react if these standards were not reached.

In a highly physical encounter at Bramall Lane, we kicked off the 1992–3 season against Sheffield United and lost 2–1. After this battle royal, I escorted the players back on to the team coach while Barry Davies, the BBC sports commentator, tried to reassure me: 'Not too much to worry about, Ned. It'll get better.'

'I can't agree, Barry. I've got that feeling of doom already,' I replied.

We fared even worse at our next home game, against Everton, and were thrashed 3–0. After the match I went to the Amblehurst Hotel to drown my sorrows with Steve Bruce and Gary Pallister. The mood was black. I allowed my emotions and frustrations to get muddled up with my lack of expertise, and I blurted out, 'We're never going to win this fucking League. There's no hunger amongst our players . . .'

The shared look of anger I received from Steve and Gary almost turned me to stone.

'So now you're a fucking expert on football, are you?' blasted Steve, who then proceeded to tear me apart further. 'I've been longer in the toilet than you've been in the game.'

I felt certain that Gary would have done the same if only he could have got a word in edgeways. I felt terrible for having opened my big mouth. What gave me the right to lash out at a great pair of players like Steve and Gary? If I could have found a stone big enough, I would have crawled under it at that moment in time.

'Come on, Gary, we're off,' said Steve, with a nod to his team-mate, and the pair left me standing there like the idiot I was. I never forgot that embarrassing episode, and the next time I met up with them I immediately offered them profuse apologies. They were both great about it, however, and Steve even admitted, laughing: 'As it happens, Ned, we *were* shite.'

Gary bought the drinks and, much to my relief, we were all pals again.

Gary in particular was a larger-than-life character. A down-to-earth bloke, he was a great defender, but would be the first to admit he was the doyen of training dodgers. In fact Fergie had, a number of times, accused him of being too laid back. Gary had immense respect for his manager, except for one occasion, when, after a defeat on the pitch, Fergie blasted him in front of his team-mates, blaming the defender for the fact that the team had lost the match. Not surprisingly, Gary felt aggrieved at being made to take complete responsibility for being beaten, and he called Fergie over the weekend to arrange a meeting to discuss it on the following Monday. Although Gary had been ready for a showdown, the manager apologized to him immediately, and as far as Gary was concerned, the matter was resolved.

The 1992–3 season marked the start of the new Premier League. It was much more than just a revamp of Football League Division One, as BSkyB's millions would change the game for ever. The revolution took place under the guidance of Rick Parry, the Premier League's new chief executive. It was a period of change for every club, and the Manchester United board were determined to be in the forefront of English football's new era.

Not every move was popular. The government's demand for all-seated stadia after the Hillsborough disaster saw United implement a very major building programme that involved tearing down the famous Stretford end.

The forward-thinking Rick Parry had broken the mould with the new TV package that put BSkyB in pole position with the rights to the lion's share of matches. The BBC still had its highlights programme *Match of the Day*, while ITV secured the rights to broadcast the FA Cup, but the satellite channel was temporarily the king of the airwaves.

I had worked alongside various television crews for years with no problems, disputes or attitudes – with a single exception, when on one occasion I saw a camera technician repairing his equipment in the goalmouth at Old Trafford, only four hours before kick-off. I couldn't believe that this idiot was scattering his spare tools and equipment all over the playing area, when behind the goal there was enough room in which to build the *QE2*.

'Excuse me. Move your tools, please,' I asked him, politely. 'The players will be rolling around here in an hour or two. Use a bit of common sense.'

'When I'm finished, mate,' he replied, without giving me a glance.

As politeness was obviously wasted on him, I decided on a more forceful approach: 'If you don't move yourself and your equipment now, I'll have you out of this stadium before your feet have touched the ground.'

He now took the trouble to look round, and though he must have realized that his 5-feet-7-inch, 10-stone frame would come off a poor second to my 6-feet-4-inch, 18-stone build, he still couldn't resist arguing.

'We pay millions to be in here; we can do what we like,' he snarled.

He had been given ample warning, and because he had made no attempt to move, I had little alternative but to march him, his camera and his tools up the players' tunnel where they were all dumped on the steps of his outside-broadcast unit. Within minutes I was surrounded by an assortment of apologizing producers, directors and commentators, who were all now fearful of having to watch the match from the stands. I thought it prudent to inform Ken Ramsden of my confrontation with the technician, and went up to the directors' office to discuss the matter with him. Ken backed me up completely, and told the TV guys never to put anything on the pitch again. It was a relief to have had the backing of the board, as I could just imagine the furore if Peter Schmeichel, when diving for a ball, had ended up with a piece of camera equipment jammed in his kneecap.

Though our form was showing little sign of improvement, new boy Dion Dublin was looking good. It seemed as though the club's failure to sign England's top striker, Alan Shearer, during the summer would soon be forgotten. In the dressing room, however, the talk was not of our current form or, indeed, Dion Dublin's goals. The chat was all about the proportions of Dion's member, which, according to the players was the size of a baby's arm, prompting Alex Ferguson to joke: 'No way that man could wear a kilt!'

Dion took the banter well, but Steve Bruce summed it up best: 'It's like a tin of Vim with a Jaffa orange on the end of it. Don't let my wife see that, for God's sake.'

As a young man, Dion once had a landlady who became very intrigued by local gossip regarding the size of his manhood. One day, curiosity got the better of her, and she went into Dion's room, while he was sleeping, and slipped her fingers under the duvet. Suffice it to say, she discovered a lot more than the hot-water bottle.

A few games into the season, Dion broke his leg and was out for the rest of the campaign. He never really recovered from that unlucky start to his Old Trafford career, and by September 1994 he had moved on to Coventry City. Football can be a cruel game, but at least Dion had something to fall forward on . . .

As well as continuing to fare badly in the Premier League, we also went out of Europe in the first round of the UEFA Cup. The first leg of the tie against Torpedo Moscow saw us disadvantaged once again by the four-player restriction on foreign players. Schmeichel had to be dropped and we just couldn't score any goals. The match ended 0–0. Not surprisingly, Fergie was desperate to sign an English striker – any English striker, it seemed.

It appeared that I was out of favour with Ken Merrett, and was told my services were not required for the return leg in Moscow, but as a true Red, I travelled with the troops this time. I found Moscow a depressing place, even worse than Poland, which I would have never thought possible. The weather didn't help matters, as it rained from the moment we arrived until the second we left, but the football was dire too, culminating in a 0–0 draw and then on to penalties. It was a wet and bedraggled Gary Pallister who sent us crashing out of Europe when he missed his spot kick. It had been a dismal end to a dismal trip, but it had been an important lesson for me to see things from the fans' point of view.

I had been talking to Fergie about the team's form (but was careful not to give an opinion, having learned my lesson) when he suggested giving the squad a break, organizing something different for them to do; not a holiday, more of a diversion.

I suggested that I try to arrange a team outing down to the SAS barracks in Hereford for an 'awayday', and Fergie laughed: 'You're kidding, Ned. Do you think the SAS would have you back, even for a day?'

Ignoring his cheek, I thought it was worth a try, so I rushed to my office to make some calls. Eventually I got hold of the camp's RSM, a great guy whom I'll refer to as Billy X. I explained the situation, reminding Billy of all the kindness shown to us by the Manchester United guys over the years, and he replied: 'Well, we had the English rugby team here recently, so I don't see why there would be a problem. Let me check it out and I'll call you right back.'

I told Alex Ferguson that we were in with a chance, and he asked me a favour: 'Try to make it a Monday, then it won't get in the way of training and matches too much.'

Billy phoned me back with the great news that he had been given the green light from the powers that be, so we agreed that Monday 19 October 1992 would be the day of the 'Great Reds Invasion' of the SAS HQ at Hereford. I sorted out the logistics of the trip with Fergie, and it was decided that we would all meet at the Four Seasons Hotel in Manchester on the Monday morning at half-past eight. There were more than a few wails of dissent at this 'early kick-off', but if the Boss said they were to be there, they would have to be there.

Fergie decided to follow the team coach in his own car and Brian Kidd, his assistant, joined him. Norman Davies, the kit man, travelled with Danny McGregor, head of the commercial department, in another car, and the motorcade headed south. Peter Schmeichel, Bryan Robson and Lee Sharpe could not travel with us, as they were back at Old Trafford, receiving medical treatment for various injuries.

Former player Norman Whiteside asked me if he could come along, and so I told him to clear it with Fergie. He was reluctant to approach the Boss directly, so I asked the question on Norman's behalf, and was pleased to tell him that he could join us on the jaunt. On arrival at Stirling Lines, the formal name of the SAS headquarters, we passed through the gates, and were led to the car park area. It felt strange to be returning to this place that had been such a big part of my life for many years.

After eating lunch in the cookhouse, we were directed to the briefing room, where the SAS lads explained what lay ahead for the unsuspecting celebrities. First of all, the United players were briefed on the regiment's history, and its wonderful achievements, and then there was a sharp intake of breath from all, and a few worried looks appeared on the guests' faces, as Billy announced ominously to them: 'Right. Now let's go to the Killing House!'

The Killing House is a building where the SAS practise hostage rescue, room clearance and, if necessary, the killing of terrorists. The United squad were to play the part of the hostages, while my former colleagues were to burst in and rescue them. There was considerable apprehension in the Manchester ranks as the SAS boys revealed they only ever trained with live ammunition.

I shot a quick look around the room and saw a few faces that looked as though they would have been happier lying on the Old Trafford treatment table alongside Bryan Robson and Co. The boys all survived their 'rescue', however, and then it was on to the shooting ranges, where they were all given a variety of weapons to shoot at targets. The results were interesting to say the least. Gary Pallister was easily the best shot, while Brian McClair appeared to me a little uneasy on the trip. I felt that perhaps his days with Celtic, and their strong Irish ties, made him a little uncomfortable in the 'home' of the SAS.

Next was the helicopter ride and, with fortuitous timing, Fergie received a phone call reminding him of a dinner that evening where he was expected to make a speech, so he made his apologies and headed back to Manchester, leaving a nervous-looking Brian Kidd in charge. The boys all enjoyed their bird's-eye view of the Herefordshire countryside, while I left it until last to take my turn and joined Ryan Giggs and Paul Ince in the chopper.

The pilot gave me a knowing smile as we lifted off. I didn't know if he wanted to test me, and see if my bottle was still up to SAS standard or whether he just wanted to give two of Britain's best players a heart attack, but in any event, after giving us the tourist-trap tour, the heartless bastard then cut the engines. The helicopter plummeted earthwards at a tremendous speed. After 350 parachute jumps and countless similar free-falls in choppers, I'd seen it all before, but Paul Ince froze, and Ryan Giggs looked as if he had been dead for a fortnight. The pilot was smiling maniacally at this point, and I sincerely hoped the engines would fire up again or we would all be in terrible trouble. Still, at least death would have spared me from explaining to Alex Ferguson how I had lost £20 million-worth of players on a day trip. During the frightening episode, Paul Ince squeezed my hand so hard, I swear I thought he had broken it. Seconds later, the pilot fired the chopper up again and we landed safely, the nightmare over.

After the death-defying helicopter stunt, the players and I moved on to a nearby pub to steady our shattered nerves. While the ale was flowing, word soon spread that some of the Manchester United team were in town, and after a while, groups of kids began to arrive at the pub in the hope of meeting their footballing heroes. The lads dutifully signed autographs for the youngsters, before heading back to the camp for the evening meal, where they enjoyed a fantastic buffet banquet. The players had a great time chatting to the SAS guys who had turned up, swapping footballing stories for SAS tales of derring-do.

We stayed overnight at the barracks, nursed very sore heads in the morning, and after breakfast, said our goodbyes to Billy and the wonderful guys at Stirling Lines, Hereford. They had all been magnificent and treated us like royalty.

Brian Kidd informed us that Fergie wanted everyone back at Old Trafford on our return to Manchester, as a team photograph had been arranged for midday. Alex was waiting for us on our arrival, and we all walked towards him thinking how smart and refreshed we looked. Alex took one look at the lot of us and barked to Norman Davies, the kit manager, 'Run the bath, Norman. The guys look terrible.'

A spick, span and shining Manchester United team duly lined up for the photograph session half an hour later, none the worse for their trip to Hereford.

The next day the team was focused once again on League business, unaware that Manchester United Football Club was about to enter a new phase in its long and varied history, following a development that would ensure that the club's rise over the next few years would not be so much rollercoaster as meteoric.

In late November 1992 I was having my normal midweek security briefing with Ken Ramsden, where I received specific instructions for the forthcoming games. We broke up the meeting at around 1.00 p.m. and I decided to have lunch in the Red Grill Room in the South Stand at Old Trafford. On my way to the bar to order my meal, I noticed Alex Ferguson with a group of people. The ever-hospitable Alex called me over: 'Ned, I want you to meet Eric Cantona. Eric, this is Ned Kelly, our head of security."

'Nice to meet you,' smiled Eric.

'And you, Eric,' I replied.

While I ate my lunch, Alex, Eric, Martin Edwards, Maurice Watkins and Eric's interpreter left the bar and moved to a table in the far corner of the room. Danny McGregor joined me at my table, and so I asked him what was going on.

'Eric Cantona joined us from Leeds United this morning for a million pounds,' Danny revealed.

'That's strange,' I replied. 'Alex never mentioned it when he introduced me.'

'I think they're working on personal terms now,' said Danny. 'You know what Alex is like. It's never done until it's done.'

'True enough,' I agreed. As far as I was concerned, nobody knew more about transfer deals than the Boss.

The rumours were that Leeds United chief executive Bill Fotherby had called Martin Edwards and asked him if Manchester United were interested in selling Denis Irwin. Fotherby was given short shrift. Fergie had been standing alongside Edwards while he was on the phone, and he wrote down on a piece of paper that Edwards should ask about Eric Cantona. The Frenchman had displayed elements of amazing skill playing for Leeds in their title-winning season, but despite having been part of a successful team, Fergie had got the impression that Cantona was unsettled at the Yorkshire club. Fotherby said he would ask the Leeds manager Howard Wilkinson about Cantona, and so when Wilko said they might be interested in selling the player, Fergie was quick to make his interest known.

Eric undoubtedly had a reputation for his fiery temper. He made his first-team debut for Auxerre in 1983, before moving on to the then giants of French football, Olympique Marseille, in June 1988. Unfortunately, after making some insulting remarks on television about the French coach Henri Michel, Eric was banned from the national side by the French FA. When he was substituted in a match against Torpedo Moscow, in January 1989, he tore off his jersey in a fit of dissent, and duly received a suspension from his club. After a spell on loan to Bordeaux, Eric signed for Montpellier in July 1989 and received yet another suspension – lasting ten days – for fighting a team-mate in the dressing room. He moved to Nîmes in 1991, becoming club captain, but following an incident in which he threw the ball at a referee during a match, he faced another French FA disciplinary committee, where he received a one-month ban; a punishment which was doubled to two months after he called each member of the committee an 'idiot' to their faces. Eric retired from French football in December 1991, seemingly in a fit of pique.

Not long after, he was persuaded to move to England, where Sheffield Wednesday initially offered him a trial. However, the South Yorkshire side were beaten to his signature by Leeds United, who got in ahead of their local rivals on 31 January 1992. In his first season with them, he played a small but significant part in helping the club to win its first Division One championship title since 1974.

Eric's feisty temper was still very much in evidence on the pitch in England – he was constantly in trouble with English referees – but Fergie clearly believed he could manage that aspect of Eric, and felt it was worth taking a chance on the volatile player, to have his skills available for the good of the club.

Prior to the purchase and transfer of Cantona, Fergie had offered the Sheffield Wednesday manager, Trevor Francis, £3 million for striker David Hirst, by fax. Wrongly assuming that United's manager was taking him for a mug, Francis took this as a personal insult, and so declined the offer. If Francis hadn't reacted negatively to the offer, and Fergie had bought Hirst, I couldn't help but wonder whether he would have had the money to afford Cantona as well. Would he even have considered buying the man who, more than any other player, inspired United's rise to fortune in the 1990s?

At the time of my first meeting with Eric Cantona, I could never have imagined how important he would become to the Old Trafford faithful, nor indeed had I any idea of how close I would become to Eric and his family.

Cantona made his Manchester United debut against Benfica in a tribute match for their greatest-ever player, Eusebio, the famous 'Black Pearl of Europe'. In his League debut at Old Trafford, he came on to the pitch as a substitute in a derby game on 6 December 1992, and scored the first of his many vital goals against Chelsea at Stamford Bridge two weeks later, ensuring an important 1–1 draw.

On the social scene at this time, Viv Anderson, one of the funniest guys in and around any dressing room, who had left Manchester United to join Sheffield Wednesday two years previously, was one of the regulars on our Sunday night jaunts. Fergie used to quip that he only bought Viv from Arsenal for his joking and fooling around which, he felt, lifted the atmosphere in the squad. He was still a character at Sheffield, and when he came to Manchester for our nights out, he would often bring along Danny Wilson, Chris Waddle and David Hirst. The Wednesday boys were always welcome on our Sundays.

Another of my drinking buddies, Kevin Moran, was a former United player who, after eighteen months playing in Spain with Sporting Gijon, had recently returned to England to join Blackburn. I'd always had a good rapport with Kevin and I remembered well the story of his parting shot to Alex Ferguson as he was preparing to move to Spain in 1988. Fergie had given Kevin a free transfer in recognition of his services to United, a 'free' being one way in which a player could be rewarded for his services, as it meant he could negotiate his own signing-on fee. In a rare moment of indecision, Fergie had said in an aside to Kevin, 'I don't know whether to sell you or not now.'

'Better make your fucking mind up quick, because I fly to Spain tonight,' Kevin pointed out, jokily.

It was one of the few occasions that I heard of Alex Ferguson being trumped verbally. Kevin was also a players' man and was especially helpful to David Hirst when he was intent on leaving Sheffield Wednesday, advising him that he should never let the fans know that he wanted to leave, 'Otherwise they'll crucify you from the stands.'

On one of our nights out, David Hirst confided in me that he'd always dreamed of playing for Manchester United, and being an ex-Barnsley player, he would have become only the second footballer in the English game to join United with the same Barnsley origins. The first was the legendary Busby Babe, Tommy Taylor, who tragically lost his life in the Munich plane disaster in 1958.

When David Hirst retired from football in January 2000, the press asked if he had any regrets and he said he had only one: the fact that he had never worn the red shirt of Manchester United.

In the second half of the season, League business was the club's number-one priority. Alex Ferguson had moulded Manchester United into a confident, attacking team, and all around the stadium I was sure that the fans sensed a wind of change.

At our game on 6 February against Sheffield United at Old Trafford, the crowd and players observed a minute's silence for the Busby Babes who died in the 1958 air disaster in Munich. Gone but not forgotten might be a much overused cliché but, at Old Trafford, they will always mourn the young men who died in the plane crash in Germany.

We beat the Blades 2–1, and two days later we faced a tough away game at Leeds. It is never easy for a player to return to his former club in opposition colours, and I knew that Eric would be given a difficult time by the crowd. Prior to the match I shadowed him every minute, especially in the Holiday Inn where the team were lunching before the game. During the 0–0 draw with Leeds, Eric was subjected to relentless abuse, and foolishly, he was seen to spit in the direction of a Leeds fan, which later resulted in a £1,000 fine by the FA, a portent of greater trouble ahead.

After exiting from the FA Cup, following a 2–1 revenge defeat by Sheffield United, it was time to put all our energies into winning the League. In April, as the season neared its end, the home game against our bogey team, Sheffield Wednesday, took on huge significance. In the best tradition of encounters between the two sides, the Yorkshire side won a penalty and went one goal up. Despite a barrage of attacks on the Wednesday goal, their keeper, Chris Woods, stood firm, and we retired to the dressing room at half-time with our heads down.

My drinking buddy, and Wednesday midfielder, Danny Wilson, had been substituted midway through the second half, and was leaning over the dugout wall chatting to me: 'Trevor Francis is desperate to win this, Ned, to fuck Ferguson's title challenge.'

'Well, fuck Trevor Francis, Danny,' I replied, in defence of my beloved team. 'It's not over until that whistle blows.'

With only minutes to go Steve Bruce headed home a cracker to bring us level at 1–1. Earlier in the second half, the referee had pulled up with a muscle problem in his leg, and had to be substituted by his linesman, which meant that eight minutes of injury time was due to be played at the end of the ninety minutes, to compensate for the time lost during the change of officials. Once again it was a Steve Bruce header that changed our fortunes, and we were winning 2–1. With the exception of the visitors' end, the whole of Old Trafford erupted. Thanks to Aston Villa's draw at Coventry, we had overtaken them and were now top of the League with only five games remaining. Alex Ferguson and Brian Kidd ran on to the pitch – Kidd did an insane dance of delight – and there were tears in everyone's eyes. Although our lead was slim, we could not help but get excited at the thought of winning the first Premier League championship.

Subsequent United victories over Coventry, Chelsea and Crystal Palace meant that if Aston Villa lost their home match against Oldham on the following Sunday, then Manchester United would be the League Champions for the first time in twenty-six years.

While we were waiting for the dice to roll in our favour, I was called to a very strange briefing by Ken Ramsden and Ken Merrett, which I couldn't help but think might be tempting fate.

'Ned, we need to discuss the collection of the new Premier League Cup from the jewellers, Garrard & Co. in London, as well as all the players' medals,' said Ken Ramsden. 'We need them at Old Trafford on the Friday before the final home game against Blackburn on Monday.'

I was surprised and honoured. This was quite a responsibility, and it would be a great thrill to handle the silverware before the named champions. However, I was worried that making such arrangements could be a bit premature, as Aston Villa was still in a position to take the title if they won all their remaining matches and we dropped points.

'We're merely acting upon the FA's instructions, Ned,' added Merrett. 'That's the way they want it done and you are the man for the job.'

Technically it was true that Manchester United looked more likely to win the League than Aston Villa, but until it was confirmed beyond all possible doubt I still wouldn't let myself believe it.

In accordance with FA orders, I drove down to London with one of my staff and presented myself at Garrard & Co. On arrival, I was ushered into a side room while a TV programme called *Standing Room Only* was filmed, which the FA had produced, to promote the new Premier League. Eventually, when filming was finally complete, I was able to take possession of the trophy and medals, load them into the car, and dash back to Manchester.

When I arrived at the ground, Ken Ramsden and I were seen by the press as we unloaded the precious silverware. We locked the goods up in the Manchester United safe and said our goodnights, arranging to meet up on the Monday for the Blackburn Rovers game.

On Sunday the tabloids were covered with pictures of Ken and me taking the new Premier League Cup into Old Trafford, and later that day we received confirmation that in fact we hadn't been presumptuous in picking up the trophy from London. To the shock and sheer delight of all the Old Trafford faithful, on Sunday afternoon Oldham Athletic had beaten our title-race rivals Aston Villa, making Manchester United champions of the new Premier League. It was official.

Fergie heard the news on a golf course in Cheshire, having been unable to watch the Villa match on television because of the unbearable tension. On the seventeenth hole a complete stranger ran up and told him the result, and then the victory jig began. I knew how he felt, for when the final whistle went I was dancing around my flat with joy. All the doubters had been silenced and we were back where we belonged – at the top. My phone didn't stop ringing, as everyone involved at the club was phoning everyone else to congratulate each other. Then Ken Ramsden called: 'Ned, get down here fast. Fans are coming in droves.'

I couldn't wait to see our faithful supporters enjoy their moment, and was in the car in seconds. When I arrived at Old Trafford it was like a match day. Those great fans had waited twenty-six long years for this day. The whole jamboree passed off peacefully and without incident, with the masses of fans singing their hearts out. It was an incredible and unforgettable sight to behold. Only one over-enthusiastic supporter climbed on to the roof to show his delight. I just waved him down but I actually felt like climbing up there beside him and waving a Manchester United scarf myself.

The majority of players had gone to Steve Bruce's house to celebrate. They were wise to stay away from the ground because their shirts, socks and Y-fronts would doubtless have been ripped from their bodies and taken as souvenirs.

On the Monday morning Ken Merrett called me and told me that huge crowds were gathering outside the ground once again, filling the forecourt and chanting Alex Ferguson's name. 'Get at least twelve men down here, Ned, will you?' said Ken urgently. 'Alex is due to arrive in the next hour and when he does, God knows what will happen.'

An hour later, I positioned myself amidst the throng of excitable supporters, along with fifteen of my men, ready for the inevitable hysteria. When Alex and the players began to arrive the mood reached fever pitch. We had to dig the manager and various team members out of the crowd of backslapping well-wishers, but there were no troublemakers, and the fans were just happy to be there to share the historic occasion. As the crowds subsided, the next step was to prepare for the evening match against Blackburn and the official presentation, which would be a moment to savour for every Manchester United fan.

Playing the penultimate match of the season as champions we beat Blackburn 3–1. The founding chief executive of the Premier League, Rick Parry, stepped up to present the cup and winners' medals to the team, and the noise grew deafening as the boys lined up for their awards. Fergie had decided that both Bryan Robson and Steve Bruce should receive the cup together, which provoked the shedding of tears of joy around the ground. However, in the midst of the overwhelming celebrations, I noticed another side of Fergie at this time. His mood darkened when he saw the players wearing baseball caps emblazoned with the logo of a company completely unrelated to Manchester United or the club's sponsors.

'Who gave them those fucking hats?' he asked Norman Davies, the kit man.

'Dunno,' he replied, sheepishly.

'Oh, I did,' piped up Jim McGregor, the physiotherapist. 'I should have run it past you, Boss.'

Fergie just glared. I didn't know whether it had anything to do with the cap incident, but when Jim's contract came up for renewal some time later, and he was called in to discuss his future with the board, he was told his services would no longer be required.

In the manager's office there was a great tide of emotion as Denis Law, Norman Whiteside and George Best, all lost in Manchester United euphoria, offered Fergie heartfelt congratulations on this unique day in the history of the club.

Our last game of the season was against Wimbledon and we travelled to London to play before a capacity crowd packed with Reds supporters. We won 2–1, and at the final whistle, Fergie told Steve Bruce and Bryan Robson to do a lap of honour with the Premier League cup to let the London-based Manchester United fans have a look at the trophy. Both Steve and Bryan were happy to make this gesture but only if I accompanied them around the track.

'Is that OK with you, Ned?' asked Fergie.

'I'd do it in the nude, Boss,' I replied.

So we re-entered the stadium, and when Steve and Bryan held up their prize, the fans instantly went wild. Our progress around the pitch was hampered by the battalions of press photographers who built a human obstacle course ahead of us, retreating a yard at a time. It became impossible to make much headway and I could sense that the now static duo might become a target for the throng of well-wishers who could see that their heroes were only a short jump away. I didn't feel comfortable, knowing that if just five or ten of the fans came on to the pitch, the hordes would follow, and could inadvertently cause serious injury to the two players.

'Let's go back, lads. This is dangerous,' I shouted above the din.

Both players had realized that I was uneasy about the way this situation was developing, so they nodded in agreement, waved goodbye and went back inside the stadium building, all three of us exhilarated by the experience, but relieved to be back in the safety of the dressing room.

CHAPTER 7

The Road Ahead

IN THE CLOSE SEASON, Alex Ferguson made one of the most important buys of his career. The Nottingham Forest and Ireland star Roy Keane had signalled that he was ready for a transfer, and the ever-astute Fergie knew that this was an opportunity not to be missed.

Roy had been in talks with former Liverpool manager Kenny Dalglish about joining his revived Blackburn Rovers outfit, and it had looked certain that Ewood Park was where his footballing future lay. Kenny and Roy met up at a Lancashire hotel and, after almost agreeing terms, Kenny drove him to the Blackburn ground with a view to signing him there and then. It was a Friday afternoon, and when Kenny arrived at the club secretary's office, intending to pick up the signing-on forms for Roy, he discovered that the secretary had already left for the day. Instead Roy agreed to return to the club the following Monday to tie up the deal, and parted company with Kenny, who naturally thought the deal was more or less done.

Things were not destined to go Kenny Dalglish's way, however, as Fergie had got wind of the talks between the Blackburn manager and the Forest player, and managed to contact Roy Keane on Friday night. The pair agreed to meet at Old Trafford the next morning. Anxious not to make the same mistake as Kenny, Fergie also rang Ken Merrett on Friday evening and told him to go to Old Trafford immediately to ensure they had the relevant forms for Roy to sign the next day.

Fergie and Roy instantly hit it off. They agreed terms and the Boss signed him on the spot. After a hastily arranged medical at the Cliff training ground, an hour or two later, Fergie's swiftness of thought had paid off – Roy was now a Red.

Dalglish heard about the astonishing developments on Saturday night and, not surprisingly, he exploded at both losing out on the services of Roy Keane and being trumped by Fergie. Kenny phoned Roy at 6 o'clock on Sunday morning and, according to the player, began to rant and rave at him, vowing that he would never kick a ball again. The tirade was far from unexpected from a manager who had been so soundly outmanoeuvred, but Roy was unperturbed, as he had got what he wanted and was content. His response was characteristically short and to the point; he mentioned to me much later how he had simply told Kenny to fuck off, and hung up on him. Without a shadow of a doubt, Roy Keane is a man of few words, but he makes them count, as the former Republic of Ireland manager, Mick McCarthy, will confirm.

Roy always had that wonderful edge of danger to him, which I often thought was what made him so ruthlessly competitive. Women found his brooding, dark good looks irresistible and, before he married his wife, Theresa, Roy had a major fling with a gorgeous young trainee lawyer who hung around the trendier bars in Wilmslow. John Barnes, the Liverpool star, was dating her friend. At that time, in the north-west of England, it was open season on footballers as far as girls were concerned.

Working alongside him over the years, I noticed that Roy could explode at the smallest thing, and I used to joke that even an imagined slight was real enough as long as Roy imagined it. I felt that his wife became a great calming influence on him (if Roy could ever be calm), and probably saved him from himself, but her time with him was far from easy.

Later in Roy's career at Old Trafford, in May 1997, I received a panicked telephone call from Ken Merrett, the club secretary; the worry in his voice was palpable.

'Ned,' he gasped, 'I've just been told that Roy Keane is running up and down the streets of Hale with a knife and a stick in his hands.'

I couldn't believe it. Ken had managed to contact me at my gun club, where I happened to be spending the afternoon shooting with Eric Cantona. I turned to Eric and said, 'You'll never fucking believe this . . .'

Eric laughed as I filled him in on the details and, not very helpfully, he suggested that I had better take the gun with me as I might need it if Roy was on the rampage. I didn't take Eric's advice, but rushed out of the gun club and drove over to Hale as fast as I could. Roy was nowhere to be seen, however, and rather more worryingly, neither was he at home.

I called Ken Merrett and informed him the streets of Hale seemed to be clear of frenzied Irishmen, which seemed to calm him down a bit. However, it soon emerged that the police were investigating a claim by one of Roy's neighbours that he had threatened her with a knife over a dispute about whether his dogs had strayed on to her family's property.

After questioning the footballer, the police decided that there was insufficient evidence to support a criminal prosecution, but undeterred in her pursuit of 'justice', his neighbour indicated she might sue Roy in the civil courts.

The altercation apparently began when her brother suggested to Roy that he should keep his dogs on a leash and prevent them from running wild. Roy's alleged response was to lay siege to the back door of his neighbour's home, brandishing a walking stick and a knife, but he apparently departed when informed that the police had been called.

The neighbourly dispute must have been resolved amicably, as no subsequent court action was taken against Roy. Much later I asked him if there had been any truth in the story, and was rewarded with a glimpse of his wonderful roguish smile: 'Who, me Ned? Naw.'

It became clear to me that Roy's mood swings were mostly fuelled by alcohol, and in my dealings with him I found him to be a shy but hopelessly arrogant man. On match days, Roy would arrive at Old Trafford in a virtual trance, refusing to sign autographs or to speak to anyone, presumably to avoid being distracted from his mental preparations for the imminent game. Such behaviour was a major disappointment to his fans, particularly the Irish supporters who had made the effort to travel a considerable distance to meet and cheer their hero. I often wondered that perhaps it was the only way that Roy could psych himself up for the match ahead but I didn't agree with his attitude, especially as he would have doubtless expected support from the self-same fans in his high-profile bust-up with the Republic of Ireland manager, Mick McCarthy, during the 2002 World Cup finals.

On the training ground, however, I'd find a different Roy Keane again; a much more friendly and relaxed individual, always ready with a quip or a joke, which supported my long-held view that the pressures of match days simply closed him down. As I was always jokingly referred to by Fergie as 'that nosy bastard Kelly', Roy would occasionally ask me, tongue in cheek, 'Well, Ned. Who have we bought today, then?'

I'd laugh good-naturedly, but one day managed to wipe the grin off his face with the retort: 'Someone to replace you.' I decided not to prolong his agony, and a cheeky wink from me restored the smile to his worried-looking face.

There were not many United players who took defeat quite as badly as Roy Keane, especially a home loss. I've watched Roy sit in the dressing room many times after a bad result at Old Trafford with his face contorted into a mask of barely controlled aggression. After one particularly depressing drubbing by arch-rivals Liverpool, I noticed that Roy was on the verge of exploding as he observed some of the other players laughing and joking when getting dressed to go home. I assumed that he considered such frivolity no less than improper only minutes after a poor display on the pitch, and he turned toward them glaring like a maniac. I started toward him, to intervene before the situation got out of hand, but goalkeeping coach Tony Coton pulled me back whispering, 'Leave it, Ned.' He was right to stop me in my tracks, as any attempt to mediate might just have pushed Roy over the edge. As I stood back against the wall, waiting for his next move, I saw Roy shake his head and visibly relax, storming off in silence to the shower room for a spell of much-needed solitude.

Socializing with Roy was always a pleasure until he had that one drink too many. As soon as he had finished the glass, it was as if somebody had pressed the Frankenstein button, and Roy transformed into a monster. If only Roy had reserved his ravings for referees and Arsenal players, but sadly, he vented his drunken rages upon anyone close at hand. It used to sicken me when the long-suffering Theresa, loyal and kind wife that she was, became the target of his outbursts. Indeed, many times, what should have been a great night out for Theresa, as she rightfully revelled in her husband's success, became an embarrassing nightmare for her. On more than one occasion I stopped him with a look, which made me unpopular with some of his so-called friends, who would stand by lamely, and watch Roy's poor treatment of Theresa. These freeloaders were probably too afraid to intervene in case they lost their free drink at Roy's expense, but such cowardliness made me fume. Fortunately, I noticed that Roy's binges on the booze were becoming less frequent after one or two of the serious injuries he sustained later in his career, so I took it as a sign that perhaps he was mellowing at last.

Prior to the 2002 World Cup, newspaper reports suggested that

Theresa had been troubled by a mystery woman pestering her with telephone calls, asserting that she had been having an affair with Roy. Roy strenuously denied the woman's claims, and his aides announced that he would make a public statement to denounce her allegations.

In signing Keano and Cantona, Fergie chose to ignore the UEFA 'foreigners' rule, which had been revised and now allowed only three 'foreign' nationals per team in a European game. In addition, a team could also include two 'assimilated' players of foreign extraction – meaning players that had progressed through a club's own youth system; for example, Ryan Giggs. When Fergie signed up the two latest 'foreign' players, however, I don't think the rule even entered his mind – he just wanted two brilliant players, regardless of their nationality, and he got them.

We went into the 1993–4 season happy to be defending our title at last. As Champions of England we were entered into the European Cup proper, a contest that had been revamped the previous season, which meant we were now entered in the Champions League.

For our first game in this competition, on 15 September, we faced Honved away and beat the Hungarian side 3–2. Back in the Premier League, a 1–0 win over Arsenal at Old Trafford marked the start of a stunning run of eight League victories in a row, so that by January 1994 United were fourteen points clear of our nearest rivals, Kenny Dalglish's Blackburn Rovers.

After beating Honved at home in the second Champions League match of the season, we discovered that on 20 October our next opponents would be Galatasaray, the champions of Turkey. The Galatasaray side was something of an unknown quantity to Manchester United. At the time there was no doubt that Turkey was a much improved footballing nation, but the general assumption was that Galatasaray would be pushed to one side with ease, and United would march into the prestigious, money-spinning league stage of the tournament – but the Turks set out to prove everyone wrong.

The Galatasaray fans were a lively bunch, and became quite a handful as the game progressed. Hopes were high early on among the United faithful, when we scored two goals within the first six minutes, but soon after, play was temporarily halted when a fan invaded the pitch carrying a burning Turkish flag, in protest over the Turkish government's treatment of the Kurds. A group of my men removed him from the playing area, and extinguished his fire as the police marched him off, while another invading fan was dealt with sharply by Peter Schmeichel, which proves it's never advisable to tackle a Great Dane.

Throughout the match, the tenacious Turks kept coming back at us, refusing to give up, and their efforts soon paid off as they scored three times to lead 3–2. With the game slipping out of our grasp, it came as a huge relief when Cantona was on hand to snatch an equalizer, but the quality of our performance in general did not bode well for the away leg in Istanbul.

I was called in to Ken Ramsden's office to discuss how best to approach the crucial matter of security provision in Istanbul in early November. We all agreed that I would take two of my best men, Vinny Earl and Charlie Narnar, and we would be responsible for guarding the team; the dignitaries could look after themselves.

The team was a bit more subdued than normal as we flew out of Manchester, and I wondered whether the players had perhaps heard the nightmare stories about the Turkish fans. On arrival in Istanbul we were met by approximately one hundred Galatasaray fans, but unlike our previous reception committees on foreign soil, this mob sounded more like they wanted to lynch us than welcome us.

The noise they were making was incredible, and many were waving banners saying 'Welcome to Hell'. They were relentless in their desire to unsettle our party, and hounded the team all the way to their coach, jeering and shouting abuse. Eventually I got everyone safely to the hotel. It turned out to be an old palace of a sultan who had built a twenty-five-foot-high wall right around it, presumably for protection, which was fortunate for us at that moment.

The team chilled out and had dinner in the hotel before they all turned in for an early night. I spent the night operating a 'two-hours-on/four-hours-off' shift, patrolling the hotel corridors to make absolutely sure that no Turkish fans could disturb the lads.

The next day, the players spent their time relaxing, watching TV and discussing their own tactics for the game, and they also gave interviews to television pundits Gary Newbon and Brian Moore. At 6.00 p.m. the team headed off to the Galatasaray ground for the prescribed hour of training that takes place twenty-four hours before the game. The ground was in a terrible state, and in our Premier

League would only have been fit for use as a car park. After training, I got them safely back to the hotel and, after dinner, it was another early night for the boys.

At breakfast on the day of the match, I was summoned to the two Kens' table and asked to accompany them to the UEFA security briefing that was due to take place at Galatasaray stadium later that morning. I sensed that they were quite nervous at the prospect of going anywhere alone, and were relieved to have my support while in Turkey. After the meeting, which was amicable enough, I went back to the hotel and snatched a few hours' sleep, as did Vinny and Charlie, and got up in the late afternoon to prepare for our trip back to the stadium for the match.

With kick-off time only a few hours away, our 'Mr Kit', Norman Davies, left for the ground with all the strips, boots and other gear, accompanied by Vinny. In the meantime Charlie and I were posted at the hotel's front door, awaiting the players, before escorting them on to the coach and guarding them on the journey to the ground. When we arrived at the stadium, a welcoming committee even more aggressive than the first we had experienced awaited us. As we exited the bus we were surrounded by spitting and snarling Turkish fans who looked like a pack of wolves, ready to pounce at any second.

We managed to lead the team safely into the building and they got dressed in what passed for a dressing room. Rather unsettlingly, what sounded like the reception usually reserved for the Christians as they were fed to the lions could be heard coming down the tunnel from the fans. As we walked out on to the pitch, the riot police raised their shields in an arc to protect us from missiles, flying debris and miscellaneous items that were being hurled down at us.

It was a unique experience, and not one that any of us wished to repeat. I was desperate for the match to be over, just so I could get the team out of the hellish environment, and back home to safety in Manchester. The highlight of what turned out to be an uneventful game of football was when Eric Cantona pushed a Galatasaray player over, which sent the Turkish players and their fans into even more of a rage. It was perfectly clear that Eric had shoved the guy, but to see the player rolling about on the ground for an eternity, you think he'd taken a bullet. Following a dire ninety minutes, the match ended in a 0–0 draw, which brought our European aspirations to an end for another year as the three away goals scored by the Turks at Old Trafford took them through to the next stage.

At the final whistle, I ran on to the pitch and started shepherding the players into the tunnel, dodging what seemed like every empty bottle in Turkey, which rained down on us from these mobs of so-called fans. As I was doing this, Eric was making hand gestures to the referee, Kurt Rothlisberger, using international sign language to make it very clear exactly what he thought of him. Seconds later, although the match had ended, Eric was shown the red card for dissent.

Then something unbelievable happened: on his way down to the tunnel, the Frenchman was attacked by one of the riot policemen, who beat him on the head with a baton. When Bryan Robson went to Eric's defence, he too was assaulted, having a riot shield brutally smashed over his head. In an effort to protect himself Robbo had put up his hand to deflect the blow, and ended up with a deep gash in his hand that would later require stitches.

Eric was also badly cut. It took another Turkish policeman to pull his maniacal colleague off the Frenchman to save Eric from any further injury. In the meantime, unaware of the mindless attacks on two members of his team, Fergie was ranting and raving at the players lucky enough to have reached the safety of the dressing room, about their poor performance. As Paul Parker entered the room, Fergie was just about to launch at him, when Paul asked, 'Have you seen Eric and Bryan, Boss? They're cut to fuck.'

Seconds later both wounded players burst into the room, looking in a terrible state. Fergie took one look at them and screamed at me: 'Ned. For God's sake, get Ken Merrett.'

I waded through the sea of people trying to leave the ground and managed to get to the VIP area to find Ken. Having explained what had happened, I told him that Fergie wanted him in the dressing room immediately.

'I hope Alex doesn't try and appeal against the result because of this,' said Merrett. This statement struck me as a bizarre thing for Manchester United's club secretary to say, when surely any effort to push for another opportunity in the Champions League was worth trying. I resisted the temptation of asking why he didn't want to complain, and just led him away to see Fergie.

As I directed Ken Merrett into the dressing room, Fergie's face was a study in controlled fury. He was on the verge of exploding. I elected to avoid the inevitable blast of shrapnel, choosing instead to make my excuses and leave them to it. Whatever issues were discussed, the result of their deliberations was that the club opted not to lodge an appeal.

I got the team back to the coach, but on the way from the dressing room to the vehicle, Eric gave an interview to a French TV crew who had witnessed the farce. At the time nobody knew what was said because of course the interview was conducted in French, but we didn't have long to wait to find out.

The coach ride to the airport was far from comfortable as bricks and bottles rained down on us. Though it was reassuring to have the protection of the bus around us, the Turkish fans still managed to break a few of the windows in the vehicle, showering us all in fragments of glass.

'Where the fuck are the police, Ned?' asked Fergie, aggrieved that we were still coming under attack from the mindless thugs.

'Probably throwing the bricks, Boss,' I replied. That, at least, provoked a ripple of laughter, and we left Turkey feeling incredibly relieved to have got out alive.

Although we arrived back in England in the early hours, there were still fans waiting to welcome us home, but the majority were members of the press, all clamouring for a quote about what Eric had said on leaving the Galatasaray ground. We had no idea what they were talking about as we were mid-flight when the French TV crew's exclusive was broadcast around the world, creating a media frenzy. Eventually, all became clear. It transpired that Eric had alleged that 'some referees are bought', apparently insinuating that Kurt Rothlisberger was one such individual, with the result that Eric faced disciplinary proceedings with UEFA, and later paid for revealing his views on the Galatasaray game with a four-game ban from European matches. Interestingly, the same referee was later banned from UEFA tournaments, following serious allegations of attempted bribery; it was alleged that he had offered to influence a Champions League game between Grasshopper Zurich and Auxerre in October 1996, by suggesting he could bribe the match referee to make decisions in favour of the Swiss team.

Out of Europe, it was back to Manchester United's Premier League campaign, where we were soon privileged to see the other, better side of Eric Cantona. In the next match we faced our Manchester rivals at

Maine Road, which was always a fiercely fought fixture. Our first-half performance let us down badly on this occasion, and by the break two Niall Quinn goals had left us trailing 2–0 to a rampant City. In the second half, however, Eric capitalized on a bad back-pass to the City goalkeeper and brought us back into the match. When he popped up to score again, a draw looked likely at the final whistle, but with only two minutes to go, Roy Keane made it 3–2 to the Reds. It was one of the best comebacks I had ever seen and proved once again how the genius of Cantona could turn a game around in United's favour when we needed it most.

Approaching the Christmas period we were well ahead of our rivals, but there was still a long way to go.

In addition to the tough line I had to take with punters who had made the mistake of buying tickets from touts, I also had to work hard to put a stop to the sales of counterfeit official Manchester United merchandise. As supplies of official United merchandise expanded in range and quantity, so did those of the unofficial variety. In response, I was ordered to organize a clear-out operation outside the ground on match days, during which a few of my employees would chase away those stallholders who were selling unofficial Manchester United goods.

At the time I considered that the money Manchester United was raking in from the official merchandise was being used to bolster the team, so I felt strongly that it really was in the fans' interest to spend their money on official United goods at the megastore, or in sports stores. Looking back, however, in the light of recent accusations concerning price-fixing by some of the big clubs, including United, I wonder whether the club had been guilty of double standards all along.

In August 2003, Manchester United FC was one of a number of football-related businesses to be fined for artificially fixing the price of their replica football shirts. Under investigation by the Office of Fair Trading for two years, MUFC was accused of selling its replica shirts at prices that had been fixed in consultation with the manufacturer Umbro, as well as with a number of national sports-store chains. This meant that consumers were being forced to spend over the odds to buy the shirts, as the products were purposely sold at the same inflated prices at every single one of the chain stores allegedly involved in the illicit agreement.

Although a £1.6 million fine was imposed on the club, Manchester United FC denied any wrongdoing, and suggested it would appeal against the damning judgement.

The second half of the 1993–4 season began as well as the first, but spirits were truly dampened on 20 January when some bad news was announced. We were aware that eighty-four-year-old Sir Matt Busby had been ill in hospital, but it still came as a tremendous shock when his death was reported. The sense of grief around Old Trafford and the city, indeed throughout the entire footballing world, was palpable. For my part it was an honour and a privilege to have known the man, and the treasured memories of those Sunday mornings with him and his daughter Sheena will stay with me for ever. His funeral, a week later, was practically a state occasion, which is just as it should have been for the man who, more than any other, helped create the modern Manchester United.

Norwich City fell 2–0 to us in the fourth round of the FA Cup, in a game that displayed the aspect of Eric Cantona's personality which would bring him much infamy later in his career. During the match he launched a quite outrageous tackle on midfielder Jeremy Goss, but somehow the referee failed to witness the assault, and Eric avoided a certain sending off. He would not be so lucky in future games.

Away from the Premier League, United had reached the semi-final of the League Cup, and faced a two-legged tie against Sheffield Wednesday. A semi-final invariably has a special atmosphere, and this one was no exception. The first leg at Old Trafford on 13 February turned out to be an uninspiring game on the pitch, and as I patrolled the touchline looking out for trouble among the fans, I approached Eddie 'the Bolt' Byrne and asked him, 'Anything doing, mate?'

'All quiet, Ned,' he replied. 'Pretty dead, really.'

It never failed to amaze me how a declaration of peacefulness and calm such as this always seemed to trigger a bout of mayhem, and even before I reached the dugout, my radio glowed red hot as I received frantic messages from my troops.

'It's gone off, Ned. K Stand, and it's a big one.'

I summoned my men by radio from all around the ground and charged to K Stand, which was the old 'scoreboard' end behind the goal. We arrived to find the Sheffield Wednesday fans carrying out a few unauthorized alterations to Old Trafford, ripping out seats and throwing them into the adjoining Manchester United fans' section, at Peter Schmeichel's goal, at the police, SPS security people and, thanks to their bad aim, even their fellow Wednesday fans.

I threw myself into the crowd with my guys right behind me and it was a scene of total devastation with chairs and bodies everywhere. We managed to form a human barricade to separate the Sheffield louts, who were pulling the place apart, and our fans who, by now, were retaliating in kind.

With the help of the police, the SPS contingent and I managed to restore what passed for order and we stayed in position to prevent any further aggravation. The Sheffield 'supporters' remained contained in that man-made corral until after the game to ensure no vengeance was wrought by Manchester United fans outside the ground. Once the police were satisfied that the Manchester crowd had dispersed, we let the Sheffield fans leave.

Meanwhile, back on the pitch, the game had ended in a 1–0 triumph for the Reds, and we had to look forward to the return leg at Hillsborough in early March. I made a mental note to mention extra security to the two Kens to cover ourselves in case there was a repeat performance. Fortunately, football took precedence on this occasion, and Manchester United won 4–1 to go through 5–1 on aggregate.

At this stage in the season we believed we could be heading for glory, but would it be a double or even a treble? We were several points clear in the League, we had reached the League Cup final and were in the quarter-final of the FA Cup. The latter fixture turned out to be memorable initially for the wrong reason. It is quite a rarity to witness a goalkeeper being sent off for a foul, but Peter Schmeichel had to face just such a punishment against Charlton at Old Trafford. After a frantic, action-packed fifteen minutes of play, Peter experienced a rush of blood to the head and charged out of his goal, knocking Charlton player Kim Grant into orbit in the process.

Paul Parker was substituted, as Les Sealey came on to fill the vacant goalkeeping position, and we battled on with only ten men. Andrei Kanchelskis had a magnificent game and scored two cracking goals, with Mark Hughes scoring the third goal, which more than made up for Schmeichel's earlier aberration. We were set for a semi-final showdown against Oldham Athletic, which the FA decreed must be played at Wembley for the first year ever, primarily because Wembley had a much bigger capacity than any neutral ground in the north of England or the Midlands, and the extra fans it could house would bolster the FA's coffers.

Meanwhile, Eric Cantona's unpredictable temper was becoming increasingly more apparent following two sendings-off in consecutive matches. In an away match against Swindon, on 19 March, he stamped on opposition player John Moncur in a moment of anger, and headed for the tunnel as the referee waved a red card in his direction, while the following Tuesday evening at Highbury against Arsenal, he displayed another flash of temper and, perhaps harshly on this occasion, received another red card. With the final scores being 2–2 draws at both matches, Eric was hardly improving our chances of retaining the Premier League title.

Our League Cup-final tussle with Aston Villa saw a Wembley Stadium packed to the rafters. The travelling Reds' fans sang and shouted at the top of their voices but their enthusiasm did not rub off on the players on the pitch, and we were subjected to a 3–1 thumping, and the loss of another cup title. It concerned me that the team had begun to lose its winning ways, with the result that the hope of us winning the first domestic treble in the history of the English League had to remain a mere dream for now.

Nevertheless the double was still in our sights, having made it through to the FA Cup final after beating Oldham 4–1 in the semi-final replay. Victories in some difficult league games meant that a win over Southampton at Old Trafford on 4 May gave us the championship for the second year running. Only Chelsea stood in the way of our coveted FA Cup and Premier League double.

On a foul, wet Saturday in May, we arrived at Wembley to take on Chelsea for the FA Cup. Tension was running higher than normal with the double at stake too. A hard-fought first half should have seen Chelsea lead at the break, but fortunately for us they had been unable to convert their chances into goals.

In the second half, Denis Irwin was brought down in the box and we were awarded a penalty. Eric Cantona took on the responsibility and, as I stood in the dugout, I wondered if he realized that if he was successful he would become the first Frenchman to score in an English cup final. If he was aware of this trifling statistic, he certainly didn't show it, and in his usual confident style, Eric blasted the ball home. We were advancing strongly now and the Red fans went crazy as we were awarded a second penalty when Kanchelskis was fouled in the box. Eric stepped up to take this one also, and thus became the only Frenchman to score twice in an English cup final. Further goals by Mark Hughes and Brian McClair gave us a 4–0 victory. Not only had we won the 1994 FA Cup and clinched the double, but we had done so in some style.

While the players received a tumultuous reception on their lap of honour, I secured the dressing room prior to their return, and kept the press at bay. In the corridor outside the dressing room, the backslapping from the TV and press was overwhelming, and they all clamoured for interviews and quotes as the players fought their way through to the changing area. I had to position myself in front of the door to block the press's entrance, and gave my media chums my usual glowering stare.

After the lads had showered and taken a short time to relax, I ushered them back through the media throng and on to their coach for the trip to their hotel, with the FA Cup firmly welded to my right hand. Once we were all aboard, I asked Fergie if it was possible to put the trophy on display at the front of the coach, and he nodded in approval.

My great idea of showing off the FA Cup on the streets of London was severely tested, however, when the coach driver overshot the entrance to our hotel and, ignoring my advice to go around the block and approach the hotel entrance for a second time, decided to attempt a thirty-three-point turn in the middle of the busy Bayswater Road.

During this epic manoeuvre, two pubs full of downtrodden Chelsea fans could hardly believe their eyes as they saw the Northern bastards who had just destroyed their FA Cup hopes stuck on a coach outside, which was jammed end-on to the pavement, and well within throwing distance.

In their efforts to scramble outside, the Chelsea supporters were getting themselves jammed in the pub doors and, once they had left the pubs, they began hurling bottles, glasses, ashtrays and abuse at the coach. A few of the players were up for a scrap, particularly Paul Ince, who had begun bobbing and weaving in a boxer's stance, beckoning the Chelsea mob to come and fight. I felt we were very lucky to get away unscathed, but fortunately, when we eventually reached the sanctuary of the hotel, a great night was had by all.

The next morning, there was many a hangover being nursed, not least my own, but I was sure it had been worth it. The hotel restaurant was on the top floor and, as I stepped into the lift to travel up for breakfast, I bumped into Steve Bruce and his wife, Jan. I shook Steve's hand and said: 'Congratulations, son. You're the first Englishman this century to captain a double-winning side.' Steve looked puzzled. 'How so, Ned?' he asked.

'Well, in 1961 Danny Blanchflower captained Spurs and he was Irish. In 1971 it was Arsenal's Frank McLintock and he's a Jock, and in 1986 it was Hansen for Liverpool, another bleedin' Jock,' I explained.

While he looked on in complete surprise, Jan Bruce kissed her husband proudly on the cheek. They were a lovely couple, but they did have their moments. For example, some time later, when Steve was acting captain at a home game, Jan arrived at the players' lounge with her entourage of ladies-who-lunch. She demanded that I allow her and her guests into the lounge before the game. I had to tell her that the arrangement was 'no tickets, no passes', by order of Fergie, which provoked a hostile response from the player's wife. When she noticed Steve on his way to the pitch for the pre-match warm-up, Jan set off at pace in his direction, and proceeded to slap him about the head, demanding, 'Where are my fucking tickets?' Steve disappeared into the dressing room and returned with her 'fucking' tickets, which gave Jan and the other ladies access to the lounge areas.

Steve later had a word with me, complaining that he was the captain and I had embarrassed Jan. I refused to back down though, for I had simply been following Fergie's orders. My daughter Elaine was with me at the time and she suggested that perhaps I had been a bit too harsh. Later, after hearing that Steve and Jan had been ranting down at the Amblehurst Hotel about how I'd treated her, I decided to act quickly. I knew that even a temporary captain's wife had a lot of power behind the scenes and so to nip any animosity in the bud, I headed round to the Bruces' house with a bouquet of flowers and an apology. Jan threw her arms round me, said 'It's OK, love,' and invited me in for coffee. Thankfully, that was the only run-in I had with the formidable Mrs Bruce. Though I liked Jan a lot, I was glad she was married to Steve.

The Amblehurst Hotel was the scene of an embarrassing situation for Steve and Jan one evening and, as always, the bar had a fair number of Manchester United players and their partners among its customers that night. Out of the corner of my eye I noticed Steve in a heated argument with a guy who was obviously a bit the worse for drink. Jan appeared to me to be upset by remarks being made by the drunk, so I made my way to their table. As far as I was concerned, Steve looked to be within an ace of breaking the drunk's jaw, so I managed to get between them and pull the drunk away. I then had a word.

'Shut the fuck up, you,' I growled in his ear, while gripping his arm tightly. 'Get out of here while you can still manage it!'

After attempting to ignore my words of warning, he gave up the fight. I accompanied him to the door, and he left the premises, promising to return with his brothers, his mates, Mike Tyson – the usual. I went back inside to find Steve trying to console Jan, who was embarrassed and distressed. In my view, the event in the pub was an example of the biggest problem that the Manchester United players had to endure, living as they did in this goldfish bowl of a community, that they and their families were often subjected to bitter verbal assaults by unsavoury characters who were jealous of their success and wealth.

After getting over our cup-final hangovers, we returned to Manchester by train later that day and were met at the station by an open-topped bus for the procession through the streets. The reception was remarkable and the double-winning players were welcomed home as the conquering heroes they indeed were.

Two female fans chose to express their appreciation in a more intimate fashion with a selection of lucky players at the Four Seasons Hotel. After the celebratory tour of the city, I had met up with a few of the squad at the hotel, and while I relaxed with a drink at the bar, some of the lads were taking it in turns to receive an extra special treat in the hotel toilets, where the two girls were on their knees offering rewards of a more oral nature. The lads were young and single – well, most of them were single – so there was no harm done. While I would have been happy to have left them to it, Martin Edwards thought otherwise, and despatched me to break up this blow-job festival, so I had to make my apologies and throw the boys out of the toilet – a unique end to a rollercoaster ride of a season.

CHAPTER 8

From Heroes To Zeros

D<small>URING THE SUMMER</small>, Manchester United bought only one notable new player, spending £1.2 million on David May, from Blackburn. I was to discover that this was common practice at the club: that when they were successful, they would not slacken the purse strings.

David became a good pal of mine and, although he was a loud man whose mouth at times seemed to work independently of his brain, he had more confidence on a football pitch than the majority of players I have seen. He was also immensely popular with the other players, and was always ready to play a practical joke. The management and staff held him up as an example to the younger players of how to succeed in the world of football, he being as fearless and determined as it was possible to be. He had an opinion on everything and everyone, and it is fair to say that there was never a dull moment when David was around.

During that close season Manchester United said farewell to Bryan Robson, who had been an outstanding servant to the club and a great captain. The fact that Fergie had left him out of the FA Cup-final squad had meant that Bryan knew his days at Old Trafford were numbered. He first had talks with Wolverhampton Wanderers with a view to taking over as manager, but after much deliberation the Wolves board turned him down. He eventually settled on the player-manager role at Middlesbrough, and initially, his form in that position seemed to mirror the success he had enjoyed at United. He took the club into the Premier League at the first opportunity, and led them to an FA Cup final and two League Cup finals.

Many thought that Bryan's managerial career was heading for a fall in 2000, when he was forced to enlist the help of former England manager Terry Venables, who became head coach at Middlesbrough when the club was going through a difficult patch. In his private life too,

Bryan had also experienced problems, arising from a relationship with Sky Sports presenter Clare Tomlinson, a former media officer with the FA. The affair had been conducted in secret for eighteen months until, in January 1999, Bryan's wife Denise burst into a hotel bedroom in Leeds and found Tomlinson under her husband's bed, sporting a broken leg still in plaster.

As Fergie read a report of this fracas in a tabloid newspaper, he considered how the story had come to light, and commented to me, 'Some friends that Bryan Robson's got.'

When Steve McClaren took over at Middlesbrough in summer 2001, criticisms about Bryan's management style were levelled at him in the wake of his departure, and allegations were made that Middlesbrough had become a 'drinking club' under his leadership. Like most footballers, Bryan enjoyed a drink, but I knew that it would never have affected his professionalism in the game.

The 1994–5 season soon got under way and, as usual, the first game was for the FA Charity Shield, in which we played the Premier Championship runners-up, Blackburn Rovers, winning 2–0 at Wembley.

In the Champions League this season, the Reds had been drawn in a group alongside Barcelona, IFK Gothenburg of Sweden, and their favourite Turkish opponents, Galatasaray. The opening European match against IFK Gothenburg at Old Trafford in mid-September went our way, and we had a comfortable 4–2 win.

In a League Cup clash with Port Vale a week later, Fergie decided it was time to give some of the Manchester United Youth Cup team players an opportunity to play for the first team. As a consequence he was accused of not taking the competition seriously enough, and although there may have been some truth in that view, as Fergie was always looking to the bigger tournaments such as the Premiership and European Cup, he proved his doubters wrong.

On that night at Port Vale's ground I was privileged to watch a team of primarily young, inexperienced players who have now become established world stars. Paul Scholes, Gary Neville, David Beckham, Nicky Butt, Ben Thornley, Keith Gillespie and Robbie Savage all played their maiden game for Manchester United in the first team on that occasion, and produced a good performance with a 2–1 win.

Seven days later, in our next Champions League game against Galatasaray, it was back to the delights of Turkey, complete with maniacal fans and policemen who favoured aggression over protection. All the Manchester United party wanted to do was to play and get out as quickly as possible without encountering any trouble, but on arrival in Istanbul we faced the same scenes as on our previous visit, with chanting and hatred spat at us from the moment we hit the streets. This time, however, we were well prepared, and knew exactly how to play our security strategy. Vinny, Charlie and I just charged through the crowds, flanking the players and shoving aside anyone who got in our way.

It was another average game ending in yet another 0–0 draw, but we were grateful for a safe passage home without drama. We even avoided being assaulted by the Turkish police, and as Eric was still serving his four-match suspension and unable to create a storm among the French media, the only folk to greet us at Manchester airport this time were the baggage handlers.

The next Champions League match, in October, was one that everyone was looking forward to, rather than dreading, as we awaited the visit of Barcelona, one of the true giants in European football. We had not played them since that memorable night in Rotterdam in 1991, and though they held us to a 2–2 draw at Old Trafford, it was an honour for the club to act as host to such a footballing institution.

In the League Cup away to Newcastle United, Fergie decided to offer the young guns some more first-team experience. They played well early on, running rings round Newcastle's established senior players for much of the game, but eventually they tired themselves out, without managing to score any goals, and the Reds lost 2–0. After the match, Fergie lectured them in the dressing room, informing them crucially that it was only goals that counted. To prove his point, when Newcastle came to Old Trafford on League business a few days later, Fergie fielded the normal first team, resulting in two goals and a clean sheet for the home side. There were some very quiet young men after that game. Though our team of younger players weren't the finished article yet, it would not be long before they would start challenging for first-team places on merit, and making a huge impact on the side.

We travelled to Spain for our return game against Barcelona in early November and were hammered 4–0, but having had to leave behind many of our best players due to the limits on team selection imposed by the UEFA foreigners rule, the result was hardly surprising. The visit to Spain had not been in vain, however, as Fergie had the opportunity to study the skills of the Barcelona team during the game, with a view to future transfer possibilities. One player in particular who had caught his eye was Jordi Cruyff, son of the Barcelona manager and former footballing legend, Johan Cruyff. Some of his father's skills had clearly rubbed off on the youngster, and Fergie was not slow to take notice.

Our good League form continued with a 5–0 drubbing of local rivals City, but against IFK Gothenburg, in our next European match, we were beaten 3–1 in a nightmare game for Manchester United defender David May, who was turned inside out with every tackle by Gothenburg's young Jesper Blomqvist. Once again Fergie took note of another talented European prospect. Paul Ince's sending off did not help matters, and we left Sweden disappointed at having been knocked out of the European Champions League for another year.

David Beckham was in the line-up for the meaningless game against Galatasaray after being on a four-week loan to Preston North End. Looking back it seems hard to believe that many at Old Trafford didn't rate David at that time, and that some didn't even think he would ever have a career in football. After showing great promise initially, there were nagging doubts about David's ability and, more importantly, his desire to be a success. In my view it was the effect of his father Ted's advice and encouragement, while David was farmed out to the third-division side, that brought him to his senses, and he returned to Manchester United pushing hard for a first-team place alongside the many talented youth team players that the club had been nurturing.

In an impressive 4–0 victory over the Turks, nineteen-year-old Beckham silenced his critics by scoring his first goal for the Manchester United senior team.

En route to a third round FA Cup game away at Sheffield United in January 1995, I was driving Martin Edwards to the match when my car phone rang – it was Fergie wanting to speak to the chairman. Using the hands-free system, Martin began to exchange pleasantries with the Boss.

'Kevin Keegan's been on the phone,' said Fergie. 'He's agreed to the Andy Cole deal, but only on condition that we give him Keith Gillespie. I'm happy with that; what do you think, Chairman?'

'If the money's right, Alex, it'll be great. I'll meet you at Bramall Lane and discuss it with you there,' replied Martin.

After the conversation with Fergie, the chairman was immensely cheerful. Fergie had always wanted an out-and-out striker and Brian Kidd had been singing Andy Cole's praises for years.

On arrival at Sheffield United's ground, Fergie dragged Martin into a corner, no doubt to discuss the financial implications of the transaction. A few days later, it was announced that Cole had signed for United for £6 million, and Keith Gillespie had joined the Magpies as part of the deal.

Later that month, Manchester United's name was in every newspaper but for all the wrong reasons. Eric Cantona's assault on Matthew Simmons, described earlier, was the turning point of the season for the Reds. Without his influential presence on the pitch, as a result of the lengthy ban inflicted on him, the team lacked spirit, which I felt had a negative effect on their remaining games.

Despite a hiccup in the FA Cup semi-final against Crystal Palace, at Villa Park, which resulted in a draw, we beat the London side in the replay, 2–0, which put us in the final against Everton at Wembley on 20 May. Sadly, Roy Keane let the side down with a fierce stamping on Gareth Southgate, which earned him a red card.

Due in part to Cantona's unsettling absence, our stuttering League form had led us to a title-deciding match away at West Ham on the last day of the season. A win would make us only the fourth team this century to win the League three times in succession, mirroring the achievements of Tottenham Hotspur, Arsenal and Liverpool. Victory was far from straightforward, however, as we were two points behind Blackburn, who were playing Liverpool at Anfield. If we could beat West Ham, we had to rely on Liverpool winning or even drawing with Blackburn (we had a far superior goal difference) to guarantee that the Premier League trophy remained in Manchester.

On the day of the Premiership decider, we drove into the parking area at Upton Park and were engulfed in sea of West Ham supporters spitting venom at us. They knew that their team had the power to dash our hopes of a third successive title, and if they could manage victory, that would be achievement enough for them that season. As we left the coach the noise was deafening, and as a former Hammer, Paul Ince in particular was naturally singled out for the worst of the fans' abuse.

Inside the dressing room, the atmosphere was remarkably calm as the lads changed into their kit. They had all experienced similar pressure on previous occasions, and knew exactly what they had to do. When the team made its entrance on the pitch, it was almost like facing Galatasaray, but thankfully without the violence.

Fergie decided to start with Andy Cole and Brian McClair up front, leaving Mark Hughes on the bench. We made a great start and even though I was looking through rose-tinted spectacles, I felt that we were by far the better side. No matter how well we played, however, we could do nothing to dictate matters in the Blackburn game, and so when news of an Alan Shearer goal for Blackburn filtered through from the fans down to the pitch, our spirits took a dive. A West Ham goal shortly afterwards made the situation even more dire. By half-time, we were still losing 1–0 and Blackburn were still winning by the same margin, and so it was a poker-faced Fergie who banged the dressing-room door in my face when I escorted the last of the players safely down the tunnel.

While standing guard outside the dressing room, I was approached by representatives of Carling, the League sponsors who, aware of the hatred growing ever stronger among the fans, were worried that the hostility could spill on to the pitch during the Cup presentation, if Manchester United were to win the Premier League. If there was to be a presentation, we decided to hold it under the main stand, out of the sight of the West Ham supporters. It was perfectly reasonable to plan ahead for such an opportunity, but I couldn't help but wonder that such discussion was tempting fate.

In the second half Fergie brought on Mark Hughes and the tempo of the game picked up pace with the Reds throwing everything at the West Ham defence. Goalkeeper Ludo Miklosko had the game of his life, and stopped everything that came his way, until Brian McClair eventually penetrated the Hammers' goal with a cracking header to make it 1–1. Minutes later there was better news from Liverpool that John Barnes had equalized. The Manchester United fans went crazy with delight, and in the dugout nails were being bitten, while the coolest man in Upton Park that day was Fergie. He could be volatile – explosive even – but he could also, when the situation required it, be the ice man.

Fergie decided to substitute Roy Keane, and as the player made his way past the West Ham dugout he became embroiled in an argument with Les Sealey, at the time the second-choice West Ham goalkeeper, who in his glory days with Manchester United had won an FA Cup medal and a European Cup-Winners' Cup medal, among many other awards.

'What was all that about?' I asked Roy.

'The silly bastard told me we'd win fuck all this season, because it's Blackburn's League,' Roy replied.

I was stunned. 'Never! What did you say to that?'

'I just told him to get to fuck,' he repeated, as succinct and to the point as always.

The game at Upton Park ended in a 1–1 draw, but the glory would not be ours. Although Blackburn had lost 2–1 away at Anfield, our failure to beat West Ham still meant that our north-west rivals had pipped us to the post by a single crucial point. I escorted Fergie to a press call in the tunnel where he was magnanimous in defeat, congratulating Kenny Dalglish and the Blackburn squad on their League Championship victory.

Fergie consoled the team with words of encouragement: 'You did your best, lads. The ball didn't run for us.' The great Bobby Charlton was also on hand to offer his commiserations also, and to gee up the boys for the FA Cup final, which would take place six days later.

Since receiving his ban in February 1995, Eric Cantona had been spending time working through his community service order, repaying his debt to society by coaching local schoolchildren in football at Manchester United's training ground.

During one of his trips back from France to Manchester to fulfil his community service commitment, Eric invited me to return to Paris with him for a weekend, which I agreed to without any hesitation. In true Cantona style we stayed at the Hotel Prince de Galles on the Avenue Georges V, where Eric was fêted like a king. He initiated me into the delights of Parisian nightlife in the Adam's Club, where he knew everyone and introduced me to them all, from major French film stars to renowned theatre actors, and we spent a memorable weekend in their company.

Prior to our FA Cup final against Everton at Wembley, Old Trafford played host to the first leg of the Youth Cup final, when our young team of hopefuls took on Leeds United's youngsters in front of 30,000 fans. The development of young players is crucial to maintaining the high standards of the English game, and Manchester United had always led the way in bringing on new talent, starting with Sir Matt's fabled 'Busby Babes'. Our boys were beaten in this first encounter, but were determined to make up for the loss in the second leg at Elland Road, which was always a hostile ground for any Manchester United visit.

Ken Ramsden called me in to his office and instructed me to travel with the youngsters to ensure their safety. As requested, I travelled on the coach with the team accompanied by Eric Harrison, the hard-working youth team boss.

Despite the grit and determination shown by our young players, we lost the second leg too, and it was the young lads at Leeds who deservedly lifted the trophy and collected their winners' medals.

Cup-final day at Wembley was always a memorable occasion, and to be there for the second year running was really quite special. My excitement was further boosted when I received a call from Eric Cantona informing me that he was travelling over from France for the game. When they heard of Eric's imminent arrival, the two Kens wanted him to travel from the hotel to the stadium with the directors and their wives in their coach. I managed to convince them that this was not good policy, however, as the distance from the coach to the VIP entrance at Wembley was a good seventy-yard walk. With almost 80,000 fans milling about, I thought it would be safer to take him to Wembley by taxi, so that we could be dropped off right outside the dressing-room area. I think the two men had been looking forward to making a grand entrance with Eric Cantona on Cup-final day, but for the sake of his security they agreed to my suggestion.

As we approached the stadium by taxi, Eric gasped at the mass of fans heading for the game.

'You should be playing here today, Eric,' I said, sadly. 'Was it worth it, mate?'

'No,' was his brief reply, as he shook his head ruefully.

We left the taxi and managed to enter the ground without Eric being recognized. Unfortunately, the Frenchman and I would have little to celebrate, as the day belonged to Everton after a 1–0 win, a disappointing end to a potentially double-winning season. It was a glum Manchester United crew that amassed back at the hotel, but after a few drinks, the mood began to lighten. I guarded the function suite door with Vinny Earl and Eddie Byrne, and once I was satisfied that the bulk of the scroungers and hangers-on had been warned off, I went in and joined the party.

While most of the lads had begun to unwind, and turned their attention to their hopes for next season, Paul Ince had other things on his mind, telling anyone who would listen that he'd had enough of Old Trafford, especially Fergie. He was outraged that the manager had blamed him for Everton's goal, and for suggesting that he'd not stuck to the game-plan. On and on he ranted, though he was more than careful to sound off well out of Fergie's earshot. A wise move in theory, I thought, but of course Fergie got to hear of it eventually.

In summer 1995, Alex Ferguson became troubled by matters concerning his private life, after it had been suggested to him that the press might be on to a juicy story. Knowing my SAS background, and aware of my contacts in the security industry, Fergie asked me to organize a full-scale counter-surveillance sweep of his family home and his offices – both at the Cliff training ground and at Old Trafford – as he was especially fearful that his private and professional telephone calls were being monitored.

I called in a favour and arranged for one of the most competent counter-surveillance operatives I had encountered during my time in the forces to undertake this operation. Though it was a matter of the utmost seriousness, I had to chuckle to myself when Fergie insisted that the bill for these services would be paid by Manchester United. While my old friend John Adams, a counter-surveillance expert, was carrying out the sweep of the office at the Cliff, Brian Kidd asked me what was going on, so I merely informed him that the Boss felt that too much information was getting out to the press and he was fearful that an electronic listening device had been planted in his office. Brian laughed at the idea, but told me that as long as it made Fergie feel more secure, then it could do no harm.

What surprised me most of all was that Fergie had requested that his own home should be swept for a listening device. The office I could perhaps understand, but it amazed me that Fergie was convinced that his house might be bugged. However, I soon became convinced that there was perhaps some justification for his apparently irrational fear, when it was revealed that there was some evidence that private conversations conducted within the confines of the house had somehow been communicated to the press. Whether they had been relayed by bugs or merely passed on through idle gossip was another matter, but I was curious as to how he would explain to his wife the reason for the presence of a couple of ex-SAS men in her house.

John was soon conducting a thorough investigation, searching for concealed listening devices one evening at 'Fairfields', the Fergusons' house, named after the Clydeside shipyard in which Fergie's father had worked.

I left John crawling through the eaves and under the floorboards, while Fergie's wife, Cathy, made me a cup of tea. Cathy had always treated me very well, and in my opinion she was a true 'lady' long before her husband was made a knight. As I stood there drinking the tea, the whole situation struck me as being all too surreal: while an ex-SAS man was combing the rafters, seeking hidden surveillance equipment, here was Cathy going about her normal household chores, unaware of what was really going on.

As Fergie joined me in the kitchen I thought I'd switch the conversation to the safe subject of football, and asked him what was going on at the club this summer: 'Who's leaving and who's staying?'

He laughed and replied, 'You usually know before me. What's the gossip, Ned?'

'Well, it's an open secret that Mark Hughes wants to leave, as does Kanchelskis. But Paul Ince is trumpeting that he's off to Milan,' I revealed.

Fergie started to laugh. 'Is that so? What would you do if someone offered you seven million for Incey?'

'I'd bite their arm off, Boss,' I said, without hesitation. 'Kanchelskis would be the only one out of those three I'd keep.'

The Boss laughed and went back to his study without further comment.

On the Friday of that week in July, Paul Ince signed for Inter Milan for £7 million, Mark Hughes joined Chelsea for £1.5 million, and a month later, Andrei Kanchelskis signed for Everton for £5 million, which is why Fergie is probably the best football manager in the world – he knows everything and gives away nothing!

After a thorough three-hour sweep of Fergie's house, John declared 'Fairfields' a totally bug-free zone, and having swept most embassies and consulates in Britain in his time in the military, he certainly wouldn't have missed anything.

I also suggested to Fergie that my expert should sweep his car and scan his mobile phone, as both are prime targets for eavesdroppers. After extensive technical investigation, we found no evidence to suggest that anyone was listening in to Fergie's personal and professional life via his private telephones.

Just as I was beginning to think that the whole matter had been dealt with, I received a call on my mobile phone a few days later. Once more it was Fergie, with another request for me as bizarre as his previous one. He asked me to arrange a similar surveillance sweep of another person's property, to check for any listening devices. His suggestion was deemed unnecessary, however, for the person in question declined his kind offer with the comment, 'Fergie is overreacting', and so the matter went no further.

I duly reported all of this back to Fergie. He thanked me for my thoroughness, and that was the end of my involvement in this intriguing affair.

CHAPTER 9

From Zeros To Heroes

THE SUMMER OF 1995 proved to be one of my busiest periods of work. Aside from the services I supplied to Manchester United personally, my company, SPS, was expanding at an enormous rate, employing 700 people, and providing security at racecourses and cricket grounds.

I spent what little leisure time I had shooting with Eric Cantona. He would fly over from France periodically and we would meet up and head for Hereford, where one of my SAS mates arranged for us to shoot on a private estate; we spent some lazy, hazy days bagging partridges, wood pigeon and pheasants. Eric was a very good shot, and on a few occasions when he brought his father over with him we three would lose ourselves deep in the English countryside.

I was in the process of preparing SPS for the start of the new season when I received a call from Ken Merrett. He explained to me that Andrei Kanchelskis was moving to Everton for £5 million but that the deal had hit a snag. Apparently, when Manchester United bought Andrei from Shakhtar Donetsk in May 1991 the purchase price had to be made in three stages: an initial payment of £650,000; a further payment of £300,000 after he had played a certain number of games; and a final payment of £250,000. Reports that Andrei had been in trouble with the Russian mafia abounded subsequently, but the events of the next few days convinced me that the information had to be true.

His old club was now claiming it had never received the second or third payments, and was consequently blocking Andrei's move to Everton or anywhere else. 'It's all nonsense, of course,' added Ken. 'But I don't want Maurice Watkins going to the Ukraine on his own to sort this one out, so I'd like you to go with him.'

I made my way to Maurice's office to make arrangements for the trip, knowing that the allegation against the club was completely without substance as Manchester United always paid their bills. I was also aware that dealings over football in the former Soviet Union were often less than straightforward. Given the potential for trouble, I was concerned for Maurice's safety.

After enduring a number of irritating delays on our journey we eventually arrived at Kiev International airport late in the afternoon. As we neared customs and passport control, we were approached by two young girls who, in perfect English, assured us that for ten US dollars each they could have our passports stamped without us having to queue. I considered the delays we would face if we joined the back of the long snaking queue ahead, and reached into my wallet for the money. The risk paid off and we breezed through the control with stamped passports.

We were met at the airport by Yuri Ramazanov, the company lawyer for Shakhtar Donetsk, and accompanied him in his car to meet with the club's officials. His driver pulled up outside an old grey building that resembled a Victorian hospital.

'It looks like a KGB building,' I joked to Yuri.

'It used to be, you're right,' he smiled.

We followed Yuri into the building and climbed the stairs to a first-floor office, where we sat down around a large oak table, and waited. Upon hearing the ominous 'clump-clump' of footsteps coming up the hall, I couldn't contain myself, and in an effort to make light of the tense situation, I laughed and said to Maurice, 'Someone's coming . . . !'

Mercifully, the man who entered the room looked relatively normal. He was about six feet tall with blond slicked-back hair, and was immaculately dressed, like a tall James Cagney. Yuri then introduced him to us as Boris Mirdan, a representative of the club. Boris spoke no English, so Yuri appointed himself translator. The meeting was soon under way and discussions began in earnest about what had happened to the second and third payments from Manchester United to Shakhtar Donetsk. Maurice could prove that the money had been paid as he had brought documentation that provided irrefutable evidence of the transaction. Boris reacted less than positively to this news, and began hitting the table and shouting loudly. Yuri looked worried and Maurice was embarrassed, but I wasn't going to accept his behaviour. I looked straight into Boris's eyes and told Yuri to tell him to stop banging the table.

At this Boris stopped his assault on the furniture, picked up the telephone and started shouting at somebody on the end of the line. After a few minutes he slammed down the phone and, through Yuri, invited Maurice and me to be his guests at a football match that evening. Having had quite enough of Boris for one day, we declined.

Maurice had made his point successfully, and the meeting was now over. To our surprise, we were given a police escort away from the building, a gesture that obviously made a big impression on Maurice. He later wrote about his Ukrainian experience in a law journal: 'I came out of their offices with Ned Kelly, the head of security at Old Trafford, surrounded by armed police. We were amazed. It transpired the police were there to protect those at the meeting from the Russian mafia. It was certainly a dangerous time.'

After a sleepless night in a draughty hotel, Maurice and I flew home the next day, mission accomplished. It had not been a pleasant experience, but it was at least rewarding to see that the matter had been resolved.

Andrei Kanchelskis did indeed make the move to Everton but didn't stay long. After a spell at the Italian club Fiorentina during the 1997–8 season, he settled in Scotland with Rangers. At the time he was playing in Italy I was approached by George Scanlon, Andrei's former interpreter during his Manchester days, who pulled me to one side during an away game against Everton and whispered: 'Ned, have a word with Fergie, will you? Andrei wants to come back to United.'

On hearing the news, Fergie exploded and said he would not take up the kind offer, though not in such polite terms.

'OK, Boss. Calm down, mate,' I laughed. 'Don't shoot the messenger.'

With Mark Hughes, Paul Ince and Andrei Kanchelskis all having departed Old Trafford during the close season, the onus would be on young hopefuls like David Beckham to step into the shoes of the more seasoned professionals. On the first day of the season, playing away at Aston Villa, I drove Eric and Steve Bruce down to watch the young stars of Old Trafford perform at Premiership level. Not everyone shared the faith that Fergie placed in these youths, and his team choice led BBC pundit and former Liverpool captain Alan Hansen to pronounce famously: 'You will never win anything with kids.'

Even those closely associated with the club were not entirely convinced that the team would be a strong enough presence in the new season's competitions. While driving to a game I asked Eric Cantona whether he thought that we could win the Premier League title this year.

'Not without buying a few new players,' he replied.

United were still hampered by the Frenchman's absence on the pitch, but while he was unable to play an active role in matches, he continued to travel to games and offer invaluable support to his team-mates.

Our Premier League campaign was in good shape as we travelled to Russia to play Rotor Volgograd in the UEFA Cup in September 1995. Like us, the Russians had been runners-up in their national league in the previous season. I flew with the team and officials into Volgograd, formerly known as Stalingrad under the old Soviet communist regime. We arrived late in the evening and checked into our hotel.

It was a rule at Manchester United that whenever we were drawn away against Eastern European teams we would take our own chefs and food, as the majority of their top hotels were the equivalent of our YMCAs. This one in Russia was no exception. When we came down for breakfast, Steve Bruce presented himself at Fergie's table covered in insect bites. At first the team physician blamed his condition on bed bugs, then decided they were flea bites. What was strange was that although Gary Pallister was sharing a room with Steve, he was completely bite-free. After much mattress-changing, the rooms were declared free from infestation and the team spent the day acclimatizing, and resting. For relaxation they asked each other Trivial Pursuit questions, which culminated in a challenge match between Fergie, who was known for his command of general knowledge and quick wit, and Steve Bruce. Not surprisingly, the Boss was the eventual winner but, as quizmaster, I must confess to trying to help Steve to victory by asking him what I thought were the easier questions.

On the morning of the match day, Fergie and I decided to take a walk around the city, during which the conversation veered towards tales of his early managerial career.

'After Jock Stein died, did you really want the Scotland manager's job for the World Cup in Mexico, Alex?' I asked.

'Nah, I didn't really want to do it, Ned,' he said. 'But I'd worked with Jock on the team and I felt I had to go on with it after he died.' Fergie then went on to say that Jock was years ahead of his time in football management, but Celtic treated him abominably: 'He made them one of the most famous clubs in the world and they did nothing for him.'

'Do you think Kenny Dalglish will end up managing Scotland?' I asked.

'Who knows? Kenny Dalglish is only out for Kenny Dalglish,' he replied.

There was clearly no love lost between these two Scotsmen, a mutual sentiment that apparently existed even before Kenny fell out with Fergie and didn't go to Mexico for the 1986 World Cup. Their opposition may have developed from a Celtic-Rangers-based rivalry – Kenny played for the former just after Fergie left the latter – and as managers they had already clashed over the signings of Alan Shearer and Roy Keane.

The match kicked off later in the day. Unfortunately, there was little to celebrate as it was a dull and uninspiring game, which was reflected in the 0–0 score. Two weeks later, the Russians came to Old Trafford and with United once again unable to field all their best players due to the UEFA ruling, the result was a 2–2 draw and we were out of Europe on the away-goal rule.

The following Saturday, Fergie fielded another youth-filled team against Bolton and another player full of promise made his debut. Terry Cooke had been fascinated by stories of my SAS days and about the survival training I'd undertaken. As he ran on to the pitch I smiled as I recalled how he had become extremely squeamish when I told him that if we were stranded on a desert island, I would have no compunction in eating him for survival. Phil Neville told me later that the young lad had really taken fright at this until he had told him that I was only joking.

'Was I?' I replied, leaving them both wondering.

Happily my ghoulish stories hadn't adversely affected Terry's footballing skills on the pitch, and he had a cracking debut, helping Manchester United to a 3–1 win. It was sad that Terry never fulfilled the promise predicted for him at Old Trafford, as a cruel injury nearly finished his career, but he didn't give up and moved to our City rivals in April 1999.

With lowly York City having dumped us out of the League Cup in the autumn, the future looked a little bleak, but just when we needed a saviour, Eric Cantona's long suspension came to an end.

'Eric's back!' The banners around Old Trafford were lifted high and once again shouts of 'Ooh . . . Aah . . . Cantona' echoed around the ground. It had been a painful eight months for Eric, while his absence had been pure torture for the fans.

The atmosphere around the stadium was buzzing as we prepared to play our arch-rivals, Liverpool, on 1 October. In anticipation of the special day some fans were arriving at 8.00 a.m., eight hours before the 4.00 p.m. kick-off. The turnout was unbelievable, although I wondered just exactly who they thought they would see at that early hour; not Eric, that was for sure.

I received a call from him at 11.15 a.m. asking if I could pick him up from his home and drive him to Old Trafford, which I was more than happy to do. The thought of seeing him in a Red shirt once again was overwhelming. Eric became visibly excited too as we neared the ground.

'It's a great day, Ned. I can play again at last,' said Eric, the relief all too apparent on his face.

As I drove on to the forecourt at Old Trafford, it gradually began to dawn on the waiting fans just who my passenger was. The wave of emotion and spontaneous applause that followed Eric into the stadium was tremendous. I dropped him off so he could join the rest of the team for a pre-match meal, while I got back to SPS business.

The hard-fought contest ended in a 2–2 draw, but Eric left his mark on the match, making the first goal for Nicky Butt and scoring our penalty. It was official – the King was back.

A month later, Bryan Robson brought his Middlesbrough team to Old Trafford. The fans gave him a tremendous reception, even though he now occupied the away team's dugout. Manchester United won 2–0, but Bryan was undoubtedly growing in stature as a manager, and it was strange for me to watch him congratulate Fergie after the match.

At the beginning of 1996 we were trailing Newcastle United in the Premier League. I was still on strict 'Cantona watch' at away games, as Fergie was worried that some lunatic fan would try to provoke him again after his Crystal Palace martial-arts show.

For the fourth round FA Cup game at Reading, Eric had invited his father over from France and had asked me to take him to the game. I arranged to meet M. Cantona Senior at Wilmslow railway station during some of the worst weather we had experienced that winter and, after much changing of trains due to line blockages, we finally arrived in Reading. We took a taxi to the hotel and lunched with the team, and then travelled on the club coach to the ground. Eric's father watched Manchester United storm to a 3–0 win and progress to the fifth round of the Cup for a derby tie against Manchester City. The elder Cantona seemed to enjoy his day out and I think he was justifiably proud to hear the family name being chanted around the stadium.

Our next Premier League game was away to Wimbledon, who shared Crystal Palace's ground at Selhurst Park, which gave certain sections of the press an opportunity to whip up a frenzy regarding Eric's return to the 'scene of the crime'.

Consequently, there were all manner of mischievous reports that the police were going over the top in their preparations for Eric Cantona's return to Selhurst Park. It is true that roadblocks were erected around the ground, but that was simply a precaution against an attempt by any of Crystal Palace's more thuggish fans to get tickets for a game that didn't concern them. Thankfully, the match was played without any off-field incidents, and we won 4–2.

As far as our Premier League prospects were concerned, having trailed Newcastle United by sixteen points earlier in the season, we had clawed our way back, and soon closed the gap to nine points. This meant that after a 6–0 thrashing of Bolton Wanderers, we faced an away game against Newcastle in early March, the outcome of which would play a vital part in settling the destination of the League trophy. The Manchester United dressing room was full of tension before the game as the boys knew that we had to win the match if we were to stay in the title race. I asked Eric what he was thinking, and with a nod and a wink he replied, 'Ned, if we win this game we will win the League.'

Newcastle battered us mercilessly for the whole of the first forty-five minutes, fortunately without scoring any goals, but in the second half we stepped up a gear and began to take control. It was a young Phil Neville who found Eric unmarked on the far post, and to the immense relief of the United fans, Eric banged it straight in. We led 1–0 and managed to hang on to the lead to take the three vital points. Manchester United had far from given up on this championship, which was definitely going down to the wire.

Hopes were still very much alive in the FA Cup as well, as yet another cup-final appearance beckoned after David Beckham scored a decisive goal against Chelsea in the semi-final played at the end of March.

By now Eric Cantona was in imperious form and the goals just kept on flowing from him. Going into the League game against Southampton on 13 April, we had played one game more than Newcastle, but found ourselves six points ahead of our north-east rivals, knowing that if we won the last four games we would be champions. However, the biggest talking point of the match concerned the grey away strip that the United lads were wearing. After a disastrous first half, during which United had conceded three sloppy goals, the Boss decided to change their kit to the club's third choice blue-and-white away strip. Nobody even bothered to check if the rules allowed a change of colours at half-time – Fergie was determined to do it anyway. Despite his unorthodox efforts to change the team's fortunes, we still ended up losing 3–1. The 'unlucky' grey strip never reappeared and cost the club a small fortune in lost merchandising.

Four days later we managed a 1–0 home win against Leeds, thanks to a late Roy Keane goal, but the day was perhaps more memorable for Fergie's comments during the post-match interview, in which he mused on whether the Leeds players would try as hard against Manchester United's principal championship rivals, Newcastle, when the teams met the following week. In the light of Fergie's controversial suggestion, after Newcastle had in fact recorded a win at Elland Road, the Magpies' manager, Kevin Keegan, revealed how Alex Ferguson had gone down in his estimation. In an over-emotional outburst, Keegan admitted: 'This has really got to me . . . It's not part of the psychological battle when you do that with footballers – like he said about Leeds,' thus proving that Fergie's mastery of the art of playing mind games with fellow managers was unrivalled.

A win at our final game of the season against Middlesbrough would secure us the title, and so it was with a 3–0 victory that we won our third Premier League Championship in four years. Both sets of fans gave the team a great celebratory round of applause as the players did a lap of honour, before taking part in a press conference and photocall.

The double was within our reach again for the second time in three years, and our collective nerves were frayed. We were off to meet Liverpool in the FA Cup final at Wembley on 11 May, and I spent the week beforehand making security arrangements with Ken Ramsden. We decided that I would accompany the directors and their wives down to London with two of my best men. The players would leave two days earlier and travel on their own.

'There's something else, Ned. A very delicate matter that I need to discuss with you,' Ken said, unusually secretively. 'At the after-match party, please keep an eye on Martin Edwards. His visits to the Ladies' are becoming more frequent.'

I stifled the urge to laugh. Both Ken and I knew the press would have a field day if they discovered that Martin had been caught in the women's toilet at a Manchester United function.

'No problem, Ken,' I assured the worried-looking director. 'I'll keep steering him towards the Gents'.'

The meeting over, I chuckled all the way back to my office. Looking back, it seems unbelievable that, in the days leading up to the game that would make history for United as the first club to do the 'double double', we were preoccupied with the disturbing fetish of our chairman. I had been aware of it since my SAS days, of course, when the United party had visited Hereford. It had been a constant source of amusement to the players and ground staff, but it was undeniably embarrassing.

Some months later, Danny McGregor, the affable commercial manager, asked me into his office and informed me that one of his female staff had been followed into the toilet at Old Trafford by a male, whom she was able to identify positively as Martin Edwards. Danny had assured me that the young lady in question was not going to the police, but he was at a loss as to how to deal with this intolerable situation. I assured Danny that I would take up the matter with the other directors, and to that end I made my way to Maurice Watkins's office at James Chapman, Solicitors. Maurice sat visibly wilting as I recounted Danny's tale, and added some other anecdotal evidence of my own, gained from various hotel and nightclub owners within the Greater Manchester area.

There was little doubt that this was not an occasional misdemeanour, but a serious and ongoing problem that had massive implications legally, morally and commercially for the club and the other directors. I felt this sat very uneasily with the family image of Manchester United, which they tried so desperately hard to convey and protect.

Martin Edwards joined the Manchester United Football Club board in 1970, courtesy of his father, whose association with the club had begun in the 1950s, when Matt Busby encouraged Louis Edwards, owner of a meat-packaging company, to invest in the club. On his father's death, in February 1980, Martin replaced Louis as chairman of United. His peeping-tom activities were already well known within the club by the time of the 1996 FA Cup final, yet Edwards was in an unchallengeable position as the majority shareholder. Eventually his sexual deviations would contribute to his downfall, but before the 1996 final they appeared to be a minor concern, certainly in comparison to what he and the board would have to deal with in the hours before the kick-off. Major trouble was brewing, and the source was Alex Ferguson.

The players left Manchester on the Thursday before the big game, while I stayed behind to accompany the directors and their wives on the train journey on the morning of the final. The plan was that the players would go directly to Wembley from their hotel and after the match would cross London to the Royal Lancaster Hotel, where they would either be celebrating or commiserating with each other. The whole Manchester United outfit was then due to return home the following day.

I accompanied the directors, their wives and girlfriends on to the coaches when we arrived in London, and made sure they were all checked in and on their way to change for lunch before leaving for Wembley. In the meantime Eddie Byrne was dispatched to the jewellers, Garrard & Co., to collect the League Championship trophy, as it had been sent away for some repair work after being damaged in a previous celebration. We wanted it back at the hotel for the revelries should we win.

I escorted the Manchester United party on to the coach and over to Wembley. On arrival, Ken Ramsden asked me to take him to meet Fergie in the dressing room, as he had some urgent information for him. As requested, I accompanied Ken down through the tunnel area and guarded the door to ensure that no one entered. As I stood outside, I noticed Martin Edwards and Maurice Watkins walking down the tunnel with two of their guests. Martin looked nervous and so I asked him if he was all right. He directed me to the toilet area and we went into the Gents' to talk privately.

'You won't believe this, Ned, but Ferguson telephoned Maurice

Watkins at his hotel and told him that unless he got his bonus and pay rise he wouldn't be leading the team out today,' Martin revealed, clearly upset.

'You're having a fucking laugh, Chairman,' I replied, incredulous.

'He was serious, Ned. He told Maurice Watkins that *he* could lead the team out otherwise.'

I dreaded to think what the Manchester United fans would have thought at the sight of the company lawyer leading the team on to the Wembley turf for a cup final.

It transpired that Maurice had tried to calm Fergie down over the phone, and told him that they would sort it out the following week, but that wasn't good enough for the Boss. The alternative was unthinkable, so a deal was eventually agreed, and Fergie would fulfil his managerial duties as expected.

I wondered just how much Fergie had been rewarded for his outrageous attempt at brinkmanship. I also wondered if, when he was honing his negotiation skills as a shop steward on Clydeside, he could have dreamed that one day they would stand him in good stead on the eve of a Wembley cup final.

Manchester United won the pre-match toss over who would wear the red strip, which to me seemed like a good omen, but the final turned out to be a dull game with only Roy Keane in brilliant form. Indeed, it wasn't until the eighty-second minute that David James, the Liverpool goalkeeper, pushed a David Beckham cross out to the edge of the goal area where, fortunately for United, Eric Cantona was lurking. After checking his pace, the Frenchman volleyed the ball into the Liverpool goal to give us a 1–0 lead that turned into a one-goal win. Manchester United entered the history books as the only team in the history of English football to win both the League Championship and the FA Cup double twice in three years.

After the match, as I kept an eye out for any possible threat to Eric while we crossed the lush Wembley turf, I asked him about the game. 'It was like a game of chess, and both sets of players simply waited for the other to make a mistake,' he replied, the classic definition of boring football.

The after-match party was a predictably high-spirited affair. Eddie Byrne had ensured that the repaired Championship trophy had been brought back in time, so that it was a great sight to see the two glittering cups on the top table bedecked with the red and white ribbons of Manchester United.

Eddie, Vinny and I took up our positions on the doors before the guests showed up. As the official party and guests began arriving, some well-known celebrities turned up uninvited, including Angus Deayton and Jennifer Saunders. They had heard where the party was being held and decided to invite themselves along. They approached the door alongside Lee Sharpe, who, when I quizzed him about the group, quickly replied that he had only met them up in the lobby, and they had simply followed him to the celebrations. When they reached me and tried to gain access to the banqueting room, I had to inform them that this was a private party and only invited guests were welcome: 'I have already checked the guest list and your names are not on it, therefore you will not be allowed entry into this function.' Deayton and his mates were outraged. They hung around the place for at least forty-five minutes, before eventually giving up hope.

I managed to keep the freeloaders out of the party and the chairman out of the Ladies', so a good night was had by all, with the exception of Theresa, Roy Keane's wife. At 6.00 a.m. she was sitting at the hotel bar in floods of tears, having failed at her thirtieth attempt to get Roy to leave his brothers and cronies at the bar and go to bed.

The close season for me was a busy time as it coincided with the Euro '96 Championship, during which Old Trafford played host to the world stars all the way to the semi-final. My planning and preparation went like clockwork, and on 9 June Germany played the Czech Republic in the first game played in Manchester. Everything went well, but the following weekend was a different matter entirely, when the IRA blew up the Arndale Shopping Centre in the centre of the city at noon on Saturday 15 June, injuring more than two hundred people, and causing widespread chaos and devastation.

Ken Ramsden contacted me within minutes of the blast and asked me to seal off Old Trafford. By 12.20 p.m., SPS had secured the stadium with great help from an obviously stretched police force. I also asked my men to carry out a thorough inch-by-inch search of the ground as my SAS training had taught me that where the IRA are concerned, lightning can certainly strike twice.

We found nothing in our searches and so the following day, with an afternoon kick-off looming, crowds of supporters started to drift towards the ground. Along with the police, we searched the bemused German and Russian fans' bags and satchels but nothing was found, and the game went ahead with Andrei Kanchelskis playing for Russia. Unfortunately for the former Reds' favourite, his side lost 3–0, but my main concern was we had got to the end of the game and that everyone would be going home safely.

CHAPTER 10

The Rise of the Young Pretenders

B Y THE SUMMER OF 1996, with a little help from the Manchester United board, I moved business premises at Old Trafford, and was relocated to an empty outbuilding. By now, my dream of building an empire had finally been realized; I had come from nothing, I was working in a business I loved, for the football club I loved, and I now had sizeable premises at Old Trafford. I was a lucky man indeed.

During the close season the club had to deal with some court action concerning Nicky Butt, one of the new rising generation of players, who was eventually cleared of assaulting a man in a restaurant.

I had known Nicky since his days as one of the star youth players. An amusing guy, and a practical joker, he was a down-to-earth local lad who just liked to get on with his life after the match or the training session. It was always perfectly clear that Butty was a player full of passion who liked to get stuck in on the pitch, but, as far as I was concerned, he was not the sort of man to start a brawl in a toilet.

The bare facts of the case were that Peter Oldbury, a twenty-six-year-old unemployed builder, who had used to go out with Butt's girlfriend, Shelley Barlow, had alleged that Butt had broken his nose in an 'unprovoked attack' in October 1995. But the truth, according to Nicky, was that Oldbury had been giving him grief for years and it was the supposed victim who had started the fight. I had not been aware of Nicky's problem with Oldbury, or else I would have advised him how to deal with the matter.

In July 1996, a jury at Manchester Crown Court took just forty minutes to find Nicky not guilty of assaulting Oldbury in the toilet at the city's Charlie Chan's restaurant. Nicky's innocence had been rightly proven, and he was able to resume his relationship with Shelley in peace. Most weekends I would see him after a game, out for a quiet drink with his girlfriend, and occasionally I'd be invited to join them.

Nicky Butt was a genuine guy in all the time I knew him at Old Trafford, but if he could find himself in trouble, what chance did the rest of them have? It occurred to me that I would have to start keeping my eye on this new generation wherever possible, to make sure that they kept their noses well and truly clean.

During the summer a number of new arrivals joined the club, including a footballer who would become one of my favourite Manchester United players. Ole Gunner Solskjaer arrived at United from the Norwegian side Molde for £1.5 million. I had all the time in the world for the 'Baby-faced Assassin' as the Norwegian would affectionately become known at the club.

He was a quiet man who kept himself to himself, was brilliant at his sport and loved United with a passion. He would turn up on time, play his heart out and then go home to his family. There were no dramas, no scandal and no tantrums. Ole had turned down many offers to move to other clubs where he would have been guaranteed first-team football on a more regular basis – but his heart belonged in Manchester.

July 1996 also saw the arrival of Karel Poborsky, who came to Manchester from Slavia Prague in the Czech Republic for £3.6 million after a brilliant performance for the Czech national side during Euro '96. I used to joke with Karel about his difficulty in speaking English properly, and to make a point, one of the first things he learned to say in English was 'How's your Czechoslovakian, Ned?'

His wife Marcella spoke English well enough for both of them and she really was his mouthpiece during his time at Old Trafford. When he arrived in England, Karel had teeth like a row of condemned houses, but once in the spotlight on the pitch, he had extensive dental work carried out, and it became a standing joke in the dressing room that the dental bill wiped out his signing-on fee.

Despite being at the club for almost eighteen months, I can honestly say that Karel came and went without anyone really getting to know him. His move to Benfica was notable for the Portuguese club's transfer cheque 'bouncing' when it was paid, but the financial niceties were sorted out eventually. It was not long before the other players were referring to him as 'Karel who?' as nobody in the dressing room could summon up any outstanding memories of him.

A world-famous name joined the Manchester United ranks a month after Solskjaer and Poborsky but, unfortunately, it was the son, not the father. Jordi Cruyff, son of the legendary Johan, arrived in August 1996 from Barcelona for £1.3 million. Jordi had started his playing career with the Ajax youth team in Amsterdam but followed his father to Barcelona in 1988. He then joined the Barcelona youth system and went on to play for the senior team for two seasons: 1994–5 and 1995–6.

His time at Old Trafford was never particularly happy and I always felt that he was cursed by his father's reputation. He did genuinely try his best to be his own man, but he was constantly compared to his father and felt compelled to try to live up to the standards the latter had set on the field, which was an impossible task.

When it suited his purpose, however, he was not above using his father's name to help him further his fortunes. Martin Edwards once revealed to me that Jordi had asked his father to try to negotiate a better deal with United than the one being offered by the club. Martin laughed as he told me that one of Cruyff Snr's opening gambits during the discussion was, 'Hey man, don't you know this is Johan Cruyff you're dealing with?'

The chairman knew exactly whom he was dealing with, but despite the stature of the footballing giant, it would have made no difference to the figures that Martin had laid on the table in the first place.

Jordi was not much liked by the other players and was destined never to fit in at Old Trafford. He did not feel he was getting a fair chance from the manager either, but if Fergie thought a player wasn't good enough, regardless of his pedigree, nothing could be said or done to change the manager's mind. Jordi eventually returned to Spain in June 2000 on a free transfer to Alaves.

While these international stars were making headlines by signing for the club, a youthful defender, Wesley Brown, also joined the squad in the summer of 1996. He was another young player whom I felt Fergie watched closely, and once he began earning big money at the club, after becoming a first-team regular in the 1998–9 season, the manager insisted that he move out of his family home and buy a house of his own.

Alex asked me to keep an eye on Wes and, even though it was not part of my job, I agreed to do so. On one or two rare occasions, when I felt he was taking a step in the wrong direction and keeping undesirable company, I shared my concerns with Fergie. I really liked the lad but he was, in my opinion, easily led astray and could have got himself into trouble – probably more by accident than design – and so I was certain that a fatherly blast from Fergie would ensure that Wes kept on the straight and narrow.

★ ★ ★

The start of our League Championship campaign had to wait until after the Charity Shield match against Newcastle at Wembley on 11 August 1996. We defeated the Magpies 4–0 and it was great to see the Reds do so well with so many of the young players I'd watched since their youth-team days. It was a superb youth-team policy that had produced these youngsters, for which credit must go to Brian Kidd and Eric Harrison. A great many youth players in the team of the early 1990s progressed to establish themselves in the world of professional football, including David Beckham, Nicky Butt, Gary Neville, Ryan Giggs, Keith Gillespie, Paul Scholes, Robbie Savage, John O'Kane, Ben Thornley, Chris Casper and Kevin Pilkington.

Our first League game was away to Wimbledon, a memorable match in which David Beckham scored a sensational goal from his own half, which marked his arrival on the Premier League scene in no uncertain terms.

In the European Champions League, after a loss and a win against Juventus and Rapid Vienna respectively in September, we headed off to Turkey once again, this time to play Fenerbahce. Manchester United's visits to Turkey were never without incident, and this occasion was no exception. Before the match Peter Schmeichel and Gary Pallister both received death threats: Gary Pallister's threat was made straight to his face when a Turkish fan came right up to him and threatened to cut his throat. Peter Schmeichel was a supposed target as a result of his actions in a previous game against Galatasaray, when he had wrestled a Turkish supporter to the ground at Old Trafford, after the man had run on with a burning flag.

I don't think Gary was really scared, but he was certainly affected by the whole experience, telling reporters at the time: 'For the sheer noise, not to mention the hatred from the terraces, it is hard to beat.'

I stood with Vinny Earl behind the Manchester United goal for the whole match, keeping an eye out for any trouble, but the only threat to Schmeichel came from a UEFA official who told him to take his lucky Umbro towel down from the goal netting as Umbro were not one of the official sponsors.

After goals from Beckham and Cantona, we left Turkey unscathed as 2–0 winners, but two weeks later, during Fenerbahce's return visit to Old Trafford, disaster struck when a deflection off Gary Pallister flew over Peter Schmeichel's head, and we were beaten 1–0. Worse still, our forty-year record of being undefeated by a European team at Old Trafford had been broken by a team of virtual unknowns, and not by one of the European heavyweight sides such as Real Madrid, Barcelona or Bayern Munich.

Juventus followed Fenerbahce's example and also triumphed with a 1–0 win at Old Trafford in November. Consequently, our qualification for the quarter-finals rested on defeating Rapid Vienna on Austrian soil early the following month. Fortunately, a goal each from Giggs and Cantona, combined with a clean sheet, guaranteed our progression to the next round, but the match would be best remembered for the hideous injury that Roy Keane sustained when his lower leg came into contact with a Rapid player's studs, which left his shin bone sticking out through his skin. As I followed his stretcher into the dressing room, people were either fainting or turning away in horror at the sight of his injury.

'Only a fucking scratch,' I joked, and winked at Roy, who smiled through the pain.

Fergie asked me to bring down Theresa, Roy's wife, from the stand, and they spent a few minutes alone together. A private man, Roy looked highly embarrassed by all the attention he was receiving.

'He'll live,' Fergie winked at Theresa, and I escorted her back to the VIP area to rejoin her party.

'Will he be all right, Ned?' she asked as we climbed the stand staircase.

'He'll be OK. The Devil looks after his own,' I assured her.

On the way home, I made it my job to ensure that Roy was as comfortable as he could be on the plane. After take-off Fergie came up the aisle and asked me how Roy was doing.

'I never thought I'd say this, Ned, but I think Roy is a better player than Bryan Robson,' Fergie added, and on that bombshell he headed back to his seat. I was surprised at Fergie's words as I had always believed that he thought Bryan was number one. The incident confirmed what I had already suspected, however, that Roy Keane would always be regarded as Fergie's lynchpin.

Roy was out of action for a while, but our League form was not too badly hampered, although, entering 1997, we were still behind Liverpool. With other players recovering from injuries as well, including Andy Cole – out with a double leg break – and David May, we also had an early exit from the FA Cup against Wimbledon, after a replay went the way of the London side. By March, however, we were just about ready to play host to FC Porto in the first game of the knock-out stages of the Champions League, and were under no illusion as to the Portuguese team's ability, knowing they were the only team in the competition to have remained unbeaten in the group stages.

There was a real party atmosphere at Old Trafford that night, and a magnificent performance from the Reds gave us a 4–0 advantage for the second leg.

In Portugal, a 0–0 draw was enough to put us in the semi-final of the Champions League, but what should have been a great night for Manchester United was marred even before a ball was kicked. The turnstile operators at the visiting team's end of the stadium were overwhelmed by the mass of Manchester United supporters trying to get into the ground. This led to long queues of singing Manchester United fans falling foul of the young and inexperienced riot police, who mistook the noise for trouble and charged into the supporters with batons flailing. I had travelled with about twenty of my staff to ensure security and order for the fans, and my men bravely put themselves between the police and the loyal United followers. Many were injured for their trouble, including my operations manager, Ian Bridges, who was badly beaten about the head, and who would joke that, after the beating, puddles would form on his head when it rained.

On our return to Manchester we were met by the press, desperate for a scoop, and hoping to raise the issue of the hooligan element among the Manchester United fans. There was simply nothing for them to report, of course, as our fans had been innocent victims.

Our Champions League semi-final first leg away to Borussia Dortmund in Germany was a tense, nail-biting ninety minutes: Nicky

Butt hit the post, David Beckham had a shot cleared off the line and, in the cruellest twist of all, Borussia Dortmund scored courtesy of a Gary Pallister deflection to win the tie by that single lucky goal.

Back home ten days later, in what the press called the Premier League decider, we travelled to Liverpool. However, some three weeks prior to that game my former SAS Brigadier, Andy Massey, sent me some drawings of artillery fire plans and asked me to pass them on to Fergie, as he believed these particular directives applied in battle could also be useful on the football field.

Fergie looked bemused at first, but soon became enthralled by the principles behind the Brigadier's plan. For set pieces the theory was really quite simple. The gun (in this case David Beckham) fired the shell (the ball). The shell would land on the target area (goalmouth) where they were aiming but the shell would not land in the same place every time as, obviously, air and other factors affect its flight path differently on each occasion. To counter this fact of ballistics, more targets (players) must be put in that general area. The players are duly kept bunched together tightly until the moment of delivery, then as the shell arrives within the target area, the players disperse with the aim of getting to the shell.

Fergie elected Eric Cantona, Gary Pallister and Ronnie Johnsen to be the 'targets' and, in the Liverpool game, they employed this method so successfully that from the first four corners, we scored twice (Gary Pallister on both occasions), had a shot cleared off the line, and another skimmed the crossbar on its way into the crowd. We defeated Liverpool 3–1 that day, and in the dressing room after the game, Fergie and Brian Kidd both sat beaming widely.

'We used your Brigadier's plan, Ned. It worked a treat,' said Fergie.

'Nice one, Boss,' I laughed, but I was extremely pleased, and felt certain that Liverpool would never have believed they had been up against the might of both Manchester United and the SAS that day.

Borussia Dortmund travelled to Old Trafford on 23 April for the second leg of the Champions League semi-final, a game we had to win to overcome their one-goal advantage. A capacity Old Trafford crowd gasped as Andreas Moller scored for the visitors, catching us on the break. All of our team missed scoring opportunities, but none as blatantly as Eric Cantona. He missed chances that on any other day he would have definitely scored. It was a miserable, frustrating night for the Reds. At the final whistle, I watched the Borussia Dortmund players celebrate going through to the Champions League final, and began to doubt that we would ever get a shot at victory in this competition.

I saw the lads safely out of the park and noticed that Eric was looking very bleak and despondent. He was marching towards the tunnel at the Stretford end of the pitch with his shirt off, dressed only in his shorts and boots. That sight was odd in itself, but much more unusual was the fact that he was completely ignoring the Manchester fans, which was most unlike him. Knowing that something was wrong, I called out to him but he just stormed down the tunnel, ignoring me too. It was much later that Eric told me the truth – that was the night he decided to retire from football because he felt that a European Cup win would always be out of his reach. He strongly believed that to become a legend at Manchester United it was essential to win the prestigious European competition, and he truly felt then that it would never happen for him. He had also been dropped from the French national side and knew he would not be back in the team for the World Cup in France '98. If Eric couldn't perform on the biggest stage in football then he would have to find himself another one.

Three draws and one win from our last four games was enough to make us League Champions again. It had been a great season for everyone connected with Old Trafford, but it was tinged with sadness for me, my SPS men, the players and many, many fans, as it was the last time that Eric Cantona would appear competitively in his famous number-seven shirt as a Manchester United player.

A week after winning the championship, the whole of Old Trafford, indeed, the world of football as a whole, was stunned by the announcement that Eric was quitting football to pursue a new career in the film industry – he had found another stage.

In a brief statement he explained that after thirteen years in the game it was time to move on to other challenges: 'I always planned to retire when I was at the top and at Manchester United I have reached the pinnacle of my career. In the last four and a half years I have enjoyed my best football and I have had a wonderful time.' He went on to thank his team-mates, manager and the Manchester United staff, before wishing them every success in the future.

And with that, he was gone, enigmatic to the end. The King had retired from the battlefield, and it was time for the young princes to show what they could do.

Although Eric was, on the face of it, a very family-oriented man, there was never any doubt about his love for women. He was never a heavy drinker and would only really let himself go when partying hard back in France. Very occasionally he would go on a serious bender when friends like Pascal Carbone or Jean-Jacques Bertrand came over to Britain to visit him.

I always had a ball on these nights out, but on a few occasions my old skills came in very handy. One night in a Manchester bar, Eric and Pascal were flirting with two pretty women who were clearly relishing the attention of the Frenchmen. Sadly, their husbands did not share their enthusiasm, and in no time they were squaring up to Eric and Pascal. I felt obliged to intervene to avoid any nastiness, and offered sincere apologies to the well-built husbands, assuring them that the guys were only having some innocent fun. After Eric bought the two couples champagne, calm was restored, to my relief. In all honesty, Eric rarely 'played away' during his time in England, but in France the gloves, or rather the pants, were often off.

One of Eric's few extramarital dalliances in England was with a female employee at a club to which he and I belonged. The woman in question was very attractive and was extremely hospitable to both of us – especially Eric. She was always ushering him into her office, and while I socialized with fellow club members, he would be taking advantage of the more exclusive member services on offer to him alone behind closed doors.

Afterwards, when we were saying our goodbyes, she would insist on planting a big kiss on my lips as we left. Eric would wink at me as she kissed me and I would almost throw up – the rascal had me convinced I had given him a blow job by proxy.

While at Manchester, it is fair to comment that Eric had a quite basic lifestyle; indeed, it was only at my suggestion, following the incident at Crystal Palace in January 1995, that he and his family were moved from the ex-council house they had been provided with by Manchester United, to a more comfortable home in Cheshire.

His choice of clothes, often a mix of extraordinary colour schemes, may have suggested he was a man who dressed with the light off, but back in France Eric led the lifestyle of a hedonistic prince. He would appear almost unrecognizable to his fans at Old Trafford were they given a glimpse of Eric at his château, walking the grounds or driving through the village streets in his Rolls-Royce or on his Harley-Davidson motorcycle.

In his choice of friends, too, Eric was more selective, mixing as he did with the crème de la crème of café society, including major film stars and directors, who enjoyed the company of this international football star, and who also shared in some of his excesses. Eric knew perfectly well that the privacy laws in France gave him and his circle of friends licence to fuck with impunity, which is exactly what he did whenever the opportunity arose.

On one occasion I was out on the town in Paris with Eric when he insisted we end the night at his favourite watering hole. We met up with a couple of Eric's friends, whom I shall call Pierre and Luc, and soon we drank our way down the three levels of bars into the den of iniquity which was the basement. The club offered wall-to-wall porn, beaming down from strategically angled TV screens, but, in the basement bar, the action was strictly live. In the centre of the floor was a huge circular bed, and to enjoy the sexual favours of other willing customers, all one had to do was to climb on to the bed and wait to be joined by another enthusiastic participant, to have sex while everyone else looked on.

After a few bottles of champagne, the club owner, also a friend of Eric's, joined us at the bar, where there was much laughing and joking. Not long afterwards, the owner beckoned to a stunning woman to come over and join us. He introduced her as his wife, though it struck me that the chemistry between her and Eric was electric. Seconds later, I couldn't believe my eyes as I watched her lead Eric and Luc towards the bed. Eric flashed me a wink and stuck his tongue out like a cheeky schoolboy.

'What the fuck . . . ?' I said to Pierre, but I was speaking to the back of his head as he was also en route to the bed wrapped around a tall blonde girl. I was left nodding pleasantries to the club owner as Luc and Eric enjoyed a threesome with his wife. My mind was racing and I didn't know where to put myself. I was out of my depth and really felt like Cliff Richard at a Caligula party. My embarrassment was not helped by Pierre's efforts to invite me to join him and the blonde. Attempting to wave me over, mid hump, the ever-generous Eric also tried to encourage me to join in with his romp. But I just lifted my glass and joked, 'I'll hold your feet, but that's it!'

I later discovered that the club-owner's wife was a former star of the porn film industry and it was obvious to me that she had lost none of her talent. It was the most erotic yet surreal experience of my life, and one that I will certainly never forget.

Eric knew his way around the privacy laws that the French took advantage of on their home soil, and he reaped the social benefits that many major stars in France enjoyed. One evening in another Paris nightclub, Eric was on the dance floor smooching the night away with a Parisian beauty. Eric's brother, Joel, and I were enjoying a glass of champagne at the bar when I noticed a photographer snapping away at Eric and the young lady. Joel and I made a lunge for the snapper and I removed the film from his camera. The club bouncers arrived on the scene and promptly ejected the photographer from the club. I remember thinking that if it had happened in Britain it would have blown into a far bigger story with potentially damaging repercussions.

At the time, and even now, I believe that Eric Cantona should have been offered a position with Manchester United in the coaching/management field, as I felt he had the ability to become one of the great managers in the game. When Brian Kidd left Old Trafford in December 1998, I called Eric and asked him to phone Fergie about the vacancy. I tried to convince him that if he wanted to be taken seriously as prospective management material, he should stop playing beach soccer and put some effort into working for his UEFA coaching certificates. Typically, Eric declined my suggestion, claiming he did not want to be a number two to anyone – not even Fergie. I shared my thoughts on the subject with Martin Edwards, who gave me a sympathetic hearing but advised that should Manchester United need a new manager, they would require someone with real experience, not just real charisma.

I also told Fergie of Eric's ambitions and he very kindly suggested that Eric should come across to Old Trafford and help coach the team for a couple of weeks to gain some valuable experience. Eric was to have stayed with me in my home during his fortnight of coaching with Fergie, but at the last minute he decided not to take up the manager's offer. In my view it was a missed opportunity to further his football career, but Eric seemed content to pursue other interests, away from the sport that had made him a legend.

Eventually, Eric applied to register his name, shirt number and the phrase 'Ooh Aah Cantona' as commercial trademarks in 1997, taking action similar to Denis Law's many years earlier, fearful that Manchester United would exploit his name and image for their merchandising ends. Little did he know that he was soon to be replaced by the 'Brylcreem Boy', David Beckham, as the club's golden goose.

When he retired from football, Eric chose to live with his family in Barcelona, and in spring 1999 he invited me to spend a weekend with them all. On the drive to his home we talked about old times, and laughed at some of the scrapes we had been through and the antics we had got up to together. At his home his wife, Isabelle, greeted me, and I was amazed to see how much his little daughter Josephine had grown. His son, Raphael, was at the American School in Barcelona, from where we picked him up and surprised him that afternoon. Eric lived in some style in the Spanish city, in a luxury complex that was also home to former Barcelona star Ronald Koeman, and we spent a pleasant afternoon talking football. I was surprised to learn just how au fait Eric was with current team personnel around the globe, and it seemed to me that his desire to be part of the game had not diminished. I was not convinced that the movie world was living up to his expectations.

Knowing Eric's reputation as well as I did, I could not resist the temptation of asking him if he had tried his luck with Cate Blanchett while filming *Elizabeth* – his first big-screen break. He gave me a wicked smile and said, 'Non,' but I was not sure I believed him. He did, however, say that Sir Richard Attenborough had been very supportive, offering him help and encouragement throughout the filming process.

That evening, Eric declared that the two of us must go out on the town. I was curious to discover if his *joie de vivre* had abated any in his retirement, but I was soon to find out that nothing had changed. Our adventure began at a bar in the centre of Barcelona with a commanding view of the city. After a few drinks, the conversation, as always, turned to women and, when we had shared a few reminiscences, I stopped Eric in his tracks.

'I know who you were shagging in my flat when you borrowed it for your secret liaisons,' I revealed with a wink.

Eric was dumbstruck but, after a large gulp of his drink, regained his composure. 'Who told you?' he asked.

'Nobody, mate. I just followed the clues,' I replied, tapping the side of my nose, knowingly.

'Who was she, then?' Eric asked, calling my bluff.

I raised my glass and named the wife of a former Manchester United player, whose car I often used to see parked outside my flat whenever she and Eric met for their regular bit of fun.

'Fuck me! How did you find out?' he asked.

'My business to know everything, Eric,' I laughed.

I wondered whether the move to Barcelona might have calmed him down, and made him change his ways. To satisfy my curiosity I asked him whether he had stopped chasing women, and without giving me an answer, his actions in the next couple of hours left me in no doubt.

After finishing our drinks we left the bar, and Eric drove us to a seedier part of town, where we parked outside a bar in a dimly lit street. I followed him dutifully as we walked through the bar, exited through the back, and ended up in an underground car park.

'Follow me, Ned,' said Eric, heading for the lift. Three floors later, he was knocking at an apartment door that opened to reveal wall-to-wall hookers. The women were absolutely stunning and all wore numbered badges. It was like a kinky pick-and-mix! Eric chose his girl and I mine, and the ladies led us to adjoining rooms where the fun began. Recalling various carnal discussions that I had shared with Eric over the years, I knew he had a penchant for slapping women's bottoms, and from the noises coming from the room next door, it sounded as though this lady had been particularly naughty. Once Eric and I had had our money's worth, we headed for his favourite karaoke bar. The reception he received from punters and staff alike made it clear he was as popular here as he had been at Old Trafford. The place erupted. After far too many drinks, Eric headed for the low stage, grabbed the microphone and proceeded to murder the Beatles' classic 'Yesterday'. Despite his dire rendition, the assembled crowd loved him, which left me thinking that Eric could do no wrong in Barcelona.

After a day of sightseeing, I returned home to Manchester the following morning. It had been an entertaining weekend, and an eye-opener as always, and I very much looked forward to my next encounter with the great man.

Back at Old Trafford, an exciting summer signing prior to the start of the 1997–8 season was Teddy Sheringham, who was bought for

£3.5 million from Spurs in June. Most people saw Sheringham as a straight replacement for Eric Cantona; indeed, many pundits viewed him as an intelligent player who was the closest thing to Cantona in an England shirt. When Martin Edwards had told the Boss, who was on holiday at the time, that Sheringham was available, Fergie jumped at the chance.

At the time of his transfer, Sheringham was going out with Nicola Smith, sister of that well-known Lolita of the pop world, Mandy Smith, the erstwhile teenage bride of the wrinkly rocker and Rolling Stone, Bill Wyman. My first encounter with Teddy's group of friends was at an after-match party at the Royal Lancaster Hotel which was strictly VIP pass only, and my instructions from Fergie were that there were to be no exceptions. Halfway through the proceedings Teddy beckoned me into a corner and rather sheepishly asked if I could let in his girlfriend's sister and her new boyfriend.

'No fucking way, Teddy. She's not on the list,' I had to tell him. 'I can't do it, mate. She's not getting in.'

Teddy shrugged and returned to his friends. A few hours later Vinny, my man on the door, contacted me to say that Mandy had turned up and was causing a fuss, claiming that she had been invited. I arrived on the scene and told her to leave, but she refused to move. Half an hour later, after some frantic phone calls from Mandy, Teddy and Nicola came to the door and began pleading her case. With Teddy in such an awkward position, I didn't have the heart to refuse him, so I relented and let her in. I made it clear that she could only stay in the reception area, and could not enter the banqueting suite where the dinner was being served, but my restrictions were not to her liking.

No sooner had Mandy got her feet under a table than she snarled at me as I passed by: 'What's your problem?'

I wasn't sure if I'd heard correctly, so asked her to repeat what she had said.

My reply was short and to the point: 'Not half the problem you'll have with me if you don't keep quiet. You'll be back out of that door before your feet touch the ground.'

She darted a look in Teddy's direction but I was quick to snap: 'Don't think he'll save you if I throw you out.'

Teddy and the rest of his company suddenly took a great interest in the pattern of the carpet, while she sat there defiantly, desperate to say something but unsure of the response she would get. I just turned my back and went back to guarding the adults.

During his four years at the club, I felt that Teddy never really settled in Manchester. At every opportunity he would be down the M6 like a bat out of hell towards London, maintaining strong ties with his own 'manor'.

Much has been said about Teddy's relationship with Andy Cole, but the truth of the matter is that they didn't get on from the start. Yet it was unusual for two major players in the England and United set-ups not to have made an effort to tolerate each other in a professional manner. When they were playing in a match together, and Coley made a mistake, Teddy couldn't ignore it and would have a go at him. It was this sort of behaviour that started a feud between the two men, which still goes on today, as they refuse to speak to each other. Teddy also had a problem with Andy Cole's attitude, and found him immature. I wondered whether their dispute had its origins in their North London rivalry, as Andy was on Arsenal's books as a schoolboy and Sheringham was, of course, a Spurs legend.

Teddy's girlfriend, Nicola Smith, was a pretty girl but it struck me that she was someone who always wanted to be the centre of attraction. On one occasion she asked me if I would ban the well-known model Jordan from the players' lounge, who had been invited along by Dwight Yorke. As Dwight could invite whomever he liked as his guest I couldn't possibly ask Jordan to leave, so I had to refuse Miss Smith's request.

When the opportunity arose at a later party, however, she took matters into her own hands. Nicola and Victoria Beckham were on the dance floor when the DJ played the song, 'Who Let The Dogs Out?' The two of them started to dance next to the table where Jordan was sitting and soon began singing the song out loud. It was quite clear to Jordan and everybody else standing nearby, that they were directing their petty behaviour at the model. Sometimes the Manchester United girls could be harder to handle than the lads.

Then, at a New Year's Eve party in Manchester in December 1999, when the clock struck midnight Teddy got down on his knees and proposed to Nicola. Looking on with a beer in my hand and my mouth wide open, I stared at the couple in disbelief, thinking, 'What's he doing? He's gone mad!' I was sure he must have been drunk, especially since they had split up earlier in the relationship, although despite my reservations, I wished them all the best. I wasn't surprised, however, when they split up again, this time for good, after Teddy left Old Trafford for a second stint with Spurs at the end of the 2000–1 season.

As the World Cup was to be held in France in summer 1998, the Premier League kicked off earlier than usual at the start of the 1997–8 season. In addition to Teddy Sheringham, Henning Berg also joined Manchester United, and with their input the Reds got off to a great start in the Premier League campaign. We were drawn away to Slovakian side FC Kosice in the European Champions League in September, and won 3–0, which was the first positive step in our quest for the trophy that everyone at Old Trafford now saw not only as our ultimate ambition, but also a realistic target.

In September, the Premier League match between Chelsea and Manchester United at Old Trafford, which was usually a happy hunting ground for the visitors, became better known for the furore off the pitch than for the bad-tempered behaviour on it. Chelsea were going through a 'mad, bad and dangerous to know' period, which eventually got them a warning from the FA. Their previous match against Arsenal had been an ugly affair, and they carried on in similar fashion against us, but the United of that era did not take things lying down. The game was full of off-the-ball incidents involving Roy Keane, Nicky Butt and Andy Cole from the Reds, and Chelsea's Dennis Wise, Dan Petrescu, Frank Leboeuf and even manager Ruud Gullit, who kept jumping out of the dugout. In the end, nine players were shown yellow cards and it was surprising that nobody was sent off.

Approaching half-time I became concerned that the mayhem might continue off the pitch. When the referee, Gary Willard, blew the whistle for the break, I was already in place, having made my way to the tunnel to wait for the players coming off the park. As they reached the halfway point inside the tunnel, the verbals started, and within seconds it appeared to me that a total free-for-all had broken out. Fortunately I had brought the SPS Quick Reaction Force (QRF) with me – the elite team I had trained to deal with crowd troubles within the stadium. I hadn't expected to be using them on the players, but needs must. We all rushed in to try and break up the fracas, but not before Dennis Wise had been hit in the face and sent tumbling to the ground. Soon there were other bodies on the tunnel floor, and Roy Keane required four stitches to a head wound.

Eventually both the QRF team and the regular stewards managed to break it up, and the players were kept apart in their respective dressing rooms. The police arrived, demanding to know what had happened. To most observers it was merely a temper tantrum in the tunnel, but the police were not happy with this explanation.

One of my SPS men told me that Fergie wanted to see me, so I went into the dressing room and he asked me exactly what had gone on. I told him that, in my opinion, it was just hot-headedness that had got out of control. Fergie wanted to bring in the police, but I explained to him that involving the cops was not a good idea, not least because, as we all know, footballers quickly kiss and make up. Fergie smiled as I added, 'And think of the media attention that it would cause. It's best to let sleeping dogs lie, Boss.'

Fergie thought hard for a few seconds about what I had said and replied, 'OK, son, but I want you to stay close to our players. I don't want Round Two at the final whistle.'

'Not a problem, Boss,' I assured him, hoping that common sense would prevail.

The second half was just as exciting as the first, and the match finished 2–2 with Ole Gunnar Solskjaer snatching a late equalizer. There were no more incidents after the final whistle, but the entire Chelsea contingent left in a rage. The tunnel fight was hushed up, but I was certain that the real reason why Gullit and the players left Old Trafford in a fury that day was because they had been given a trouncing in the tunnel, not on the pitch.

After the match, the police wanted to speak to me. They asked me what had really gone on in the tunnel, so I explained what I had seen, and tried to make light of it by suggesting to them that football players were not real fighters and it was just a scuffle. In my view none of the players could box kippers. The police officers were not satisfied with my version of events, and told me so in no uncertain manner, but I had related my view of the incident and assured them there was nothing more I could contribute. Had there been a full police inquiry, both I and the members of my staff would have continued to co-operate, but the affair died a quiet death, thankfully, or else the players and officials of both sides would have been under investigation, and subjected to endless interviews, for weeks – distractions the team could certainly have lived without.

Three days later, a 1–0 defeat away at Leeds United was memorable for two reasons: firstly, the Manchester United faithful were reminded of the loss of Eric Cantona; playing at the ground of his first English club, his absence from our team was somehow magnified. Secondly, as a result of making a crunching tackle on Leeds defender Alf Inge Haaland, Roy Keane had seriously damaged the ligaments in his knee and was out for the season. While Roy lay on the ground writhing in agony, Haaland wrongly accused him of feigning injury, which the United player never forgot. Keano waited more than three years for a chance to get his revenge on the Norwegian, by which time Haaland was playing for Manchester City. Roy's assault on Haaland's left leg almost crippled his opponent, but though the illegal challenge cost him a red card, Keane was satisfied to have made his point.

During my time with Manchester United, it became quickly apparent to me that Roy Keane was someone who would not allow anyone to walk over him, with the possible exception of Fergie, whether he be a team-mate, opponent or friend. Indeed, while recovering from the career-threatening injury he sustained in the Leeds game, Keane was involved in a serious confrontation with his own goalkeeper, Peter Schmeichel, a man renowned for his outspoken opinions.

One day, during a pre-season tour, Peter, who was described in Roy's autobiography as 'a poser' and 'a show-off', stepped over the mark in one of his all-too-frequent verbal tirades. In his time at United, Schmeichel had rowed with virtually all the big names in the squad, but with Roy Keane, he had riled the wrong man. In spite of his stature, standing a head taller than Roy, Schmeichel swiftly felt the power of the Irishman's fist in his face, and from that day onwards there was no doubt as to who was top dog in the dressing room.

A couple of years after he left, I was driving in a car with Eric Cantona when I happened to mention the incident involving Roy and Peter. Eric laughingly told me that he wasn't surprised, as he had also come close to punching Schmeichel in the dressing room after training one morning, because of the Dane's attitude towards him.

In the Champions League, meanwhile, we were making notable progress in October 1997, beating the Italian giants Juventus 3–2 at Old Trafford, and three weeks later facing Dutch champions Feyenoord, again at home, and triumphing 2–1, to record our third consecutive European victory.

When the newly promoted Barnsley visited Manchester, also in October, the gap between Division One and the Premier League was made all too obvious when we thrashed them 7–0. The Barnsley manager, Danny Wilson, was a good mate of mine, and I tried to cheer him up after the game by telling him, 'You'll be all right, you'll stay up.' But we both knew that the season would be a tough one for the South Yorkshire club.

The goals were flowing home and away, in Europe and in the Premier League, for the Reds. After thrashing Sheffield Wednesday 6–1, we travelled to Rotterdam to play Feyenoord, where a great 3–1 Manchester United victory was secured by an Andy Cole hat-trick. But once again the win was blighted by fans from both sides clashing in the stands. The Dutch police had plenty of experience of dealing with this sort of violence, and so the trouble didn't last long and a few of the part-time pugilists were rewarded with a hefty thump from a Dutch police baton. It struck me that the fans were really only mirroring what happened during the game as Feyenoord's tackling was truly shocking, with one particularly bad lunge putting Denis Irwin out for a month.

A coveted place in the Champions League quarter-finals was finally assured for our hard-working team, when, at the end of November, a visit from Slovakian side FC Kosice produced a 3–0 home victory.

At home, the FA Cup and Premier League were still well within our sights. Facing Barnsley in the fifth round of the FA Cup in February 1998, the general feeling was that if we could beat them 7–0 in the League, then a cup victory was highly likely. However, this was not to be the case. After a 1–1 draw at Old Trafford, which was thought to be a mere blip on the radar, the minnows of this scenario had a point to prove and put us out of the cup competition in the replay with a 3–2 win over a weakened United side.

The European quarter-finals were upon us and we headed for the playboy paradise of Monaco, but could only manage a 0–0 draw against FC Monaco. In an uneventful trip, for me the highlight was watching Eddie Byrne in action at the famous Casino de Monte-Carlo in the main square. Dressed up to the nines, we headed straight for the roulette tables.

'Number seven never fails. It's my lucky number,' Eddie tried to convince us, as he plonked down £300 worth of chips on his 'lucky' seven. The wheel spun and the ball finally settled on the casino's even luckier number twenty-two. Eddie turned to the lads, muttering, 'It's all a fix,' before storming out of the casino, cursing his bad luck.

I had watched the away game from the dugout at Fergie's side, never guessing that Fabien Barthez, Monaco's bald goalkeeper, would one day choose to play for the Reds. In the return leg, Monaco visited a less than glamorous Manchester, and held us to a 1–1 draw. With a crucial away goal against us, we were out of Europe once again. Disappointed to have come so far once again with no reward, there were some very long faces in the Manchester United camp that March evening.

Winning the League was to be our only chance of glory this season. At the end of February, the bookmakers had closed the book on United winning the League, as we had an eleven-point lead over Arsenal at the top of the table. One bookie even paid out on United as if they had already won, but it was to prove a major error of judgement.

After a hard season, we had little to show for our endeavours. Amidst the feeling of doom within Old Trafford, there had even been talk of Fergie leaving the club, but he soon issued a statement indicating that he intended to be around for a long time to come.

Despite winning our last three games of the season, our grasp on the Premier League title had slipped away into the hands of our nearest rivals, Arsenal. Manchester United were the runners-up for the second time in the Premier League's six-year history. Having become so accustomed to success at Old Trafford, winning nothing was like experiencing a death in the family. Fortunately, the 1998 World Cup finals proved to be a useful diversion from dwelling on United's failures in the previous months, watching players who might well have been on Fergie's shopping list for the new season.

One significant highlight during the close season was the visit of the great Brazilian football superstar, Pelé, who flew into Manchester to open the Manchester United museum. I had previously met him in a professional capacity in September 1997, providing security for him on a promotional tour for MasterCard in Paris and Cairo, and so it was a privilege to see this legend again, this time on home soil.

I had a long chat with Fergie in the summer, during which time we discussed the forthcoming season, and how it could not be as bad as the last. 'Boss, is all the media speculation accurate?' I asked the canny manager. 'Is Jaap Stam leaving PSV Eindhoven and coming to Old Trafford?'

Fergie laughed. 'Trust you, Ned. You never miss a trick. Aye, he's coming, and lots more besides,' Fergie replied with a wink. It transpired that Fergie had had a showdown with the board, and had persuaded them to loosen the purse strings.

The 'more besides' turned out to be Jesper Blomqvist from Italian club Parma, whom Fergie had had his eye on since watching his performance as an IFK Gothenburg player in the Champions League in 1994, and, after a drawn-out transfer saga, Dwight Yorke from Aston Villa. Villa chairman Doug Ellis had kept refusing to release Yorke and only relented when Dwight had come to Ellis's office in tears, begging to be released so he could join United.

On a day out at a Chester race meeting where SPS were providing security in the summer, I bumped into Middlesbrough boss Bryan Robson, looking in very good health. Talk, as always, turned to football, and I casually mentioned that I'd heard that Gary Pallister would be happy to leave Manchester United if the deal was right.

'Christ, Ned. I'd have Gary in my team in a heartbeat,' said Bryan.

I smiled and replied that I was certain the defender would be glad to play for any club managed by his former team-mate.

Gary Pallister did return to Middlesbrough, his first professional club, not long after our chat. I always felt sad when one of the players moved on from Manchester United, especially one like Gary, whose career I had watched flourish since he joined the Reds in August 1989.

When Steve Bruce left the club in June 1996, and I mentioned that he would be sorely missed by all, Ken Ramsden told me he thought I was getting over-melodramatic: 'Ned, players at Manchester United are like ships in the night, just passing through. Just wait until you and I have been here another fifteen years . . .'

A sobering thought indeed.

CHAPTER 11

The Buggers
in the Boardroom

AT THE DAWN of the era that saw the greatest season in Manchester United's history, it is worth reflecting on how close the club came to seeing all those amazing dreams go up in smoke, for I have no doubt that, if left to their own devices, the board of Manchester United plc would have made a mess of everything. It seemed to me that they nearly drove Fergie away, and they almost sold the club to another company, which would certainly not have had the best interests of United at heart.

During my time with United, members of the board and the club's senior staff were often kind to me personally, but they were also collectively quite maddening at times. Not the least of their problems was an occasionally overwhelming sense of paranoia, a destructive lack of trust between fellow board members, which led to my being involved in surveillance checks at Old Trafford.

There were two occasions when club chairman and chief executive Martin Edwards had asked me to carry out searches for bugging devices under the 'old pals act', as, due to feelings of mistrust resulting from internal wranglings with other Manchester United board members, he did not want anyone else to know of his suspicions. The first was in 1990 at the time of major disagreements between Edwards and a former employee.

It was alleged that the man had somehow obtained a set of keys for the offices at Old Trafford, and was tapping the phones. He had, apparently, established a relationship with an Old Trafford office girl, and although he had been sacked, he was still able to gain access to club premises. Edwards suspected that this young lady was helping him enter the offices at night.

There had been a number of stories in the newspapers about United's boardroom shenanigans, ever since the days when Michael Knighton had tried to buy the club in 1989, albeit without success. Edwards was absolutely convinced that someone within Old Trafford was passing on information to the press, and without naming the former employee, he made it clear whom he suspected.

I called in some friends who specialized in counter-surveillance measures, whose company was made up of former members of a government intelligence unit, discreet and highly trained. I spoke with my contact, who was also called Martin, and he arranged to come to the ground at around seven o'clock one evening, when everyone had left for the day.

Martin, his colleagues and I met with the chairman at the South Reception door and he let us in. Edwards requested a full-scale sweep of the offices to find any listening devices, and he also wanted to bug one of the phones to try to catch the culprit. The whole job took between three and four hours, and later that night I reported to Edwards that nothing had been found in the shape of listening or video devices in or around his office. We were absolutely sure that the whole place was clean. Edwards and I then talked with the experts, before walking round the building to work out where people were most likely to go if they were making secret phone calls.

We came to the conclusion that the best place for such covert activity would be the boardroom itself. Having a lock on the door, calls could be made with the utmost privacy, without fear of being overheard or interrupted. The bug was duly planted in the telephone with a voice-activated tape recorder in a secret place near by. Although such cloak-and-dagger tactics may be considered a little extreme, Martin Edwards was determined to discover the identity of the mole, and considered these actions to be wholly justified under the circumstances.

Martin the de-bugger was sworn to secrecy and was asked to come in and check the tape for recorded calls at least once a week, after being issued with guidance about what to listen out for. For the first couple of weeks, I accompanied him to listen to the recordings. It transpired that the office girl we suspected of being involved with the former employee had, in fact, used the boardroom telephone on a regular basis, and in one of the recorded calls she was heard having a very risqué chat with a male person unknown to either Edwards or myself. We couldn't help but have a good laugh listening to what was being said between the giggling pair, whose explicit conversations left nothing to the imagination.

There was little else that was damaging to the board or the club on the tapes, and I left Martin to carry on checking them weekly. We worked on a need-to-know basis; if I didn't hear from him, I could safely assume that everything was fine. Nothing was ever reported to me that would have justified the chairman bugging his own boardroom, but such was the level of paranoia at that time that he felt he had no option but to investigate any potential security breach.

The second occasion was during the 1995–6 season, when once again Martin Edwards called me in privately to carry out a 'technical search' of the offices. The same suspicions had arisen but no prime suspect was identified. A similar pattern of events took place, but this time I had a younger crew. We decided to widen the search and explored the old and dusty attic space. This time the inspection wasn't in vain, for during our thorough checks we discovered equipment and material in the attic that indicated the place had been bugged for some time. I went to get Edwards and informed him that we had found recording equipment in the attic, and were currently following the wires to locate their origins. When my man had finished his investigation, he told us that the end of the wires were taped to the ceiling underneath Edwards's office. In the loft space above Ken Merrett's office, which was directly underneath that of the chairman's, we found a tape recorder and several tapes.

We took the evidence up to Edwards's office, and then tried to listen to the cassettes, but as the tape recorder wasn't working properly, I told the chairman that it would be best to lock it in his safe overnight and we would meet again the following morning when he came to work. The next morning I arrived at the club just after 9 a.m., and went straight to Ken Merrett's office, motioning him to come outside and to keep quiet. Ken did as I asked, albeit with an irate expression on his face, and before he could say anything, I told him of the previous night's search and its results. I explained that microphones were found between his office and the chairman's office. His face went deathly white when he heard the news.

'Have you played them yet?' he asked.

'No, we'll do that when the chairman arrives,' I said.

We then went into Ken Ramsden's office and I gave him a detailed explanation of the events of the previous evening.

It was then that Merrett told me that he was worried about what might be on the tapes. He confessed that he had little time for the finance director Robin Launders. Indeed, Launders was not well liked at the club generally, because as far as most of the old guard were concerned, he was from the City, and was viewed as a money man, not a football man. When he eventually left United there were few who mourned his departure. But at that time he was finance director and, as such, was a senior figure in the Manchester United set-up. It later transpired that Robin Launders was in the building on the evening we discovered the devices, and soon all the directors were looking decidedly sheepish, each wondering just exactly what they might have said about each other on the tapes, for all was about to be revealed. I could tell by Robin's demeanour that he, too, had obviously been talking 'out of school' about a fellow director, and was fearful of it all coming back to haunt him. The next couple of days promised to be most uncomfortable for anybody who might have been either involved in the bugging or who had said something on the phone believing their conversations to be private and confidential.

On listening, the tapes had good sound quality, and various conversations between the chairman and directors could be heard quite clearly. It was fortunate for all concerned that there was nothing of any consequence on the tapes, as conversations were deemed to be old, and all were completely innocent. Nevertheless there were many who were relieved that we had discovered the situation before any damage had been done, and I presumed that, as a consequence, everyone concerned was considerably more guarded in their telephone conversations within Old Trafford from then on.

It was never discovered who had planted the bugs and tape recorders, but the fact that they had existed proved that, theoretically, Martin Edwards and the board were absolutely right to be concerned about in-house security and confidentiality. The air of mistrust and suspicion now prevalent at Old Trafford further strengthened my view that this football club was beginning to be run along the lines of the great corporations which had, for years, endured industrial-espionage conspiracies, which was a far from ideal situation.

In 1999, the main directors' offices were relocated to the old scoreboard end in the East Stand, but the board continued their preoccupation with surveillance, employing a rigorous approach to security at the club.

Manchester United did not just monitor the performance of potential signings on the pitch through the orthodox method of scouting; the club also examined their lives off it. Almost unbelievably, in one case, involving one of the best known footballers in Britain, Manchester United instructed that a full-blown SAS-style surveillance operation be mounted. The player, Chris Sutton, the former England international who, at the time of writing, plays in a talented Celtic team alongside Henrik Larsson and John Hartson, would never have been aware that, for two weeks of his life, his every movement was watched twenty-four hours a day by two former SAS covert-surveillance experts.

The then head scout at Manchester United, Les Kershaw, wanted the report on Sutton to help him evaluate the young player's suitability for joining the club. The board of Norwich City had decided to put Chris Sutton and Ruel Fox up for sale, and Sutton was of great interest to Kershaw. I contacted two of my former SAS colleagues and gave them the details of this strange mission. Both of these individuals had followed some of the most important figures in both the IRA and UDA for months without detection, so trailing a young, unsuspecting footballer would be a breeze.

The surveillance team duly went over to Norwich and started following Chris Sutton after a City home game. They tracked and photographed his every move – where he went, whom he met – and then they checked out his associates. They shadowed him to pubs, clubs, the training ground and shops. They even followed him as he visited his son Jordan, whose mother was an air hostess from Warrington. Their surveillance was so intense that if Sutton had farted, these guys would have smelt it.

After two weeks, I submitted the report to Les Kershaw, and told him that we had found nothing to substantiate the rumours of illegal substance abuse surrounding Chris Sutton, concluding that the young footballer had been wrongly suspected all along. Kershaw nodded and walked off with my report under his arm.

Chris Sutton never joined Manchester United. Instead, Blackburn

Rovers received the benefit of his great talent, and after a brief spell at Chelsea, he moved to Celtic in July 2000.

There was now little doubt in my mind that certain individuals within the hierarchy of Manchester United had allowed the sheer size of this club to lead them to lose sight of the right and proper way to run the 'company', and were beginning to display certain egocentric characteristics both in their professional dealings with prospective players and also in their personal affairs.

Maurice Watkins was a pleasant enough man who has done much for Manchester United in his capacity as company lawyer, and who had worked very closely and diligently with Martin Edwards to take the club to the very top. In his personal life, however, circumstances were less than straightforward. For some time he had been having an affair with a woman who had become a regular visitor to Old Trafford, and by December 1994 they had had a child together. Now a proud father to their son, he would attend Old Trafford matches with his family one week, and his lover the next. I found the situation quite uncomfortable, and often wondered how he squared this with his conscience as a major figure in a so-called 'family club'. As a consequence of her relationship with Maurice, his lover, Elaine, appeared to think that she was entitled to the same rights and advantages as members of the Watkins family, which I found difficult to comprehend and to deal with.

After Alex Ferguson's testimonial game in October 1999, in which the United players faced a World XI side, there was a reception in the Europa suite for the footballers who had come from all over the world to play that night to honour the manager. Even though Maurice was not attending the event, Elaine had decided that she would go, and that she would bring a number of friends along with her. I was on duty at the door to the suite and had to inform her that neither she nor her entourage could join the party as none of them were on the guest list. Needless to say, the news was not well received by Elaine and tensions soon mounted. After Maurice's private secretary, Marion, joined in the debate, insisting that I stand aside and let them in, Elaine then called Maurice on his mobile phone.

I agreed to speak to Maurice, and I explained to him that I was under strict instructions not to let anyone in without a pass. I could not turn a blind eye on this particular occasion as she had turned up with a party of six and the place was already full. I handed the phone back to her offering my apologies but insisting that my instructions were non-negotiable. It was a highly embarrassing situation that I had found myself in, and further brought home to me just how unsavoury certain aspects of life at the club had become.

A couple of weeks later Maurice tracked me down in the players' tunnel and demanded that I apologize to both Elaine and Marion. I explained to him that I was only following orders and thus had done nothing that required further apology, although I assured him I had a certain sympathy both for his position and Elaine's humiliation. Maurice would not look at me, never mind speak to me, for a period of time, but eventually common sense prevailed and we put the episode behind us.

Far more important matters loomed when BSkyB's original bid of £570 million to buy the club was raised to nearly £624 million in September 1998, which meant that Martin Edwards stood to make £85 million if the deal went through. The fans and ordinary shareholders organized a very loud campaign against the sale, with the backing of some MPs and even government ministers. It all came to a head at the annual general meeting of the plc in November. Martin Edwards, in particular, received a very hard time at the meeting and there were genuine fears for his safety as feelings and emotions were running high. At all times Martin insisted that I accompany him in the Manchester Suite in the North Stand. To my relief he was only attacked verbally, most poignantly by one elderly supporter who told the board that Manchester United had been built by the 'blood, sweat and tears of the people of this city'.

The plc chairman, Professor Sir Roland Smith, used his not inconsiderable expertise to maintain some semblance of order during the meeting, and for more than two hours managed to keep it from boiling over. His graciousness almost veiled the fact that he was in favour of the deal, knowing well that the large sum of money would allow Manchester United to expand beyond anyone's wildest dreams.

Few people realized that Sir Roland Smith was not just a high-powered executive with an impeccable pedigree in business, he was also a life-long Manchester United fan. It was Sir Roland who sorted out the 1998 debacle surrounding Fergie's future at the club: at a time when speculation was rife that he was about to resign, Fergie had returned from the World Cup to explain to the board that he wished to continue as manager. Furthermore, in 2001, Sir Roland also increased the offer made to Alex Ferguson by the board if he were to resign as manager and take the position of ambassador for Manchester United, from £100,000 to £1 million a year.

After the November meeting Martin Edwards told the press: 'I felt that a lot of supporters who were against the bid would turn up and voice their opinions and that's what happened. I'm used to being abused at this club, I have had it for twenty years, probably longer, given my family involvement. It's something you have to accept. You know you are going to have to make decisions which aren't popular with everyone, but you have to do what you feel is in the best long-term interests of the football club.'

The government eventually vetoed the BSkyB bid, but United continued to expand anyway, due largely to the vast increase in television money in the 1990s – most of it paid by BSkyB.

Many saw these developments as a sign that Martin Edwards was losing his grip on the club, and it was clear that new blood was infiltrating the boardroom.

Eventually, the former deputy chief executive, Peter Kenyon, was appointed as the new chief executive in August 2000 (taking over the role from Martin Edwards, who had been the club's chief executive, in addition to his role as chairman, since 1991) and earned the eternal gratitude of the vast majority of fans through being credited with persuading Alex Ferguson to stay at Old Trafford until at least 2005. Fergie himself had admitted that life was more straightforward with Kenyon than it had been under Edwards.

★ ★ ★

When my official presence as head of security was not required at away games, I would still always attend as a fan; a VIP one, admittedly, but a fan nonetheless. Occasionally I would give a lift to David Gill, who had succeeded Robin Launders as the club's finance director in December 1996, and on these social jaunts I found him to be a witty and charming man. We had many conversations about various subjects and personalities at the club, but more often than not Fergie featured large in our chats. I got the strong impression that David was more than wary when dealing with the Boss, and knew all about his love of money.

He once got a call from Fergie about buying a player, but told me that in his honest opinion it was just a smokescreen, as Fergie had no real interest in the player he was talking about. The real reason for the call, according to David, was that Alex wanted his bonus early, but had called about the player as an excuse to bring the conversation around to his own financial situation. David never spoke highly of the Boss. He was also less than happy with Ken Merrett and Ken Ramsden, and over the years he slowly eroded away most of the power they had had at Old Trafford.

From everything that I saw and learned within the walls of Old Trafford, I will always hold the view that Manchester United became great in spite of itself, and only the greatness of managers like Matt Busby and Alex Ferguson, and players like Eric Cantona and George Best, made it the most famous club in the world. The tragedy was that the board had begun to believe their own press releases, and started to think that they, not the players, were responsible for the club's meteoric success.

On the day before the final game of the 2000–1 season, Fergie and his assistant, Steve McClaren (who replaced Brian Kidd in early 1999), went to Old Trafford for a meeting with the board. According to someone who attended the meeting, it developed into more of a showdown between Fergie and Steve, and Peter Kenyon and David Gill, regarding who was going to take over from Fergie, as he had declared his intention to retire.

It transpired that Fergie recommended that Steve McClaren should be his successor, but the board did not agree. Both Steve and Fergie felt that the board already had a successor in the wings. Fergie was in no doubt that Martin Edwards was behind this plot and the general feeling was that if the two men had offered to resign there and then, the board would have accepted their resignations. Fergie advised Steve to go into full-time management elsewhere as he was convinced that the Manchester United board would never accept him as manager at Old Trafford. Eventually Steve McClaren moved to Middlesbrough, where, with far fewer resources than those at Old Trafford, he began a successful role in management.

Ultimately, it was Sir Roland Smith's careful stewardship that helped avert a crisis at the club. The Manchester United board eventually put together a deal that rewarded Fergie with a huge pay rise for what everybody supposed would be his last season in charge, and on his eventual departure, he was promised a handsome retirement package.

Sir Roland's intervention was also instrumental in keeping Roy Keane at Old Trafford, as he spearheaded the board's attempt to satisfy the Irishman's demands in a new contract. It was an open secret that most major clubs in Europe were queuing up to secure the services of Roy, if and when he finally decided to leave the club. Fortunately the situation was resolved before the January deadline, and Roy Keane remained a vital part of the Manchester United team.

Away from boardroom scuffles and security problems, one of my more pleasant duties was to ensure that George Best was taken care of on his visits to Old Trafford. He was always made more than welcome by the fans as they, better than anyone, knew what George had contributed to the folklore surrounding United. In my view he was a living legend, and whenever he turned up at the ground I made certain that he passed through to the VIP suites with as little hassle as possible from the adoring hordes.

Sadly, the board had a different attitude towards George. It struck me that they considered his public association with Manchester United was somehow damaging to the club's image. It seemed that they were also concerned about his potential influence over current players, as on many an occasion Fergie insisted that I kept George out of the player's lounge when he was visiting Old Trafford. As Fergie had spent a long time ridding the club of its drinking culture, he didn't want young players being set a bad example, even though George had always been the perfect gentleman during his visits.

When George arrived with his wife, Alex, on one occasion, I met up with them in the Grill Room before the match and noticed a large scab on his head. Innocently I asked how he had hurt himself and, with tongue firmly in cheek, George replied, 'Oh that. That was the wife. She hit me with an ashtray last night.'

'Christ, George. I never knew you smoked,' I replied, laughing at the improbable scenario being suggested.

We continued joking as we walked back to the executive area, before George settled down to watch another impressive United performance, his passion for the club undiminished.

CHAPTER 12

The Glorious Treble

BEFORE WE COULD LAUNCH our next Champions League campaign in the 1998–9 season, we had to play LKS Lodz of Poland to qualify for a place, having ended the season as Premiership runners-up two months previously. Following a 2–0 victory at Old Trafford and a 0–0 draw in Poland, the team had done enough to qualify for a place in the draw of the Champions League proper, which was made towards the end of August. After United was drawn in the same group as Barcelona, Bayern Munich and Peter Schmeichel's old team Brøndby, the press immediately christened it 'the group of death', but the team were not unduly concerned by the quality of their competitors, and were merely looking forward to the start of the new season.

The first test of our endurance and skill came in a home game against the mighty Barcelona in mid-September. Prior to kick-off the Old Trafford crowd was buzzing with anticipation, while the football certainly lived up to expectations. By half-time we were leading 2–0, but Barcelona stormed back into the game in the second half and levelled the score. Although a moment of David Beckham magic made it 3–2 to the Reds, again Barcelona stepped up a gear and scored another equalizer. On the down side, Nicky Butt was sent off for a handball offence, but it was certainly a memorable night of top-class football. The lads were more than aware, however, that a tough time lay ahead in their Champions League campaign.

Two weeks later, a 2–2 draw away at Bayern Munich proved upsetting, but more for events off the field than on it; the team's plane had developed a fault before they were able to fly out of Germany, which brought back memories of the 1958 tragedy, as well as causing major delays to their return to Manchester. Fortunately, the team bounced back from the two drawn European games, as well as the trauma of the flight from Munich, to beat Brøndby 6–2 and 5–0, in their respective away and home matches, ensuring that the Reds' European dream was very much alive.

Our progress in the League was good, but when Blackburn Rovers came to Manchester in mid-November, the football took second place behind the rumours that Fergie's assistant, Brian Kidd, was set to replace Roy Hodgson as Blackburn manager. Though we beat our north-west rivals 3–2, the Kidd situation was of much concern to the Old Trafford faithful.

On 25 November the Manchester United contingent was escorted to the Nou Camp stadium in Barcelona by thirty SPS security men. Knowing that the famous stadium was nicknamed 'the cauldron', Ken Ramsden thought it best to be prepared. It turned out to be a trouble-free match and, again, a stunning game, for although the teams once more drew 3–3, football was the real winner.

The following month we were then sent crashing out of the League Cup by Spurs at White Hart Lane, losing 3–1. So, I thought, no quadruple then, we'll just have to settle for a treble of League, FA Cup and European Cup. I wished . . .

After the draw against Barcelona, we faced a home tie against Bayern Munich in the last game in our Champions League group, and it was a match we could not afford to lose. A draw would suffice, but defeat would put us out of Europe once again. Thankfully, we managed a 1–1 draw so we were through to the quarter-finals, where we would face Inter Milan.

Now able to concentrate on the Premier League, the team experienced a few ups and downs, but by the end of the year, we were just about holding our own in the championship race.

After one match in December, Ken Merrett pulled me aside and said that Fergie needed a favour from me: 'He wants you to drive him to Glasgow tomorrow on some urgent family business.'

I tracked the Boss down and told him that I was ready to go to Scotland with him at a minute's notice, and we agreed I would meet him at Old Trafford at 10.00 a.m. the next day. It transpired that his brother Martin's wife, Sandra, was terminally ill with cancer, and Fergie was desperate to go north and visit them, as her condition was rapidly deteriorating.

Having encountered horrendous traffic en route to Old Trafford, I was late arriving at the ground, but eventually I picked him up and we were on our way, bound for Scotland. As the Ferguson clan was a traditional close-knit Scottish family, Fergie was anxious to be with his brother and sister-in-law in their time of need, and so I drove as fast as conditions would allow.

Despite the sombre mood, the conversation soon moved on to the topic of football. I asked Fergie about how he thought his temporary assistant coach Jim Ryan was doing, as many at Old Trafford had thought Brian Kidd would be a difficult man to replace. The rumours that had been circulating when Blackburn Rovers came to play at Old Trafford had not been proved groundless, and Brian had made the decision to leave United to manage Blackburn earlier in the month. I knew that there was no love lost between Fergie and Brian, and when he left there were certainly no tears shed by the hard-nosed Scot. He had known that Brian was after the Blackburn job, and as many felt the latter had virtually made a career out of bad-mouthing Fergie, and even harboured ambitions of taking over from him when he retired, I came to the conclusion that the Boss was glad to see him leave.

I was often infuriated by Brian's behaviour on match days, after Fergie had informed each player whether they would be playing, or on the bench or in the stands. As coach, it would be Brian who was responsible for telling the manager who wasn't performing adequately in training or who was not 100 per cent match fit and, acting on this information, Fergie would make the team selection. What I found difficult to understand was the way Brian would dispense sympathy to the dropped player, backslapping and proclaiming his surprise that he hadn't been selected, despite the fact that Fergie's decision had been based on Brian's own recommendation. He would also suggest that Fergie's unpredictability was the cause of their failure to make it to the team. It bothered me why the coach wasn't more up-front with the players but, in time, they realized he was putting on a show and just laughed at his attempts at camaraderie.

After Brian had parted company with the club, Fergie would become uneasy when his former coach's name came up in conversation, so I made sure that I rarely mentioned him when the Boss was around. This time, however, Fergie merely said that Jim Ryan was doing well and made no further comment on the subject.

The journey to Scotland seemed to fly by, and I took Fergie straight to the Glasgow hospital where his sister-in-law was being treated.

While I waited in the car, I listened to radio commentary on the game between our main Premier League opponent that season, Arsenal, and Aston Villa. Arsenal were leading 2–0, which was just what I didn't want to hear, so I switched off the radio, feeling depressed. After an hour, curiosity got the better of me and I turned the radio back on to hear that Aston Villa had pulled back three goals to win 3–2.

Eventually, Fergie emerged from the hospital, and the minute he got in the car, said: 'Great news for Villa. Suits us, eh Ned?' He had heard the result from one of his cousins.

I smiled and drove him out of that bleak hospital car park, thinking to myself that the Boss never missed a trick when it came to football, no matter where he was, no matter what the circumstances. Even so, the return journey was much quieter as the hospital visit had been most upsetting. I asked how Sandra was doing, but Fergie was subdued, and suggested the prognosis wasn't good. After a while our thoughts returned to lighter topics of conversation, as we gravitated towards the subject of Martin Edwards's rather unusual habit of visiting the Ladies', hot on the heels of any attractive woman intent on using the facilities.

'It's unbelievable, Ned. The press would have a field day with this. Mark my words,' said Fergie.

'I know, Boss. I must be the only security chief in football who has to keep an eye on the chairman and stop him going into women's toilets,' I replied, completely unable to understand Edwards's motivation.

Fergie was a walking encyclopaedia where the subject of football was concerned, and missed nothing that went on in the game. From many of our conversations, I got the distinct impression that he was greatly frustrated by the financial constraints imposed upon him by the board, which prevented him from signing people like Gabriel Batistuta, Marcel Desailly and even Alan Shearer. Often Fergie would hear of the private 'deals' that some of the personnel who ran the various departments at Old Trafford seemed to organize for their own benefit, and I genuinely felt that Fergie was disgusted by their behaviour as he believed the fans would be the ones eventually out of pocket.

We finally arrived back at Old Trafford at 10.30 p.m. and after Fergie gave me some petrol money for the lengthy round trip, we said our goodnights.

It is hard to believe, but while I was at the club it is true to say that Alex Ferguson spent as little time as possible at Old Trafford. The man who is synonymous with Manchester United would only go to the ground on match days and for management meetings. It appeared to me that he mistrusted the directors and the administrative side of the club, and that as far as Fergie was concerned it was him against them. Explaining this to me one day, he said: 'I want nothing to do with any of them, Ned. I just want them to stay out of my way. If any of them try to stick their noses into the running of the team, I'd be off.'

Most of the board were only too aware of his views in this regard and, more often than not, they let Fergie get on with his job unhindered. The only exception to his general mistrust of the board was Ken Merrett, but Fergie was still wary of disclosing too much to him. I was the original 'piggy in the middle', as Ken would, on occasion, moan to me about Fergie's guests at Old Trafford, especially those from the world of horse racing, telling me that the manager's apparent infatuation with them could result in some of them abusing his hospitality.

'You can always judge a man by his friends, Mr Kelly. And Fergie will be judged by his,' he warned me.

I nodded my agreement but felt compelled to stick up for the Boss: 'Fergie is nobody's mug, Ken. And he's not backward at coming forward. He knows exactly what he's doing.'

Fergie was a strong man and a great manager. With him it was always a case of 'his way or the highway', so I always thought Ken's genuine concerns were well-meaning but unnecessary.

Fergie's commitment to the success of his team was such that he was normally the first to arrive on Saturday match days, usually showing up at around 10.30 a.m. Before beginning his preparations for the forthcoming game, he'd head straight for Ken's office and collect his allocation of match tickets and directors'-box passes for his guests.

I usually met up with Fergie immediately afterwards to check whether he had any VIPs to be looked after or any other special requests. I always made a point of asking him who was in and who was out of the team for that day's match, which became something of a standing joke between us. It is true to say, however, that Fergie never once revealed to me the team, or even replied, for that matter. An occasional 'Fuck off, Ned' would bring my enquiries to a swift end.

★ ★ ★

At the beginning of 1999 our Premier League form was looking good, and a fourth-round FA Cup tie against Liverpool at home beckoned in late January. Always a hard-fought match against our bitter rivals, defeat was seemingly on the cards after a Michael Owen goal gave the visitors the edge throughout the game. With less than two minutes left on the clock, however, Andy Cole headed the ball across the face of the Liverpool goal and Dwight Yorke beat everyone to it and scored. The United crowd was ecstatic. A 1–1 draw would suit us perfectly, happy to settle for a replay now. Ole Gunnar Solskjaer had other ideas though, and with seconds to go he sent the Liverpool keeper, David James, the wrong way to snatch a late victory.

The Liverpool players and fans were incensed. The club's assistant manager, Phil Thompson, was beside himself with rage and raced on to the pitch to confront referee Graham Poll, apparently still furious at the circumstances surrounding the free kick, from which Dwight Yorke had equalized two minutes earlier. In complete contrast, the United camp were elated following one of the club's most memorable cup victories. It had been a narrow escape, but such a tenacious display proved United's commitment and focus, and would stand the team in good stead for an even greater test later in the season.

On the forty-first anniversary of the Munich air disaster, Manchester United rose to the occasion by beating Nottingham Forest by an extraordinary margin of eight goals to one. Ole Gunnar Solskjaer earned the nickname 'super sub' that day by coming on the pitch and scoring four times in twenty minutes, a feat that has yet to be bettered by a substitute in the Premier League.

A month later it was time to play host to Inter Milan in the quarter-final of the Champions League competition. After a confident start, two Dwight Yorke goals, both set up by some superb play from David Beckham, gave us a crucial 2–0 lead by the end of the first half.

When the referee blew the half-time whistle, I was walking towards the tunnel when I watched one of Inter Milan's vice-presidents approach the referee and put his arm around his shoulder as if they were old friends. It surprised me because UEFA rules strictly forbid any contact between club representatives and the match officials, for very obvious reasons. Any communication between them would have to be made through the designated UEFA official.

I marched straight up to the senior UEFA official and told him what

I had witnessed. He assured me that he would attend to the matter, so I decided not to inform Fergie, as I didn't think that a distraction of this nature would have been particularly useful or indeed welcome during his half-time pep talk to the team.

At the start of the second half, two Inter players attacked the same ball; one pushed the defender while the other got a free run with the ball. It was an old trick, and worked well as the second player, Diego Simeone, scored, but it was disallowed because of the earlier foul made by his team-mate. The Italians failed to score any legitimate goals and we couldn't add to our first-half tally, but we felt comfortable going to the San Siro stadium with a two-goal advantage.

Two weeks later we were on our way to Italy for the return match with Inter. Several days before we were due to leave, however, Ken Merrett accosted me outside his Old Trafford office and suggested to me that my presence would probably not be required at the game.

I shook my head in disbelief. 'Ken, are you saying that you don't think you need to take security to the San Siro stadium? Are you having a laugh?' I asked incredulously.

He considered my shocked reaction to his statement, and revised his views rapidly.

'Maybe you're right, Ned,' he replied cautiously. 'OK – go ahead and organize it,' and turned to walk away.

I couldn't understand his attitude towards me, and wondered if perhaps he had heard about my complaint to the UEFA officials. Or maybe he was underestimating the likely number of fans who would be travelling to the game. In any event, I took a contingent of SPS guys with me, both for the players' protection and for the safety of the fans, 10,000 of whom would make the journey in support of their much-loved team.

On the day of the match, just before kick-off, I was in the dressing room when Fergie pulled me aside: 'I want you in the tunnel, Ned. I need to speak to you in private.'

I waited outside as requested and wondered what was on his mind.

'Ned, I want you to watch the referee's dressing room,' he said, 'and if any Inter Milan officials go in, let me know immediately.'

I agreed to his request readily, recalling what I had seen at Old Trafford, and realizing that Fergie must have been informed by other sources of that moment of improper conduct. It was not the only issue that was bothering Fergie, as he even revealed publicly his fears that the Inter players would be diving and play-acting during the game; an opinion that caused the Italian club to accuse him of playing mind games with the referee, who eventually turned down three penalty claims on the night.

All was quiet on the Italian front until I heard an argument behind me in the tunnel between Nicky Butt and Fergie. The manager had decided not to pick Nicky for the big event, and so the young player, devastated by the news, was remonstrating with his boss in the fiercest possible terms.

I kept an eye on the referee's room before kick-off, as directed, but saw nothing untoward, which was a great relief. The game got under way amid the shouting and screaming of almost 80,000 fans, and I reported to Fergie in the dugout that nobody resembling an Inter Milan official had entered the referee's quarters. I took up a position behind one of the goals and settled down to watch the feast of football.

Inter Milan had brought out the big guns in an effort to redress the balance from the first leg, and included Ronaldo in the starting line-up for the first time in months. Fortunately for the Reds his presence on the pitch was short-lived as he was substituted after a crunching tackle by Gary Neville. The young Italian player Nicola Ventola, who was brought on in his place, caused even more trouble, however, and ended up scoring a goal for the home side. Our one-goal advantage was now under serious threat, but our concerns were short-lived, as an Andy Cole header directed downwards for Paul Scholes to shoot home made it 1–1 on the night and gave us a 3–1 win on aggregate.

After the full-time whistle was blown, the fun and games began. When the team left the pitch they were pelted with a range of fruits, from tomatoes to apples and oranges. I positioned myself at the mouth of the tunnel at the end of the protective cover to make sure the boys came home safely. As a grinning Paul Scholes came running towards me, an Inter fan must have recognized him as the goalscorer who had ended his team's chances in Europe, and lobbed a two-litre bottle of water at him. It fell short of its target, however, and hit me squarely between the shoulder blades. The force of the missile knocked me over but I got back on my feet quickly and spun round to face the crowd, hoping to challenge the culprit. I could have taken my pick of the thousands of screaming Inter supporters baying for Manchester United blood. To add insult to injury, as I threw the bottle away, I realized that it hadn't contained water at all, but a liquid that had most likely passed through an Italian fan's kidneys before it had been propelled through the air at me.

Just as I was heading for the comparative safety and sanity of the dressing room, Peter Schmeichel approached me with a sad, worried face, begging a huge favour from me: 'Ned. It's my lucky towel. I left it in my goal. Will you get it for me, please? It's my lucky one. I must have it back.'

'For fuck's sake, Peter. We've got more towels than the Hilton. Just get another one,' I replied, trying to reason with him.

'No, Ned. Please. I want my own one. Please,' he persisted, verging on the hysterical.

I don't know who was the most crazy: Peter for asking, or me for going. I couldn't bear to see him in such a state, though, and set off for a bracing run to and from the goalmouth. The Inter fans still had plenty of fruit left, which continued to shower down about my ears, but at least I had rescued the precious towel, and on my way back to the tunnel, covered in rotten fruit, I couldn't resist giving a cheeky wave to the disappointed Italians before joining the celebrations in the dressing room.

Having progressed to the semi-finals of both the FA Cup and the Champions League, as well as maintaining our grip on the Premier League, we were still on course for the treble.

Juventus travelled to Old Trafford for the first leg of our European contest on 7 April, and took an early lead. They protected their one-goal advantage until almost the end of the match, but the Reds refused to give up and Ryan Giggs snatched a deserved equalizer.

Four days later, the semi-final of the FA Cup against the holders, Arsenal, was upon us and, after a 0–0 draw at Villa Park, in which Roy Keane had what seemed a perfectly good goal disallowed, we faced a tense replay. It was an extraordinary match. David Beckham gave the Reds an early lead, only for Dennis Bergkamp to equalize in the second half. Arsenal attacked us as though war had been declared, and when a Marc Overmars strike directed toward Manchester United's goal was blocked strongly by Roy Keane, the fiery Irishman was sent off following his second bookable offence of the day.

When an Arsenal penalty arose from a mistimed challenge on Ray

Parlour by Phil Neville, I thought that we were doomed. The tension was unbearable as Dennis Bergkamp ran up to take the kick. Nine times out of ten, Bergkamp would have been running to the fans in glory, but not this time. Peter Schmeichel saved the shot and Paul Scholes swept up the loose ball. The Manchester United fans were ecstatic and the game went to extra time. Then the crowd was treated to one of those rare but unforgettable goals when Ryan Giggs took off on a wonder run past five Arsenal players to slot the ball past David Seaman. We held on to our 2–1 lead until the final whistle, which put us in the FA Cup final against Newcastle at Wembley Stadium on 25 May.

The second leg of our other semi-final cup fixture soon came round, and we arrived in Turin with immense trepidation: not only was it thirty years since Manchester United had last reached a European Cup semi-final, but the Reds had, unbelievably, never before won in Italy.

We received a high-spirited but well-behaved reception at the stadium but I knew how the mood would change if we were to leave the ground victorious. The game began badly for the Reds and within eleven minutes we were two goals down, thanks to Filippo Inzaghi.

When I heard the cheer that boomed around the stadium after Juve had scored a second goal, my heart was in my boots. From my position behind the Juventus goal, where I desperately wanted to witness some on-target action from the United strikeforce, I couldn't help but wonder whether yet another opportunity to reach a European Cup final was slipping out of reach.

I tried to keep positive, and even commented to a UEFA official standing near by that at least the Italian side hadn't scored two *late* goals, and so we had plenty of time to get back into the game, but deep down I was devastated.

Twenty minutes into the game, however, we finally began to settle down and started to match Juventus in style and pace. Some Roy Keane magic kick-started our revival, and his beautifully headed goal seemed to change more than the scoreline. The Italians suddenly looked more nervy, and the United players seemed determined to capitalize on their opponents' dip in confidence. Dwight Yorke picked up an Andy Cole cross and headed it home to make the score 2–2 on the night, 3–3 on aggregate, which would have been enough to send us through on the away-goal rule. The excitement continued when a Juventus goal scored on the break was judged to be offside, but the

After Bryan Robson's testimonial match against Celtic on 20 November 1990, dozens of well-wishers ran on to the pitch to congratulate the United captain during his lap of honour, and I had to step in to keep him safe from the hordes of enthusiastic admirers.

In the more spectacular surroundings of Rio de Janeiro, during the World Club Championships in January 2000, it was my privilege to keep an eye on David Beckham away from the pitch.

Manchester United's finest:

Since his debut in March 1991, Ryan Giggs has been a loyal and dedicated servant to Manchester United. Razor-sharp, confident and a reliable goalscorer, he has been invaluable to the club's success over the past decade.

Although he has now left the club, David Beckham's contribution to the recent triumphs enjoyed by United has been extraordinary. Ever reliable in the deadball situation, he amazed the crowds and silenced critics with an array of spectacular goals.

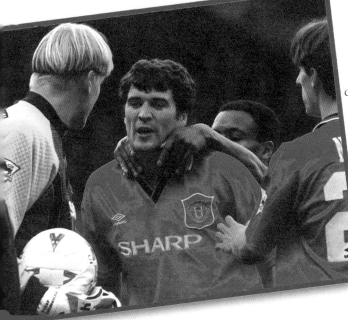

Fiery, controversial and ruthlessly competitive, Roy Keane has been Fergie's lynchpin at the club since the day he was signed in summer 1993. He is pictured here involved in an angry exchange with goalkeeper Peter Schmeichel; it was not the first time the two had clashed either publicly or privately.

Paul Scholes is one of the most successful graduates of the youth team; though passionate in his ardour for the club, he is a private young man, with a dislike of the limelight, and is only interested in putting his heart and soul into every performance.

Champions in Europe:
Victory in the European Cup-Winners' Cup in May 1991 gave Manchester United its first European trophy since Matt Busby's triumph in 1968.

United's veteran striker Mark Hughes hit the back of the net twice to give the Reds a 2–1 win against Spanish giants Barcelona, in Rotterdam.

The first of many:
After the heartbreak of missing out on the Division
One Championship title in 1992, United bounced back in the 1992–3
season to win the country's first Premier League title in May 1993. Steve
Bruce and Bryan Robson (*top*) celebrate their achievement parading the
trophy across the Old Trafford pitch.

The following season, the Manchester United players surpassed themselves by winning the League and FA Cup double in May 1994. In the dressing room at Old Trafford I was proud to pose alongside young guns Ryan Giggs and Lee Sharpe (*top*), keeping a firm grip on the Premier League cup.

It was a distraught and disbelieving Ruud van Nistelrooy whom I led away from the press conference at Old Trafford in April 2000. Due to a serious ligament problem in his knee, he had failed his medical, and his transfer from PSV Eindhoven was put on hold.

A year later, however, Ruud returned to Manchester under more positive circumstances: his cruciate ligament injury had healed, and he was physically fit and more than ready to pull on a Manchester United jersey. I led a much happier Dutchman away from the press conference in April 2001. It was an arrival worth waiting for, as he has proved beyond any doubt his measure as a truly great player.

Treble champions:
A unique achievement in
Manchester United's history, the
Reds were triumphant in the
Premier League, FA Cup and, most
important of all, the Champions
League European Cup in May
1999. Thousands of fans crowded
the streets of Manchester city
centre to welcome the victorious
team and catch a glimpse of
the trophies.

Ever responsible for the safety
and protection of the silverware
(*pictured in 1990 with the FA
Cup*), I could never have
guessed at the number of
trophies I would have to
keep an eye on throughout
my twelve amazing years
at the club.

honours would eventually go to United, when a superb Andy Cole goal put the result beyond all doubt to give the Reds a 4–3 aggregate win.

The only downside to a fantastic night of football for Manchester was the fact that both Roy Keane and Paul Scholes had been booked during the match, and had to miss the next European game, which meant that neither could play in the Champions League final against Bayern Munich at the Nou Camp in Barcelona. Celebrations in the dressing room were understandably blighted by this, but the squad was certainly big enough to make up for their absence, and there would be plenty of players jostling to take their places.

Throughout the latter stages of the season, our triumphs in Europe were mirrored by our successes in the Premier League. By Sunday 16 May, the last day of the season, we were a point ahead of our nearest rivals, Arsenal, and faced a visit from their north London rivals, Spurs, while the Gunners were due to play Aston Villa at home. The lads played their hearts out and took all three points with a 2–1 win. Manchester United were champions again for the fifth time in seven years.

The Marriott Hotel in Worsley was wall-to-wall celebration on the Sunday night as the players toasted another Premier League title win. Amidst the revelry, Roy Keane approached me with a request: 'Can you supply a couple of your lads for Tuesday night? Me and the boys are going out on the piss.'

'No problem, Roy. You know that,' I replied.

'Good, Ned. Have a word with Nev. He'll fill you in on the timings and the meeting place.'

Gary Neville (known as 'Nev' to his team-mates) had taken over the role of party organizer-in-chief, although Dwight Yorke would also help out. (At Christmas, they would let me know where they were going, usually the Reform Club in the city centre, and I would visit the management and insist on the removal of all CCTV videotapes, and in return promise the club a quiet and very lucrative night. No details were ever revealed about the antics of the players, which, on their one private night of the year together, was the way I thought it should be. The only time a Christmas party at the club was marred slightly was when all the wives and girlfriends turned up and barged their way in. Luckily for the lads, most of them were sitting down and only the odd player was caught on the dance floor with a good-looking girl.)

Later that night at the Marriott Hotel, I asked Gary about his plans for the following Tuesday, and he suggested we all met up at Mulligan's, the Irish bar in the centre of Manchester, at around 2.00 p.m.

'I'll send two of my best men with you, Gary. To make sure you get a bit of peace,' I assured him, smiling.

'But you'll be coming too, won't you, Ned?' asked Gary.

'No need, mate. My men will provide all the security necessary. I'm really not needed,' I replied.

'No, not for security, silly bollocks. I meant to join us for the piss-up,' he laughed.

I agreed without a moment's hesitation, looking forward to a social night out with the lads.

The players began arriving in twos and threes and I positioned Alvin and Graham at the side of the bar so that they did not get in the way of the other customers, but were near enough to stop any idiots annoying the players. The banter was good and the lads were all in high spirits, while the conversation inevitably turned to football. There was much concern that Jaap Stam would not be fit enough to take part in the FA Cup final and everyone agreed that would be a major drawback, so vital was Jaap's role in defence. Teddy Sheringham and Dwight Yorke were in a heated debate over Clare Tomlinson, the Sky Sports presenter, who had apparently turned down Dwight's kind invitation to join him at the celebratory bash on the previous Sunday. With Dwight's reputation in mind, it seemed that she was not too keen on becoming another notch on his bedpost.

Roy Keane arrived later in the day with a friend, his glazed eyes letting us all know that he had started his drinking en route to the Irish bar. The pub-crawl proper began and we made our way from venue to venue on Manchester's wine-bar circuit, eventually arriving at Henry's Bar later in the evening.

I was standing with Peter Schmeichel, Ollie Solskjaer and Ronny Johnsen, and was quite taken aback at the vitriolic attack Peter unleashed on anyone who would listen to his views on Roy Keane. From my conversation with the talented goalkeeper, I was left in little doubt that he had developed a rather low opinion of his fiery team-mate.

Most of the lads standing around Peter were slightly embarrassed at his tirade and I was glad that Roy was at the other side of the bar, otherwise Peter might have had to endure yet another physical encounter with the Irishman. Little did the Dane know, but I was well aware that his previous confrontation with Roy had come to blows some months earlier, and that Peter had come a poor second. I presumed his pride was still wounded, and I simply put his latest rant down to Scandinavian sour grapes.

Thankfully, the topic changed to the other great love in footballers' lives – women. Soon the lovelies of Manchester were flocking into Henry's as word got around that the boys were enjoying a night out on the town. Roy Keane and his friends were in a group making a lot of high-spirited noise in the corner of the bar when a few girls joined them and, initially at least, everyone seemed in good humour. It was short-lived, however, and on hearing a commotion of breaking glass and screams from the girls I rushed over to investigate. Apparently, one of the girls had taken offence at a risqué comment made by one of the lads, and a row had ensued. A glass was thrown at Roy, cutting him below the eye.

Having witnessed the incident in full, the landlady at Henry's threw the girls out and barred them from the establishment but, as they were leaving, one of them was heard to be shouting that they were going to the press, which would have been an easy sell.

The police soon arrived and one of my men explained what had happened. In the meantime I went looking for Roy, fearing that in his current state he would not have been too co-operative. I grabbed him and spirited him out of a side door into the night. He wouldn't be told what to do, however, and together with his friends, full of belligerence, he insisted on going his own way and disappeared into the darkness. I tried to reason with him, but he paid no attention. With a touch of overkill, the police had requested van-loads of back-up, presumably fearing a backlash on the scale of a riot. One of my men started to remonstrate with the excessive response shown by the police, and the staff from Henry's bar joined in too. The police brought a speedy conclusion to the argument, however, by threatening to nick the lot of them.

I telephoned Fergie at his home and left a message on his voicemail outlining the night's events. There was nothing of any use I could do at Henry's, short of continuing the futile argument with the police, so I decided that I had had enough and headed for home.

I was woken by the telephone ringing. It was Fergie. It was daylight and with my head feeling as if it would burst, I realized I had the hangover from hell. The fact that Fergie was ranting and raving down the telephone, screaming about the fact that Roy had been arrested the previous night, didn't help.

'Why the hell did you let him wander off into the night?' blasted Fergie. 'Get yourself down to the Cliff right now, Ned. Then we'll try and get Roy bailed.'

I stumbled into the shower, dressed and drove to the Cliff training ground, where I parked my car and jumped into Fergie's vehicle.

'We're going to James Chapman's offices,' he explained. 'Maurice has a lawyer on stand-by who is a bail expert.'

On arrival at the solicitors, we discovered that James Chapman had agreed bail terms for Roy with the police so all that remained was for Fergie and I to go and fetch him. We parked in a garage adjacent to the police station and, as expected, were met by a media scrum. Fergie and I shoved our way through them, barged into the police station and asked for our boy back. I was left waiting in a corridor and the Boss was taken down to the cells to speak to Roy first. I laughed to myself, thinking that if I were Roy, I'd rather face a prison sentence than deal with Fergie in a full-on rant.

The formalities and the paperwork signed, Roy was free to leave. He was released without charge and bailed to reappear at the same Bootle Street police station on 13 July. Fergie sent for a club car to collect him and, with Roy on his way home, the Boss and I headed back to the Cliff with him still seething inwardly, his face red with rage. I suspected he remained angry with me for letting Roy out of my sight, but on the night I didn't feel as though I had any choice in the matter.

Certain newspapers went overboard on their coverage of the incident at Henry's, but one or two pointed out that the two women in question had been making a nuisance of themselves by pestering the players for a drink. Furthermore, after the glass was smashed in Roy's face, it was the two women who were thrown out, and not the victim or his friends.

'The two girls in question caused offence to both staff and customers, and were ejected in line with company policy,' said a spokesman for Henry's in a newspaper the following day.

But the two women also made a basic error. Rather than calling the police first to report any 'crime', they called a newspaper to sell their story, which meant that legal proceedings were out of the question; no prosecutor would touch the case after such an ill-advised action.

The whole affair petered out quickly, but the memory of Detective Chief Inspector John Davis's statement to the press after the event when he was asked about Roy Keane, always brings a smile to my face: 'He is totally in control of himself and not distressed. Shall we say, in football parlance, he isn't over the moon, but certainly not distressed. Ask me about his innermost feelings and I have to say I don't know.'

After all the excitement died down it was back to business as usual to prepare for the small matter of the FA Cup final on 22 May. The day dawned with everyone at the club now hyper-aware that the treble could be ours. This fact added even more pressure to all concerned and stretched already taut nerves.

It wasn't a classic match, and once again Roy Keane found himself in the wars, having to be substituted early on after experiencing a dreadful foul against him. But his replacement, Teddy Sheringham, promptly scored and then set up Paul Scholes for the winner.

With a 2–0 victory against Newcastle, we had completed the second part of the potential treble and Wembley was a sea of Red. As always I left the stand area five minutes before the end and, collecting Ken Ramsden, we made our way to the bottom of the steps to watch the players on their way to the medal presentation. While the Newcastle players collected their runners-up medals first, I had a quick word with Teddy Sheringham, congratulating him both on his goal and on winning the double.

'There's no way you'd have won this lot with Spurs,' I told him, winking.

With a huge grin on his face, he had to admit I was right.

Roy Keane led the Reds up the thirty-nine famous steps to be presented with the FA Cup trophy and medals, and I noticed Alan Shearer also paying close attention to the presentation. I smiled at Ken Ramsden and nodded towards Shearer. The Newcastle player was looking up at Roy Keane and seemed to be lost in thought. I wondered whether he was thinking if it could have been him up there, had he joined Manchester United, and taken up the opportunities offered to him to join the Reds. Later, I mentioned my observations to Fergie and he merely shrugged uninterestedly: 'He had his chances, Ned. Two of them, in fact, so he's only himself to blame. Fuck him.'

And so on to Barcelona, for the third and most important leg of the treble. It had been thirty-one years since Manchester United had last won the European Cup. If we were going to do it this time round, we were going to do it in style, and so we travelled to the Spanish city on Concorde, courtesy of British Airways' generous sponsorship, which stood us in good stead for the rest of the trip.

It seemed that half of Barcelona had turned out to greet us. We received a fantastic reception and the carnival atmosphere continued on the drive through the city to the hotel. We set up camp quickly. Dave Fevre and Doc Stone had a room dedicated to medical attention for the players, as some of them needed treatment after the FA Cup final. Albert Morgan, the new kit manager, even had a room put aside for the kit, and the Manchester United floor of the hotel was soon a hive of activity.

Fergie, Steve McClaren and Tony Coton (the goalkeeping coach) were huddled in another room discussing tactics. Everyone concerned was aware that the team faced an enormous challenge against Bayern Munich, but it was, nonetheless, a tremendous opportunity. On Tuesday I travelled with the team to the Nou Camp stadium for their training period before Wednesday night's final. While standing on the touchline, taking in the magnificence of the empty stadium, I had the distinct impression that someone was watching me. I spun around to find myself face to face with Gérard Houllier, the Liverpool manager, who, it transpired, was one of the game's UEFA officials. We exchanged pleasantries before I returned to my preparations for the next day's big event.

Before we left the stadium, Fergie pulled me to one side and asked me to keep an eye on Roy Keane in the bar later in the day: 'I think it's just hit him how big a game he's missing out on, and I don't want to have to deal with any dramas. Watch him, son.'

'Sure, Boss,' I replied.

Within minutes, Doc Stone made the same request. I assured him that I would look out for Roy but, privately, I knew he wouldn't listen to Fergie, me or anyone if he wanted to get drunk. In the event I sat in the bar with Roy and Henning Berg, talking and drinking until 4 a.m. The evening remained trouble-free, but I was exhausted by the time I went to my room to grab just a few hours of much needed rest.

Earlier on the Tuesday, I received a telephone call from Eric

Cantona's new agent, Pascal Carbone, asking if he and Eric could have six tickets for the match, and I made a call to get the go-ahead for this request before telling Carbone to come over to the hotel to collect them. I also managed to have a good chat with Eric on the phone. I hadn't seen him since he had visited Old Trafford for the testimonial for the survivors and relatives of the Munich disaster, which took place at the start of the season. By then he was making his name as a movie star, having played the French ambassador in *Elizabeth*, among other roles. For that particular match he had flown in to Manchester by private jet from Marseilles with Isabelle and their children, looking fit if a little heavier, but certainly not as big as some people had predicted.

As it would be difficult for Eric to wade through the sea of Manchester United fans, he asked me to organize a car-park pass for the stadium. I asked Ken Ramsden to sort out the pass for Eric, and we both went to speak to a UEFA delegate who had been assigned to the Manchester United team on our arrival in Barcelona. He issued me with a 'pass' of sorts, and I left it along with the match tickets at our hotel's reception under Eric's name.

On match day I spent much of my time checking on my own SPS troops as I had 200 men and women accompanying the fans on the journey over to preserve the great reputation the club enjoyed abroad. Nobody reported any trouble, either on the coaches or on the planes, and so around lunchtime I gave the order for them to make their way to the Nou Camp stadium and take up their positions around the ground as the fans began filtering in for the evening's game.

There was a strange mood among the whole Manchester United contingent as anticipation grew at the thought of the task that lay ahead. The pre-match light meal of pasta was eaten in the same subdued atmosphere and even our own resident jokers were quiet for once. The briefings were over, the team talks were finished and each player knew who was playing and who was on the bench. It was time to go.

On leaving the hotel, I called up the team coach and began loading it up with the players. As the coach approached the stadium we came through a tunnel and the magnificent Nou Camp came into sight, dominating the view over Barcelona. But what made it seem even more spectacular than normal was the carpet of red and white that seemed to roll down from its walls to greet us. From that distance it looked as if our fans had laid out a path for the coach. It was an unforgettable sight.

I hit the VIP car park tarmac running, as I had one-hundred-and-one jobs to do. Everyone wanted something. It was relentless and, after I had escorted the players safely into the dressing room, I made my way to my team and we went through our final preparations. When I had a spare moment I went outside to the car park to try to find Eric Cantona and Pascal Carbone, but I couldn't see them nor could I get through to either of their mobile phones. A radio call from Ken Merrett had me back in the stadium trying to find some players' relatives who had got lost in the maze of tunnels that weaved through the inside of the Nou Camp.

I made sure I was back in the dressing room just before kick-off, to watch the team's final minutes together before they made their momentous entrance on to the pitch, where 90,000 screaming fans awaited them.

We started the match badly, and Bayern Munich capitalized by scoring after only six minutes. Our normal balance and flow seemed to be missing from our game, and at half-time we were lucky to be just one goal behind.

While Fergie gave his players the pep talk of his career, in which he told them to imagine being six feet away from the European Cup and not being able to touch it, to make them all the more hungry for victory, I stood guard outside the Manchester United dressing room. In the meantime, one of my staff had been despatched to check whether Eric and Pascal were in their allocated seats, but my heart sank when he returned to say that their seats were empty.

During the second half, we began to assert ourselves with more authority. Fergie had made changes to thwart the German onslaught and replaced Jesper Blomqvist and Andy Cole with Teddy Sheringham and Ole Gunnar Solskjaer. Although there were gaps in our defence, the Germans kept missing their chances while Schmeichel was also producing some fine saves.

We battled bravely throughout the second half but I couldn't help but feel it was never going to be enough. The Germans played the defensive game all too well, and kept their 1–0 lead until the ninety minutes of normal time had elapsed. I looked in despair at the fourth official as his electronic board flashed three minutes of extra time. In the VIP box I could see the German team's colours being tied to the cup and watched as the president of UEFA, Lennart Johansson, made his way down to the presentation area, preparing to award the trophy to the Germans. I turned my head back to the pitch just in time to see

Manchester United earn a corner and smiled as I watched big Peter Schmeichel sprint towards the Bayern goal.

David Beckham sent the ball into the area and everyone, including Schmeichel, went for it. A Munich player tried to clear the ball but miskicked it. The ball then fell at Ryan Giggs's right foot, hit his shin and bounced to Teddy Sheringham, who struck it far from cleanly – but no matter, as it flew straight into the net. Teddy shot a glance at the linesman who kept his flag firmly by his side. We were level.

The whole stadium erupted and the kit man, Albert Morgan, nearly broke my neck as he jumped on me, spinning like a top. The Manchester United bench were going mad but the players kept their heads and, seconds later, were on the attack again, resulting in yet another corner. Beckham again stepped up to take it, but this time Schmeichel stayed in his area. Teddy Sheringham made a run to the near post, pounced on the ball and flicked it across the Bayern Munich goal. Ole Gunnar Solskjaer, aptly named the 'Baby-faced Assassin', was in the right place at the right time, and put his foot out and connected with the ball. He put the ball in the net and it was now 2–1 to Manchester United. Nobody, particularly the German side, could believe what had just happened. The remaining seconds flew by and referee Pierluigi Collina blew the whistle to signal that the game was over and Manchester United had won the European Cup.

I found out later that the UEFA President, en route to present the trophy to the Germans, had already commiserated with Martin Edwards over Manchester United's 'defeat', which was somewhat premature when the final whistle had yet to be blown.

The United players ran over to their supporters and applauded them, and the supporters' cheers turned into a roar unlike anything I'd ever heard before.

Meanwhile, 'Team UEFA', the commercial department of the governing body, were busy ripping the German ribbons off the cup and medals, and replacing them with United's red and white ones for the presentation. I looked up into the stands to see Sir Bobby Charlton waving down at me, so I gave him the thumbs-up sign and he returned it, delighted at his beloved team's astonishing victory.

The shell-shocked German team lined up in a collective daze to collect their runners-up medals, but in comparison our joy was absolute when, after the lads had collected their medals, the captain

Peter Schmeichel went up to collect the trophy with Fergie. Together, they raised the cup heavenward, and there was scarcely a dry eye between us as about 60,000 United fans watched the European Cup head for Manchester for only the second time in the club's history. I couldn't imagine how Schmeichel must have been feeling, knowing that this would be his last game for Manchester United. It was certainly the right way to finish a successful career with the club.

After the presentations, the players returned to the pitch for the photocall, but I noticed that something wasn't quite right. Some idiot in search of fifteen minutes of fame had had the cheek to join the team for the official photographs, dressed in a khaki baseball cap and shorts. Needless to say I quickly dragged him out of the line-up and handed him over to a UEFA official.

After escorting the players on their lap of honour, which seemed to last an eternity, I ran over to Eric Harrison, the youth-team coach, the man partly responsible for developing the careers of some of the younger footballers on the field that night who had only been impressionable boys when he began coaching them. 'What a result! Now we've the treble, Eric. Can you believe it?' I asked him excitedly.

'It's great, Ned. Just great,' a choked Eric Harrison replied, with tears in his eyes.

'This will help Fergie get all the money he needs to buy new players now, eh?' I suggested.

The wily Eric shook his head, however, revealing that he felt certain the win would have the opposite effect, and that it would be even more difficult for the Boss to request more money from the board: 'They'll just assume that because he managed it this time, he'll not need any new players. There'll be handcuffs on the money now.'

Eric would be proven right; Fergie was given no extra money with which to buy new players in the close season in 1999.

When we eventually made it back to the sanctuary of the dressing room, the place was full of directors and close family members all swigging champagne from the bottles. As the players were having personal photographs taken with the trophy, I noticed Fergie sitting alone in a corner with his head in his hands, staring at the ground. It was a moving sight to see this great manager alone with his thoughts, no doubt contemplating what a remarkable feat both he and his team had deservedly achieved: the pinnacle of their respective careers.

We readied ourselves for the coach trip back to the hotel and the inevitable party, but first we had to run the gauntlet of the 'mixed zone', where the players meet with the press for one-to-one interviews. Before we left the dressing room, David Beckham and Gary Neville came over for a chat.

'Great night, lads,' I congratulated them. 'So which one of you wants to carry the cup?'

David was first to speak up. 'I will, Ned,' he replied enthusiastically. Gary smiled and winked at me.

'Let's get the fuck out of here,' I said, leading Gary and David to the door.

'Here, son,' I said to David, thrusting the European Cup into his hands before leading the two players through the mixed zone.

Within seconds the players were surrounded by a swarm of reporters and paparazzi, and before long David had begun to feel the weight of the trophy while facing a barrage of endless questions. He returned the cup to me with an unmistakable sigh of relief, and continued his post-match interview duties.

Concerned that the silverware would get snatched or damaged while in my possession, I grabbed the trophy and held it tightly to my chest.

I walked as fast as I could in the direction of the team coach, met up with Fergie and climbed aboard the bus, placing the cup on the dashboard so that it was visible to the hordes. Fergie settled into his usual place behind the driver. He was still unusually quiet, and turned to me and commented: 'Isn't it amazing that it would have been Sir Matt's ninetieth birthday today, and we won the European Cup tonight by scoring two goals in the ninetieth minute?'

Looking heavenwards, Fergie paused and said, 'Thank you, Sir Matt.'

We both sat in silence. I was speechless. After a few seconds had passed the coach started to fill up with players and the unique moment was gone.

We travelled back to the hotel through a sea of cheering fans; even the Bayern Munich fans were magnanimous in their defeat. Inside the hotel it was like a carnival with everybody clamouring for a piece of the Manchester United action. I could tell immediately that guarding the party that night would be a challenge and a half. Gatecrashers were insinuating their way into the festivities at every opportunity and hiding everywhere in an attempt to slip unnoticed into the function room.

As I set up the top table with the trophy on display, I received a disturbing phone call from Pascal Carbone, telling me that Eric was very upset. He and Eric had been refused entry to the parking area at the Nou Camp because the useless UEFA official had only scribbled something on a piece of UEFA headed notepaper, instead of giving Eric more official documentation to allow him entry to the ground. On presenting it to a Spanish policeman guarding the car park, Eric had been promptly turned away, without any opportunity to negotiate. When I heard the news I was mortified, and no amount of pleading from me would make Eric attend the evening's celebrations. It was a shocking way for Eric to be treated, and so terribly disappointing for him to have missed possibly the biggest night in Manchester United's history.

Not entirely unexpectedly, I found myself having to secure the hotel on my own. I suspected that the board's logic was such that after having paid a fortune for security during the game it ought to cut back and save a few pounds on the after-match expenses. It puzzled and frustrated me that a rich and successful club like United could, thanks to the board, take on the characteristics of an amateur pub-league side with limited funds when it came to parting with money off the pitch. It took me forty-five minutes to clear the party area of hangers-on, whereas with an extra two of my staff it would have taken only ten. At the door to the function suite I was turning people away left, right and centre. Some were famous, some were not, but my old chant of 'No pass, no glass' became my mantra once again.

During a lull in the proceedings a trendy-looking couple approached me; the man introduced himself as Simon Le Bon and the lady as Yasmin, his wife. Simon assured me that Ryan Giggs had invited them so I asked them to wait while I went back inside, found Ryan and confirmed their invitation.

I sought out Ryan and told him that the Le Bons were outside under the distinct impression that they had been invited as his guests. With a cheeky glint in his eye he said, 'Fuck him off, Ned, but bring her in.' He laughed, but I didn't. Rather reluctantly I returned to the door and apologized to this genuinely nice couple, saying that the Boss had decreed the party full.

At around 6.00 a.m. there were only a few revellers left in the function suite. They were the usual suspects: Roy Keane and Ryan Giggs among others and, surprisingly, the chairman's son, Jimmy Edwards. I saw my window of opportunity, grabbed the European Cup and ran upstairs to my bed.

I had arranged to meet up with Fergie in the hotel lobby at half-past ten the next morning, so I booked an alarm call for 10.00 a.m., climbed into the king-sized bed and pulled the cup in beside me. The alarm startled me out of a deep sleep and a dream involving Yasmin Le Bon, and I wondered why I could feel cold metal pressing against my right leg. I pulled down the bedclothes and smiled when I remembered that four hours previously I had decided that the safest place for the trophy was in bed with me.

I was downstairs five minutes early and chatting to some press photographers who were also waiting for Fergie, when a reporter approached me and whispered to me: 'What happened at the party?'

'Nothing. Why, what do you mean?' I asked, genuinely surprised.

'The chairman's son and Giggsy had a punch-up. Ryan's got a corker of a black eye. Didn't you know?'

'He hadn't got one at 6.15 this morning. It was all quiet when I left them,' I replied.

When Ryan walked past me later he was all smiles but was sporting a panda eye. I couldn't resist a bit of teasing: 'Eye eye, son,' I winked. He just laughed and walked on.

Later I discovered the cause of the falling out. Ryan's mother, Lynne, had taken exception to young Jimmy Edwards being rude to one of her guests, a drag artist known as Foo Foo Lamarr, who was out of costume on the night. Apparently, Ryan had jumped up to take his mother's side, but the confrontation became heated and the inevitable punch-up ensued. I wasn't surprised that Ryan had got involved with a bout of fisticuffs with Jimmy Edwards, as the young man often swaggered about bearing the 'I'm the chairman's son' badge of authority, which I felt could rile even the most laid-back of people.

After a buffet lunch, we all climbed into the coaches and headed for the airport and our flight home. A return flight on Concorde was completely out of the question, as the Manchester United board were footing the bill for the journey home, but the flight was comfortable nevertheless, apart from the moment when I almost had a coronary. On

Manchester United – The Untold Story

returning from a visit to the toilet the European Cup, which had never left my side since our departure from the hotel, was missing from the seat beside me where I was sure I had left it. Nobody around me on the plane seemed to have noticed anything amiss and all looked to be as surprised as I was that the trophy had disappeared. I was really beginning to panic when I heard a shout from further down the plane: 'Ned!' Teddy Sheringham was falling about laughing and, to my absolute relief, produced the cup from under his coat. I stamped down the aisle to Teddy, half-amused, half-angry, and everyone cheered when I took it from him and strapped it securely into the chair next to me.

Since the start of the flight Roy Keane had been taking advantage of the airline's hospitality and that, coupled with his obvious despair at missing the final, meant that he was like a volcano waiting to erupt.

On the approach to Manchester airport, Ken Ramsden asked Roy if he would accept the honour of leading the team off the plane and down the steps, carrying the European Cup. Unfortunately, Roy's response was in the negative. He was clearly distraught at missing out on the chance to play in one of the biggest matches of his career, and consequently had little interest in savouring the moment as the regular captain of the conquerors of Europe. In the end, Peter Schmeichel led the team off to tumultuous applause.

We boarded an open-topped bus on departure from the airport, where the team were reunited with the FA Cup and Premier League trophies, which two of my men had been instructed to bring along, to complete the glorious treble celebrations. On every street along the parade route through Manchester, the team and their trophies were welcomed with enthusiastic shouts and cheers of sheer excitement from the masses who were gathered, until the jubilant procession finally ended in the early evening. Police estimates put the crowd that greeted our open-topped bus parade at 750,000 people, but to me it looked as though at least a million supporters were lined up along Deansgate, waving anything that was red and white.

As Dwight Yorke puffed on a huge Cuban cigar the size of a cruise missile, looking as though he owned the world, Tony Coton, the goalkeeping coach, remarked prophetically, as he observed the United striker, proudly basking in his glory: 'Fergie had better watch that Dwight Yorke. This is going to his head. Look at the size of that cigar!'

[174]

The reception at the MEN (Manchester Evening News) Arena was an amazing spectacle and, at the end of a long yet successful season, I drove the chairman home, bade him goodnight and shook his hand, praising him for the club's wonderful achievement. He paused as he got out of my car and said quietly, 'Ned, you are the only one at the club who congratulated me. Goodnight.'

I watched as the chairman of the country's most successful football team slowly made his way up to his front door; a victorious member of the United board undoubtedly, but clearly upset to have received little or no thanks for the contribution he had made to the club's treble-winning season.

CHAPTER 13

Onwards and Upwards

IN AUGUST 1999, Quinton Fortune joined Manchester United from Atletico Madrid for £1.5 million. As well as being a top-class footballer, Quinton was dedicated to the development of football among the youth of South Africa, and owned his own football club, FC Fortune, in Cape Town. Before he joined the Reds in July, discussions were held to forge a mutually beneficial relationship between the two clubs, with the result that FC Fortune was appointed as United's official youth-player development representative in South Africa, and in turn a number of United players were sent out on loan to the Cape Town club.

Quinton had a great sense of humour and always called me Steven Seagal after the all-action movie-star, given my SAS background. He also had very strong views on other footballers' abilities and weaknesses, and did not mince his words when asked for an opinion. In his view David Beckham was no more than a good footballer, but one whose commercial value to a club far outweighed his worth on the football pitch, a belief I shared wholeheartedly.

Quinton knew perfectly well that he faced an uphill struggle to achieve a regular first-team place at Old Trafford, but I felt this situation merely encouraged him to give 100 per cent every time he pulled on his boots. He came from humble beginnings – his father was a cleaner at the local university and his mother worked in the neighbourhood council library. He was a big hero back home in South Africa and had been capped many times for the national team. The biggest single problem that Quinton encountered when moving to Britain was an unsettling wrangle over a work permit for him, but with Fergie's help the issue was eventually resolved. His best mate at Old Trafford was French defender Mikaël Silvestre, another player for whom I had much respect, who arrived at the club from Inter Milan in September 1999.

The young defender nearly found himself in the dog-house at Old Trafford as, when on international duty with the French squad, Mikaël criticized Fergie, which is never a good career move. He disagreed with the manager when he was made second choice to veteran Denis Irwin for a place in the much-criticized Manchester United defence. He was quoted as saying: 'I've sat through the videos of our games with the manager but I don't agree with his theories.' Such an honest but ill-advised comment could have wrecked his relationship with the Boss irreparably, but at the time of writing, Mikaël is still very much part of the Old Trafford set-up.

During my time with the club I had learned that it was never a wise decision to cross the Boss, no matter what the subject. I often had run-ins with him on the subject of the number of tickets allocated for visitors to the players' lounge. Every so often, I'd be pulled up by Fergie when he was on a mission to tighten up the number of visitors to the players' lounge. Wandering through the room, he was often unhappy with the quantity – and the quality of – the players' guests.

'I'm fucking telling you, Ned, if you cannot control the numbers getting into the players' lounge, then I'll find someone who can,' he'd rage.

'Yes, Boss,' I'd reply. 'But it really is the players who overload the system by bringing in too many guests. What can my staff do? Turn away a player?'

Fergie would shake his head, sometimes almost incandescent with rage, but he knew that none of my SPS staff could turn away £15 million players just because they had one or two too many guests. Fergie would give me a hairdryer blasting but, like all hairdrying, it was usually just hot air, and did little to ruffle my feathers.

Fiery and hot-tempered he might have been, but without this aspect of his character I doubt he would have had inspired the players to achieve the level of success that the club has enjoyed. In the dressing room before a match, he would walk among the players with little asides of encouragement: 'You're better than them. Let's do it!' or 'Keep your concentration, stick to the game plan. This game is ours.'

By half-time his tone would have changed, depending on the game's progress. Whether we were winning, losing or drawing with our opponents, Fergie's half-time talks were legendary. Half-time shouts would be a better description, especially if we were losing. The Boss could shout and bawl for Britain, but if ever a man could inspire flagging men, it was Fergie. Such was his experience as a manager, he could detect where the weakness in the team was beginning to show long before even the opposition could, and God help any player who was responsible for a stupid mistake that put Manchester United a goal behind. That player would never make the same error in the second half. Nobody would want to face Fergie's blast twice in one day.

After the game, the dressing room would fall silent once again, as Fergie began his post-match assessment – an encouraging talk if we had won or a high-decibel tirade if we had lost or played badly. Fergie's manner may have been tough, but week after week it produced results, which was good for all concerned at the club.

With such pressure on the players to perform well, they each had their own way of dealing with nerves and stress prior to a match. David Beckham was always cool before a game, but to me his eyes always said 'Let's get on with it', and his body language gave the impression that he was like a coiled spring ready to be released. Roy Keane would simply sit in his shorts and socks, staring into the abyss, before pulling on his boots and top, his face giving away nothing. Some players engaged in rituals: Peter Schmeichel would always have the kit man throw a ball to him up and down the tunnel, while Nicky Butt and the Neville brothers would pass a ball about in the dressing room to warm up before running on to the pitch. Andy Cole would always refuse to go on to the pitch for a pre-match warm-up and Paul Ince never put on his shirt until the very last moment, and would keep his shorts at his knees until it was time to go. During his time at United he always insisted on being the last man out of the dressing room and up the tunnel.

Fergie too had a pre-match ritual of sorts, stories about which were often relayed to me in post-match chats, which amused and fascinated me in equal measure. Before each game, Fergie would take up residency in the dressing-room toilets, with the match programme for reading material, and start humming a song that he had known for years. However, the musical feast would pale into insignificance as the aroma of his business permeated the air, making the dressing room an uncomfortable place to remain. From a careful distance I could only pity the players, and the dreadful assault on their sense of smell. Many a day I would laugh as they moved nearer the door of the dressing room, waiting to be saved by the bell that would summon them on to the pitch.

Once the players were through the tunnel and then safely on to the pitch, another of Fergie's affectations would appear. He chewed gum relentlessly during a match, which seemed to help his habitual nervous cough and his tendency to spit. Before Fergie began the gum-chewing ritual, there was a standing joke that you needed a life jacket to enter the dugout as a result of his unfortunate habit. Indeed, he was once politely advised by Martin Edwards that TV footage of him spitting throughout the game was hardly suitable for dinnertime viewing!

★ ★ ★

At the end of August 1999 we flew to Monaco for the Super Cup match against Lazio, the Italian holders of the Cup-Winners' Cup. After a 1–0 win, Lazio went back to Rome the victors, while we consoled ourselves with the knowledge that we would be competing for the World Club Championship later in the season.

In the Champions League we were drawn in a potentially difficult group with Croatia Zagreb, Sturm Graz of Austria and Eric Cantona's old club, Olympique Marseille, the champions of France. In our first European encounter against Zagreb, in mid-September, we were disappointed to come away with a poor 0–0 draw at home, but a week later we enjoyed better fortune by beating Sturm Graz 3–0 in Austria, and despatching Olympique Marseille 2–1 at Old Trafford.

For the return match in France, security would have to be tight as the city of Marseilles had been the scene of some trouble involving English fans during the 1998 World Cup finals. My aim, naturally, was to avoid a repeat performance. In preparation I put together a top-class team of my men, and between us we made sure the players and staff arrived at the stadium safely and without incident.

As I guarded the mouth of the tunnel, awaiting the players' imminent arrival on to the pitch prior to kick-off, I had a chat with United's finance director, David Gill. When his appointment was announced at the end of 1996, there were some accompanying sniggers within the club, owing to the fact that his previous business experience had been with the First Choice Travel Group. Consequently, there were some who were sceptical about the merits of his selection. While I had no opinion on the matter, I couldn't resist having a laugh with him about his former employment, before the game in France kicked off.

'So if any of us need a cheap holiday, you'll be the one we all come to then?' I remarked, teasingly.

Unfortunately, my joke went down like a lead balloon. 'Maybe so, Ned,' David simply replied, 'but don't forget that I'm the "man" at Manchester United now.'

He surprised me with his seemingly immodest response, and the thinly disguised warning about his management style, so I decided to get back to work, mumbled a goodbye to him, and returned to guarding the team.

The 1–0 beating we suffered at the hands of the French side ended our quite remarkable unbeaten run of eighteen games in the Champions League, which made defeat even more difficult to bear.

In October 1999 it was Fergie's turn to appear as an accused person in Her Majesty's Courts, not just once, but twice. How the young guns at Old Trafford must have laughed among themselves at this state of affairs. For once the heat was off them, and all attention was focused on that hard taskmaster in all matters behavioural – the Boss.

Eight months previously, on 6 February, following United's 8–1 victory away against Nottingham Forest, a police camera near Derby had snapped a BMW 750 saloon exceeding the speed limit, and computer records showed that the car was leased to Manchester United. The problem for the magistrates of the Derby courthouse was that Manchester United Football Club was unable to establish the identity of the driver on the day of the offence.

When it came to court on 21 October, the case against the manager collapsed, as the club was still unable to provide any clue as to the erring driver's identity, or indeed to reveal exactly which car Sir Alex Ferguson was driving at the time of the incident. The club, however, was fined the grand total of £650 and ordered to pay £35 in court costs. Fergie's lawyer on the day, Nicholas Freeman, was successful in his application to the court for Fergie's defence costs to be paid by the taxpayers' 'central fund' scheme. This action later prompted an angry comment by Bob Laxton, then MP for Derby North, who was reported as saying: 'It seems that if there is a loophole in the law then it needs tightening up. It is a disgrace that high-profile people can avoid prosecution with this get-out clause.'

More interestingly, perhaps, was the fact that the car was exactly the same model as the one in which Fergie was caught driving illegally along the hard shoulder of the M602 on the outskirts of Manchester, at the end of February. When this matter eventually reached court, also in October, it was the magistrates of Bury who had the dubious pleasure of a celebrity in the dock.

I drove Fergie and Nick Freeman to the courthouse in Bury, where, when questioned about driving along the hard shoulder, Fergie claimed that a severe bout of diarrhoea had been about to manifest itself, while the motorway traffic was piling up ahead of him on the M602. In an attempt to try and make a dash for it back to Old Trafford, Fergie elected to travel some of the way on the hard shoulder. Eagle-eyed traffic cops in a Range Rover witnessed the illegal driving act and pulled him over. They cautioned him and charged him with dangerous driving. At the time, Fergie chose not to mention his crippling diarrhoea, later citing embarrassment and the possibility of attendant publicity as the reason for his silence.

The magistrates believed Fergie's version of events and found him not guilty. So concerned were they for Fergie's well-being that, during the short trial, they offered him the rare luxury of sitting down while he occupied the witness box. Feeling slightly unconvinced about the outcome of the day's events in court, I made a mental note never to vote in favour of hanging.

As Champions of Europe, Manchester United embarked on a trip to Japan at the end of November to play Palmeiras of Brazil, the South American champions, in the Inter-Continental Cup competition. Tokyo went wild for Manchester United, but more especially for David Beckham who, at times, received the kind of adulation that would once have been reserved for Elvis. A Roy Keane goal decided the contest and, having won this cup, we now had to play in another more controversial competition in Brazil, in January 2000.

Back in England, United were having success in the League, but had suffered a few setbacks in Europe, notably in November, losing 2–0 away to Fiorentina of Italy.

During the last weeks of 1999, the main talking point in the sporting press concerned Manchester United's decision to withdraw from the English FA Cup competition, in order to compete in the inaugural FIFA World Club Championship in Brazil. This judgement caused many people to assume, quite wrongly, that those in charge at Manchester United believed the club was too grand for the domestic competition and was now only content to compete on the world stage, when in fact the truth was something else entirely. Enormous pressure had been brought to bear on the club by both the FA and certain government departments, which were intent on trying to secure the World Cup finals of 2006 for Britain, even though it would always have been an uphill struggle as UEFA had already declared that their vote would be for Germany. The powers that be were convinced that if the rest of the world could watch and enjoy the quality of footballing skills exhibited by Manchester United, then somehow Britain's chances would be enhanced.

Accompanying the team alone, I joined the Manchester United circus, and together we headed for Rio de Janeiro, where the team was to face local champions Vasco da Gama, Necaxa of Mexico and South Melbourne of Australia in the January 2000 competition. Necaxa held us to a 1–1 draw in a game in which David Beckham was sent off for an uncharacteristic foul. It was probably the case that the heat was getting to David, because as I chaperoned him back to the dressing room, he seemed to lose his head completely, booting the cool-air fans in the shower area and generally going a little mad. I calmed him down as best I could and went back to the dugout, silently praying that Fergie wouldn't explode at David when he saw the broken fans later. I worried unnecessarily because on my return to the pitch there was an empty seat in the dugout – Fergie had also been sent off. He was banished to the stands for an outburst against the referee, and so I hoped that would balance things out between the two angry men, which it did.

During the day the heat in Rio was unbearable, while in the stadium the humidity was oppressive in the extreme. It was fortunate that the match scheduling allowed the players plenty of leisure time, which was gratefully taken by all concerned. I spent most of my free time lazing around the hotel pool with Fergie, the peace only being disturbed when he discovered that he had lost his wallet, which led to the hotel being turned upside down in the course of a thorough search for it.

On the field we were knocked out of the competition 3–1 by Vasco da Gama and so our consolation win over South Melbourne became academic; we were out of the World Club Championship. We managed to rearrange our return flight to get home early, as everyone was desperate to get back to Britain and see a bit of rain. On the penultimate day, I was lounging by the pool with Fergie when he put his hand over his eyes, visor-like, and stared into the sun. I could see his attention was drawn to a group on a hilltop, overlooking the hotel, who were engaged in a spot of hang gliding.

'Fucking dangerous that, eh Ned?' he commented.

I went red but didn't disagree: 'Too right, Boss.'

I didn't dare tell him that he was watching Roy Keane, Teddy Sheringham and Nicky Butt flying about over Rio on six bits of balsa wood and two metres of canvas. I imagined that his response to the news that approximately £35 million worth of Manchester United players were throwing themselves off cliffs for fun would have been far from positive, so I kept quiet, and hoped that no injuries would befall the intrepid trio.

Meanwhile, Martin Edwards was also throwing himself about in Rio; not off clifftops, however, but at ladies of the night. Unfortunately for Martin, one particular beauty, Maria Elves, quickly realized that she would get paid more by the press for her moment of passion with him than whatever he gave her. It transpired that the enterprising Maria had an 'agent' who had negotiated a fee for her silence where her clients were concerned – absolute discretion had been guaranteed for US $250,000. I laughed when I heard about the situation and told Martin that I had deep reservations regarding the young lady's integrity, believing that she would sell her story to the press anyway.

My doubts were not heeded by the chairman, and Martin paid the price both financially, and personally. After he had paid Maria for services rendered, the press also paid her handsomely for her story, and the tabloids loved every salacious minute of it. He protested his innocence on television – 'I did not have sex with that woman' – and in the newspapers, but there were few who believed his story. There was outrage at the allegations, and calls for his resignation but, as always, he hung on.

We flew back into Manchester to an unsympathetic reaction from the media, which had decided that United had earned a well-deserved comeuppance for turning their backs on the FA Cup.

The FIFA World Club Championship was shelved after just one tournament, as most of the clubs that had competed had received a similarly negative reception in their respective countries.

Putting the misfortunes of the ill-fated FIFA tournament behind us, the team made reasonable progress in Europe, but success in progressing to the penultimate round was elusive, as Real Madrid knocked us out in a quarter-final clash in April, denying us an opportunity to take the European Cup for the second time in two years. However, another League title remained firmly within our grasp, and for each of the last eleven games of the season, a victory was recorded for the Reds every time, to guarantee a sixth League title in eight years.

Martin Edwards did not enjoy an end to his woes, however, and over the next eighteen months his problems grew ever greater. Numerous women came out of the woodwork claiming to have had relationships with him, while exposés of his alleged antics with Doug Hall, a former vice-chairman of Newcastle United Football Club, appeared in the tabloids. Yet another complaint of a misdemeanour in the women's toilet, this time at the Mottram Hall Hotel in Cheshire, in December 2002, finally brought him a police caution under the Public Order Act. There was no doubt that he had to put a stop to this behaviour before any more damage was done, both to the women who had their privacy so unpleasantly invaded, and to his own reputation and the unity of his family.

After much persuasion from his peers about the damage he was doing to Manchester United, a club he never tired of professing to love, he finally quit the board towards the end of 2002. I was sorry for him, as Martin Edwards, like many at Old Trafford, had been good to me, and had given me my first invaluable break in the security business. One night, long before the incident at Mottram Hall, in an effort to encourage him to put a stop to his unusual behaviour in or in the vicinity of women's toilets, I tried to explain to him, while having a drink together in a club in Manchester, that his behaviour had made him a laughing stock at the club. My news was less than well received, however, and he became enraged at me, shouting: 'Name me one instance!'

I was able to offer him nearly a dozen episodes, especially his visit to the Ladies' at the SAS HQ in Hereford, again when we played Spurs at White Hart Lane, and inside Old Trafford. The list was tasteless if not endless. Martin banged his glass down in a rage and left me sitting on my own at the bar. I know the truth was hard to take, and it certainly gave me no pleasure to say it, but somebody had to make an effort. It made no difference, however, for Martin Edwards could not even admit to his sexual peccadilloes, never mind control them, and perhaps he never will.

★ ★ ★

The 2000–1 season saw us crash out of Europe at the quarter-final stage yet again, this time against Bayern Munich. I had attended this game as a supporter, having been informed by the two Kens that security wasn't required, but as a fan I would still travel anywhere I could to watch the Reds, whether it was on business or for pleasure.

Next, our FA Cup hopes were to be dashed when a Paolo Di Canio goal put West Ham through to the next round at the end of January 2001. The goal would be long remembered for the moment when United's goalkeeper, Fabien Barthez, stopped playing football and stood with one hand raised in a Statue of Liberty pose, hoping to con everyone into believing that the little Italian was offside. Di Canio ignored this performance, electing instead to let the man in black make the decision, so he simply ran around Barthez and, unchallenged, stuck the ball into the back of the net. Although the goal knocked us out of the competition, I still have to admit it was a moment of pure genius.

At our next match at Old Trafford I brought along a picture of the Statue of Liberty on which I had superimposed a photograph of Fabien Barthez's face. Fergie loved the joke but I knew Barthez would have been far less impressed, so the photo stayed in my pocket. Fergie thought Di Canio was a great footballer and he told me it was a real disappointment to him when a proposed transfer deal, which would have involved the sale of Dwight Yorke to Middlesbrough to generate enough funds to buy the Italian, fell through.

In a small way, I was briefly involved in Fabien Barthez's move to Manchester United. In April 2000 I received a phone call from Pascal Carbone, Eric Cantona's agent, who mentioned that Monaco's current goalkeeper, Fabien Barthez, was keen to join Manchester United – would I mind telling Fergie? I wasted no time in imparting this information to the manager, and he organized a meeting with Pascal and Jean-Marie Cantona, Eric's brother, who also acted for Barthez. He invited them over to watch Sunderland play United at Old Trafford, and after the game the Boss told me to bring them down to the players' dressing room after it had been cleaned. I duly gave them the grand tour and they were obviously impressed by what they saw. The French contingent returned at the end of May, this time with Barthez who, at the time, was in the French national squad for the European Championships. I picked them up at Manchester airport and sped them into the city. As we approached the centre Barthez took a sudden interest in his surroundings, looking around at all the pubs and clubs as we passed them by, before asking, 'Where are the bars with all the pretty girls?'

'Paris,' I replied, and everyone laughed. The negotiations at Old Trafford lasted all day until, at 9.30 p.m., Barthez stormed out of the meeting and asked me: 'Can you get me a private jet back to Paris? Now!'

Clearly things were not going well. I explained to Fabien that he'd be lucky to get a taxi in Manchester at this time of night, never mind a private plane. He calmed down a little, and laughed, before rejoining the transfer discussions after a short break, which he obviously needed. About an hour later they all spilled out of the meeting and announced that a deal had been signed. After his medical checks the following morning, Barthez was officially revealed as Manchester United's new goalkeeper. At the mandatory press conference to announce the signing I overheard Carbone saying to Peter Kenyon, who was still deputy chief executive at the time: 'We have learned a valuable lesson here, and lost a lot of money on the deal.'

Kenyon was nonplussed, but gave a smile in reply, adding, 'Let that be a lesson to you, then.'

Not for the first time United had played hard to get and won. Though I believed that Barthez was a great goalkeeper I seriously doubted that he would ever be in the same class as Peter Schmeichel.

The arrival of Fabien Barthez speeded up the July departure of another United goalkeeper, Massimo Taibi, who had failed to live up to expectations since his arrival at Old Trafford. After signing for £4 million from Venezia in August 1999, the Italian played just four games in the autumn, conceding an astonishing eleven goals. He was loaned to Italian Serie A side Reggina for the second half of the season, and eventually moved there permanently in July 2000, the transfer reportedly handled by L'Attitude, an agency that employed Fergie's son, Jason, which received a fee of £25,000 for its role in the deal. As I always regarded Fergie as an expert on recognizing players' abilities, especially concerning their usefulness to Manchester United, Taibi's lack of success at the club was surprising.

Later that month I was travelling in a private jet with Fabien, Fergie and Mikaël Silvestre on the way back from a testimonial match in Marseilles, when Fergie revealed that some time ago Eric Cantona had mentioned to him the potential of a young player named Zinedine Zidane. Barthez raised his eyebrows, remarking in a typically French fashion, 'Oh la la.'

A member of France's victorious Euro 2000 team that had won the competition earlier in July, Zidane's talent was legendary. Fergie spoke to him through an interpreter on the night of the testimonial game, and asked him if he could play on the right side of midfield. Zidane replied that he preferred to operate in the centre. At the time, Fergie was happy with his central midfield, and decided not to pursue the matter, but he later voiced his regret at not taking things further, which could also be considered another rare error of judgement on his part.

The 'private jet' philosophy was now part of everyday life where football transfer transactions were concerned, as club and players used this form of transport as they had once used limousines, both to impress each other and to save their time. It was a commercial plane, however, that brought one of the sport's true gentlemen back to Old Trafford in April 2001, but this time for a more permanent arrangement, when Ruud van Nistelrooy bounced down the steps of the plane and greeted me with open arms.

'Hi Ned! Told you I'd be back,' he drawled, affecting a mock Arnold Schwarzenegger accent.

Twelve months earlier I had delivered a crestfallen Ruud back to his plane after he had failed his medical at Old Trafford due to a serious ligament problem. The injury had blocked his transfer from PSV Eindhoven, and many feared he would never get the opportunity to wear a United shirt. At the time of writing he is an essential part of any Manchester United attack, after showing true courage in the face of disaster and overcoming his injury problem. He now enthrals millions with his skill and expertise, but it could all have been so very different.

In April 2000, I collected Ruud from Manchester airport with his beautiful girlfriend Leontien and his agent, Roger Linse. After driving them to the Mottram Hall Hotel, where they all checked in, I took

Ruud to the BUPA hospital a few miles away where he was to have his medical examination, overseen by the Manchester United medic, Doc Stone. In the meantime, Ruud's girlfriend was being shown around the area by a Manchester United club official to see if she favoured any particular location, as a quality house was high on Ruud's list of priorities. Once Doc Stone had finished his examination, I drove them to the Alexandra Hospital, in Cheadle, where more in-depth medical tests were to be carried out. The last tests were to take place at the Carrington training ground, and it was during these physiotherapy examinations and final fitness tests that the discovery was made concerning Ruud's right knee – he had sustained a damaging injury to the cruciate ligament.

This discovery brought the whole transfer process to a grinding halt. Then came the argument. The doctor at PSV Eindhoven, Cees Rein Van Den Hoogenband, declared that the injury was not to the cruciate ligament but was merely a knee injury that was healing well. After many frantic and increasingly heated telephone conversations between Holland and Manchester, it was decided that the PSV Eindhoven doctor would fly over to Manchester the next day and discuss the problem with Doc Stone.

The next morning, I picked up the Dutch doctor from Manchester airport and drove him to the Mottram Hall Hotel to meet up with Ruud. After coffee, I drove the pair to the Carrington training ground to see Doc Stone, who by now was under considerable pressure to clear Ruud for signing, as many at Old Trafford were willing to take the risk that the injury was not as serious as the doctor had advised. But Doc Stone's strength of belief in his own diagnosis that Ruud's knee problem was major would not be swayed. He was not about to risk his reputation, and especially not when such a huge sum of money – £18 million – was involved.

After much deliberation, the two doctors still could not reach an agreed mutual decision concerning the severity of Ruud's injury. The discussions rumbled on into the following day. A press conference had been scheduled for the afternoon, but still the matter was unresolved. I waited outside David Gill's office to escort Ruud and his party to the event, but two hours after the press conference had been scheduled to start, the press still didn't have their story. Something was obviously going badly wrong, and I privately wished that Fergie had chosen a different week in which to take a family holiday in Spain. It was an inopportune moment for the manager to be away from Old Trafford, and the nervousness on the directors' faces suggested they felt the same.

I patrolled the corridor outside David Gill's office and stole the odd glance into the proceedings, where the look on Ruud's face spoke volumes. Mistakenly, I assumed that they were wrangling over money, but soon all was revealed.

I remember thinking that the media would have a field day if this transfer were to go wrong at this late stage – Ruud had been signing autographs at Old Trafford only a day or two earlier – because as far as everyone else was concerned it was a done deal. At 5.45 p.m., however, the bad news was confirmed when David Gill emerged from his office and told me to bring the Mercedes to the front door as the deal was off. I was angry about the outcome but bolted for the car, grateful to be spared the job of evacuating the press who now occupied every corner of the building. It was an extremely subdued van Nistelrooy party that I drove back to the airport. Ruud was convinced his cruciate ligament was not damaged and that he should have been signed by Manchester United, but there was nothing he could do about it.

Despite Ruud's beliefs otherwise, Doc Stone was proven absolutely right in his diagnosis of the Dutchman's injury, as only three weeks later, during training for PSV Eindhoven, Ruud collapsed holding his knee – tests later proved his injury was cruciate-ligament failure. Fortunately, as has been said, a year of patient waiting on both sides was rewarded with Ruud's eventual signing in April 2001.

Indeed the eager new player scored two goals on his home debut for the club, on 1 August 2001, in a testimonial match for Ryan Giggs against Celtic, a game played to honour and celebrate the career of the talented young Welshman. As I considered the phenomenal success that Ryan had enjoyed with United, I began to wonder where the years had gone, for it seemed like only yesterday that I had watched him make his first-team debut, and now, over ten years later, he was being honoured by his peers and adoring public.

Ryan has overcome a lot in his personal life. He has a brother, Rhodri, who has been in trouble with the police on a number of occasions: he was convicted of an assault in a nightclub (for which he served a nine-month sentence), and also faced a serious, though unproven, allegation that he supplied drugs to a tabloid reporter. In

September 1998 fire bombers attacked the house of Ryan's mother, Lynne, a home bought for her by her famous footballer son. Mercifully, at the time of the attack Lynne and Ryan's half-sister, Bethany, then only six years old, were staying with friends nearby. Rhodri was at home alone, and managed to escape the inferno by jumping out of a window. Firemen tackled the blaze, which caused extensive damage to the cottage in Swinton, Greater Manchester, and a search by officers equipped with breathing apparatus found the house to be empty. Initial police enquiries revealed that Rhodri was the intended victim.

Despite his lucky escape from the arson attack and the potentially fatal consequences it might have visited on his family, Rhodri Giggs still kept finding himself on the wrong side of the law. Many hold the view that it is only because he is Ryan's brother that he is still alive.

Ryan, on the other hand, is a 'no-go area' as far as being troubled by the gangster community in Manchester is concerned, since he is under the (unsolicited) protection of the 'Salford mob' and affiliated gangs in Manchester. He is quite simply untouchable, and is viewed as the original local boy made good.

His high living and devil-may-care attitude masks a sensitive man, a worrier and a devoted son to Lynne and brother to Bethany. In the dressing room before a match, he always rallied the troops, urging them on and going round them shouting encouragement, 'Come on Yorkie, come on Coley,' and generally whipping up a storm before the players left the dressing room for the battle on the pitch. For me, his most annoying habit was the constant nose-picking, and I would try to embarrass him by saying to him: 'Ryan, if that's a green one, give me a bit!' but it would never work, and I soon came to the conclusion that it was impossible to make the lad blush no matter how hard you tried.

Ryan and Rhodri's father was an ex-rugby player called Danny Wilson. Like many Welshmen, he had transferred from rugby union in Wales to rugby league in England. When his parents divorced, Ryan sided with his mother and changed his name from Wilson to Giggs – her maiden name. Lynne remarried, but her second husband died young. She has had more than her fair share of grief, and her vulnerability allowed some people to take advantage of her. For a time, she was in a relationship with one of my SPS stewards. She had taken him on a few holidays and had bought him various trinkets, the most expensive of these being a £20,000 BMW. It transpired that his affection for Lynne disappeared as the BMW ownership papers appeared, and within a short period of time he had sold the car and dumped Lynne. She contacted me about this unpleasant situation and I promised to try to retrieve her money. Though he had ceased to work for SPS, I managed to locate him and confront him about the liberty he had taken with Ryan's mother.

'Lynne did buy me the car, Ned, but she insisted,' he protested.

'Well, give her back the money for it. For once do the decent thing,' I argued. But it was in vain, as all the money had been spent. The worst of it, as far as Lynne was concerned, was that once he had moved to a new address, he telephoned her threatening to sell his story to the tabloid press.

It cannot have been easy for Ryan's mother, having one son whose achievements at Old Trafford brought her great pride, and another who made her life difficult by regularly getting into scrapes. It was bad enough that Rhodri would sometimes call the press trying to sell his idea of a story from Old Trafford that he had picked up from something Ryan had innocently mentioned, as well as stealing £2,000 from his brother's bank account on one occasion.

I often wondered if part of Ryan's drive and determination was simply rooted in a desire to break away from his early surroundings, as his dedication to his training and craft was absolute. It is hoped that fatherhood will help him to settle down, as Ryan and his fiancée, Stacey Cook, celebrated the birth of a baby daughter, whom they named Liberty, in April 2003.

During my tenure at Old Trafford I witnessed a few players who arrived full of promise and left with it unfulfilled. A perfect example was Australian goalkeeper Mark Bosnich who joined the club in summer 1999, and who should have matured into one of the best footballers in the world, but his personal problems were overwhelming and largely of his own making. He had a complete aversion to training and almost drove the goalkeeping coach, Tony Coton, insane with his arrogant attitude and complete lack of willingness to learn. Although I always found Bosnich to be quite a laugh around the dressing room and training ground, he really did think himself to be a wide-boy, gangster-type, despite the fact that he was a long way from living up to a tough-boy reputation.

Rumours were rife in Manchester that Mark was indulging heavily in cocaine, although my own investigations into the stories were inconclusive. When he eventually moved to Chelsea in January 2001 after his contract with United had been terminated by mutual consent, blood tests proved he had tested positive for cocaine. Though he denied using the drug, he received a highly publicized nine-month suspension from the FA, and Chelsea FC sacked him. Appealing against both the charge and the sentence, Bosnich was unsuccessful in having his protestations of innocence accepted. Few at Old Trafford were surprised. We all knew that Bosnich was hanging around with undesirables, and even the dogs in the streets knew he was a 'coke-head'. I used to joke that Bosnich would sniff the white lines along the M6 if he had nothing else.

His weight also made him the butt of some jokes among the other players as from week to week his physique really could balloon out of all proportion; indeed, sometimes he seemed to resemble an Easter egg with feet. On one occasion Nicky Butt actually bet him £5,000 that Ryan Giggs could beat him in a race – goal line to goal line. Nicky offered Bosnich a start of eighteen yards, and the contest was arranged to take place during our trip to Rio in 2000. I would have confidently bet £50,000 that Ryan would have won by eighteen yards. Needless to say, Bosnich pulled out of the bet, purely, I suspect, because he didn't fancy his chances against Giggs.

In complete contrast to Bosnich, Nicky Butt was a typical Manchester lad, a cocky git who was full of himself, as well as a great practical joker who loved winding people up. Late one evening, Nicky, Roy Keane and I were drinking in Kitty's Bar at the Four Seasons Hotel in Cheshire, and Roy was rambling on about his contract and wages, which were both up for review and renewal.

'I'm asking them for a million a year,' Roy declared.

Nicky looked shocked at Roy's audacity, and gasped, 'What? My contract is coming up for renewal too. But I couldn't ask them for that much.'

I knew that Nicky loved Manchester United and that he would never make excessive wage demands for fear of being accused of rocking the boat. Whatever he did eventually accept as a wage deal, he has earned every penny of it in his service to the club. Like Paul Scholes, he disliked the limelight and was simply content to turn up, play and go home.

I had known both Nicky and Paul since their days with the youth team, and had watched Paul develop into one of the finest players in the world. A quiet individual, he hated giving interviews and kept himself very much to himself. Even I found it difficult to have a conversation with Paul on occasions, and I could talk to a wall. If Paul was not in the mood for talking, that was that. All you would get was a grunt. He was a great family man and, after home games, when the stadium was empty, he could be found kicking a ball about on the pitch with his son while the rest of the team were either celebrating or commiserating in the players' lounge.

Gary Neville was another of the younger players who was content to play his football and stay out of the headlines. However, in spite of attempts to distance himself from public scrutiny, Gary found his private life thrust under the unwanted glare of the media spotlight after his relationship with Hannah Thornley, sister of former United player Ben, ended after six years together. In February 2002 Hannah told friends that she had split from Gary, and she was reportedly 'walking out' with Lee Howard, an old friend from her schooldays.

In Gary I was reminded that not everybody in footballing circles is driven by fame and fortune. I formed the impression that he was content to stay at home and concentrate on his next match while Hannah would have preferred them to be out on the town together. A private person, Gary wasn't much inclined towards signing autographs and posing for photographs either, and was happy to sneak out of Old Trafford by the back way after a match. Although I would count him as a committed players' man and active in their union, he would never go into the players' lounge after a match, preferring to head for home as soon as he had showered and dressed.

Mark Bosnich and Dwight Yorke, on the other hand, were the complete opposites of Nicky, Paul and Gary. I never thought it was wise to bring the Australian to Old Trafford where he could join forces with Dwight once again, as I felt that they had a bad influence on one another. Their antics had been well chronicled when they played together at Aston Villa, and it wasn't long after Bosnich arrived at the club that he renewed his unholy alliance with Dwight. The Trinidad and Tobago player's reputation in Manchester was forged more by his off-field antics than his undoubted powers as a striker. Allegations about his personal video collection (one particular film featuring

Bosnich as an onlooker), in which he appeared in various sexual pursuits with young women, together with lurid tabloid tales about his sex life, meant that he was constantly in trouble with Fergie. Dwight's guests at Old Trafford were well known around Manchester and deemed highly undesirable.

On match days Dwight Yorke would normally be the last to arrive. He'd sign a few autographs, make his way into the building and then, strangely, head straight for the children's crèche for a few hours of seclusion before the players' children and wives arrived, and sit with Andy Cole, talking on the phone and watching television. Before a match they seemed to enjoy the comparative isolation, away from the buzz in the main building.

Dwight seemed to have a sixth sense about how he would perform on a match day, and would sometimes tell me, 'I'm cooking, man. I'm cooking today,' and sure enough he'd go out and have a fantastic game. One of the more pleasant duties I would fulfil for Dwight would be when he told me that Jordan, his model girlfriend, was coming to the match, and ask me if I would escort her into the VIP areas. I always found this up-front young lady good fun and really pleasant. One afternoon, Dwight took me by surprise by asking me: 'Ned, can you make sure my missus gets in OK?'

'Missus?' I replied. The surprise on my face was not lost on Dwight.

'Oh, I mean Jordan,' he replied sheepishly. I could feel his embarrassment at his slip of the tongue, so I cut the conversation short: 'Of course I'll escort her in, Dwight. Leave it to me.' I winked, and went about my business.

When Jordan arrived at Old Trafford, I met up with her at the VIP car park and escorted her into the players' lounge. I found her a larger-than-life character and we usually enjoyed some good banter. As always, she was full of smiles and greeted me with a 'Hi, Ned. Wotcha.'

I gave her a smile and a wink, and flashed a cheeky look at her bare, but obviously expanding, waistline. The rumour mill was in full swing that she was pregnant and that it was only a matter of time before Dwight Yorke would be announced as the father of her child.

'You are putting on weight, eh Jordan?' I laughed.

She blushed momentarily but soon had her bolshie front on again: 'Fuck off, you. You cheeky bastard. I'm not putting on any weight.'

A few months later, Jordan gave birth to Dwight's son, Harvey.

There was no doubt that Dwight really loved the ladies, and most loved him right back. One particular affair (before his relationship with Jordan) which brought him considerable grief was with a stunning American woman, who could drown out almost everybody else in the players' lounge with her high-pitched drawl.

'She's driving me up the fucking wall, Ned,' he complained one day.

'Why do you put up with it then?' I asked him.

'It fits,' he smiled back.

Without a doubt she was a stunner, but Dwight knew his off-field antics were colouring his future on the field and that he had to address his weaknesses and excesses.

'Fuck the Yankee bird off, Dwight. She's causing you too much grief,' I suggested.

He took my advice and broke up with the American girl, assuring me: 'Ned, I've got my head right now. I'm back on track.'

But it was all too little, too late. Dwight was synonymous with problems and Fergie knew the cure for wayward players – he would make sure they played for some other team. What most of the high-jinx-loving players at Manchester United never seemed to understand was that Manchester was a village compared to London or Birmingham. Everything that happened within a thirty-mile radius involving Manchester United players would eventually get back to Fergie and the directors before too long.

The Boss eventually reached the end of his tether with Dwight after a meeting they had at the Carrington training ground when the player begged for 'one last chance'. Fergie replied that he'd been given about twenty-two chances to pull his socks up. That meeting took place on the Thursday and the players were due to report back on the Monday for pre-season training at 10.00 a.m. Yorkie finally showed up the following Monday at 10.40 a.m. Fergie said nothing to him, but a few weeks later, in July 2002, Dwight was sold to Blackburn for a knockdown price, having failed to take the last chance that Fergie had given him.

CHAPTER 14

All That Glitters

THE CULT OF CELEBRITY is a relatively new phenomenon. Some people have it thrust upon them and some pursue it from the cradle to the grave. Manchester United has always attracted big-name celebrity players, but massive wages, global television audiences, worldwide advertising and merchandising campaigns have served to transform football players from working-class heroes into media and fashion icons. When this cocktail is mixed with a few high-profile and, in some cases, dangerous liaisons with members of the opposite sex, the results can be unpredictable, for they may be viewed in a bad light by the masses who still struggle to pay for a match ticket. Long gone are the days when stars like George Best could command headlines by drinking too much and bedding the odd Miss World winner. Now it is more common to see the stars parading in the celebrity magazines with their glamorous designer jewellery, £10,000 suits and expensive high-performance cars.

Nobody can deny that these stars bring fabulous amounts of money into the clubs they play for, from advertising and merchandising across the globe, and consequently there is an argument for the high wages that they command. However, when one of the biggest stars in the football world joined forces financially, as well as romantically, with one of the biggest stars in the pop music world at that time, the resulting opulence surrounding their lives reached Pharaoh-like proportions.

The shy, mild-mannered, often embarrassingly quiet David Beckham that I had known since his youth-team days was to mature into one of the world's most famous and competent footballers, captaining both his club and his country. A chance encounter with Spice Girl Victoria Adams, when she visited Old Trafford in March 1997, led David to a marriage that would propel the pair into a completely different sphere of celebrity, more usually associated with younger members of the royal family. Nonetheless there were many who considered that the tasteless extravagance of their wedding would have embarrassed even Taylor and Burton.

After the nuptials, the bride and groom sat on matching thrones while, it seemed to me, a motley assortment of self-appointed VIPs and sycophants fawned over them. Photographs and details of what I viewed as an embarrassing spectacle were soon available on news-stands worldwide, since the enterprising couple had sold the rights to their wedding to one of Britain's best-selling glossy magazines.

It might have been so different for David if his early critics had been proven correct. When he was sent on loan to Preston North End as a youngster, many predicted that he would never return to Old Trafford – or indeed have a future in the game. However, David came back from his spell at Preston with his dedication and commitment renewed, and went on to enjoy great success with the youth team before joining the first team and adding his name to the history books. With his pop-star good looks, David soon achieved idol status amongst the fans, and also among women who had previously had no interest in football.

His eventual relationship with and marriage to 'Posh Spice' – Victoria Adams – was a union made in merchandising heaven; nowadays it is difficult to watch TV or read a newspaper or magazine without seeing Beckham's face promoting at least one global product, whether it be mobile phones or soft drinks.

I always found it a pleasure to be around David, even though his painfully shy demeanour could be hard work at times. I have fond memories of the young kid arriving in a red Ford to knock around Old Trafford, and find it hard to comprehend how, in ten years, his lifestyle and public persona have been transformed so dramatically.

Now when he arrived at the ground before a match, in one of his expensive and powerful cars, fans of all ages gasped, cheered and waved, and many a time I worried that the barricades might give way as the supporters surged ever nearer for a glimpse of him. Thankfully, nobody ever received any injury in the excitement, and David, who would sign every autograph that time allowed, always got into Old Trafford unscathed.

On match days, when the team were relaxing in the players' lounge, I would often approach the various groups to check whether there was anything I could do for them before kick-off. Usually, I might be asked to pick up tickets for various family members or friends, or if the lads were deep in discussions about tactics for the forthcoming game all I'd get for my pains would be a jovial 'Fuck off, Ned.' On one occasion, however, David had an unusual request for me: 'Do you think you could arrange for me to have a go at flying a fighter jet, Ned?'

David Beckham in a fighter plane, now that was a thought. My expression must have told him I thought this activity unlikely.

'I'll see what I can do,' I nodded, and walked off scratching my head. I loved a challenge though, and I telephoned contacts in the Ministry of Defence and convinced them of the publicity merits of having the captain of England fly about in one of the RAF's Red Arrows jets. Later in the season, I was able to tell David that I had got clearance for him to fly in a high-performance military jet. His colour paled slightly as he muttered a quiet 'Thanks Ned'. Despite a formal invitation, David is still to take up the RAF's kind offer, to my knowledge.

I did not enjoy the same relationship, however, with Mrs Beckham, the ex-Spice Girl. I first met Victoria when she was a guest at Old Trafford with Mel C, a fellow Spice Girl, and I escorted the pair into the players' lounge after the game. The dressing-room gossip was that the object of the girls' attentions was Ryan Giggs who, at the time, had been photographed out and about with Dani Behr, a TV presenter. It soon became clear to everyone present that David and Victoria were attracted to each other, and as she was part of the hugely successful chart-topping group of the moment and he was the Johnny Depp of football, the tabloids went wild. The headlines wrote themselves. Ultimately true love conquered all and, in July 1999, the couple tied the knot and the celebrity show hit the road.

Security was always going to be a nightmare when these two stars entwined and I had to keep reminding myself that there were eleven players in the team with families, and I should administer to everyone's security needs as fairly as possible. It was felt by David and his father, Ted Beckham, that they required rather more security than I could provide within my remit at Old Trafford, so, without my knowledge, they began paying one of my employees, Dave Greenwood, to provide extra cover. I confronted David about this when I discovered the arrangement, as no one should have been poaching my men, and it wasn't long before Greenwood parted company with SPS to work for the couple full-time.

The relationship between David and Victoria was, for a time, a matter of great annoyance to Fergie, as it was through her that David was properly introduced to the London scene, which, of course, kept him away from his base in Manchester. Fergie was adamant that David should live within reasonable distance of the stadium and training ground, and so, not surprisingly, when tales about David commuting between London and Manchester reached the manager's ears, they would send him into blinding rages. This situation was never going to be allowed to continue and eventually it came to a head on a trip abroad.

Fergie pulled me to one side in the airport VIP lounge and barked, 'Right, Ned. You know what's what. Don't lie to me. Where is Beckham living?'

His question put me in a very uncomfortable position. With a less high-profile player I could have blagged it and said I didn't know, but with David being photographed almost every other night in London I could hardly tell Fergie that his head of security was the only guy in Britain who didn't know where David was spending most of his spare time.

'He's in London, Boss, and travelling up and down to Old Trafford,' I replied honestly, though inwardly cringing at having to tell tales on David.

Fergie's face was a study in controlled anger. 'That Beckham is taking the piss, Ned,' he growled.

'Yeah, Boss. Maybe you should sell him,' I proposed, half-jokingly.

I knew it was a cheeky remark, but Fergie's blank stare told me his thoughts weren't so far removed from my own suggestion. Hearing it from me must have prompted him to realize the enormous consequences of losing Beckham, and he smiled, 'Nah. I'll sort him.'

Fergie did indeed clip David's wings and assurances were made that, for the sake of his career, the player would live nearer his place of work. Fergie knew the toll it would have taken on David's fitness if he had to face motorway journeys or flights from airports before a training session. Nobody was in any doubt, however, just which of the couple was missing London. As an observer, it seemed to me that Fergie and David's professional relationship became all the more strained with the arrival of Posh Spice on the scene, and consequently, there has never been any love lost between Fergie and Mrs Beckham; a feeling, I believe, that has always been mutual.

Fergie always supported David in times of difficulty, but never more so than when his star player set off to the 1998 World Cup finals as the conquering hero, only to return to anger and recriminations after his sending-off during a crucial game against Argentina. David was famously red-carded for kicking out at an Argentinean player while the Englishman lay spreadeagled on the floor as the result of an earlier challenge. The world saw it, the referee saw it and Beckham was out of the World Cup, closely followed by England who, one man down, lost to the Argentinians on penalties. A great many English fans blamed David for the team's exit from the World Cup, and as a consequence, the venom that followed him from game to game at the start of the season was unpleasant in the extreme. David Beckham had gone from hero to villain almost overnight, and when the new season began, I was instructed to guard him from the baying hordes.

Even his father received threats from these idiots, and David was visibly upset when from time to time I had to shepherd him through a hail of abuse at Manchester United's away games. He had never experienced this kind of treatment in his career, and when we were due to face Leeds United in an away game I felt as though I was taking a small boy to school as his face fell when the team coach approached Elland Road. As traditional rivals of the Reds, the Leeds fans were far from welcoming on this particular occasion, and held nothing back in their efforts to unsettle the unhappy player in the number-seven shirt.

Several years on, and his unfortunate experience in France during the 1998 World Cup has almost been forgotten in the wake of more recent triumphs in the role of England captain. Although it was an unpleasant time for David, I believe the episode toughened him up and gave him the strength to face any difficulty that comes his way. He may be a quiet guy, but he has proved beyond doubt that he is no quitter, a characteristic he shares with his media-savvy wife, whose single-mindedness in pursuit of money and fame has served the couple well.

Everybody at the club had their own views about the Spice Girls, both regarding their music and their individual singing ability, but as far as I was concerned the only issue that struck me as I went about my daily business was the fact that, to me, Posh Spice was nothing more than a pain.

All the players at Manchester United had wives and girlfriends, and their individual safety at the ground was of equal concern to me, but as a consequence of her celebrity, Posh would always try to demand extra protection, even at a time when the Spice Girls had passed their peak and no longer received the attention they had once commanded.

An example of this attitude was much in evidence at the 1999 FA Cup party in London, which was held at the Royal Lancaster Hotel. Everyone was saying their goodnights when David Beckham tugged on my sleeve: 'Ned, Victoria's in the foyer and she's not happy. Some paparazzi have been in the hotel. Please come out with me.'

I followed David into the hotel reception area to find Posh Spice looking far from happy.

The problem was that she and David had left the party of their own accord without asking to be accompanied, and on the way to their room they had been approached by some photographers.

'They shouldn't have been here, Ned,' she moaned at me.

'Victoria. This is a public place. They can come and go as they please,' I replied, signalling to my man, Vinny Earl, to escort Victoria and David up to their room. She refused to be so easily placated, however, and started ranting and raving about my security company. On and on she complained about how she had travelled the world with her group and how no photographers would have been allowed near her, and berated me by saying that I was not doing my job properly. While she whinged and whined, the captain of England stood, head bowed, until his wife had run out of things to moan about. I felt genuinely sorry for him – all that was missing was his school cap. We eventually got Queen Victoria off to bed and Vinny remarked when he came back downstairs, 'Blimey, Ned. She can go on a bit, eh?'

'It would have been worse if nobody wanted her picture, believe me,' I replied.

The next morning, the plan was that the directors' wives and girlfriends would return to Manchester, while the players would travel to the England training ground at Waltham Abbey. We would all meet up again on the Wednesday evening after the European Cup final in Barcelona. At the hotel reception desk, while checking out, I heard a voice that I had heard all too often over the past twenty-four hours: Posh bloody Spice.

'Ned, I want to know why you allowed the press to get into the hotel on Saturday ni—'

She never got the chance to finish the sentence. I raised my hand to signal 'stop', and just let rip . . .

'Enough now, Victoria. Listen to me once and for all,' I barked. 'I am paid to look after Manchester United personnel whenever and wherever I am asked by the board to do so. The minute you left the function suite, you and David were not my responsibility, so leave it out. Not another word.'

I turned and finished checking out – in silence.

The following day, David came over to me at the airport news-stand and asked if he could have a word. He looked upset about something, and I sincerely hoped he wasn't going to mention anything to do with his wife.

'One of the airline staff keeps giving me a hard time,' he said, almost sobbing. 'Dog's abuse. Every time I come through the airport.'

'Show me who he is,' I demanded. The mood I was in, this joker certainly wasn't going to get away with bothering any of my players.

I followed David and he pointed out a beer-bellied member of the airport staff. As I marched toward him, the overgrown bully seemed to turn pale. 'Can I have a quick word with you?' I demanded.

'What's wrong?' he asked sheepishly.

'Why do you keep giving David Beckham a hard time?' I asked him calmly. 'The next time you give *him* any grief, I'll come back and give *you* some grief.'

I turned on my heel and joined the Manchester United group to watch them having their photographs taken by airport staff before they boarded Concorde. Some time later, I asked David if on any recent trips to the airport the worker had ever bothered him again.

'No, Ned. He won't even look at me,' he laughed, with obvious relief.

The showbiz side of football raised its head again when the Manchester United stalwart Phil Neville and his beautiful girlfriend, Julie Killelea, decided to get married and I was given the task, and the honour of providing security for the big day.

Security at a wedding might seem a little unnecessary, but since the couple had sold the rights to a celebrity magazine, it was vital that no other publication should scoop them. It transpired that Posh Spice had helped the couple secure a lucrative deal with *OK!* magazine, and it was imperative that the public didn't see the dress until the magazines hit the shops.

The reception was to be held at the grand old Midland Hotel in Manchester. I met up with the staff of *OK!* magazine who would be covering the event, and with people from Revellers, the reception organizers, as well as the hotel's own security people.

Julie's big day dawned and I collected her and her father, Bob, and we drove to the church and into the large tent that the magazine had erected to preserve their 'exclusive'. Once the bride and groom and their guests were safely inside the church, the doors were locked. I couldn't help thinking how farcical it all was. My company carried out security checks in and around the church in case of lurking freelance or rival magazine photographers. My nephew, Andy, was in charge of this operation and he assured me that the place was 'as clean as a whistle'.

'Great, son, all OK then?' I asked.

'Just one thing,' he replied, laughing. 'That silly bastard Beckham turned up with a hat on and still has it on in church!'

I shook my head in disbelief and had a walk around the churchyard.

The reception was a huge success but, for me, the highlight was watching the so-called celebrities jockeying for position when the cameras started flashing.

It was Phil and Julie's big day and, like all newlyweds, they must have looked forward to seeing their wedding pictures, especially as they were to grace the front cover of *OK!* When the magazine came out, the happy couple were indeed beaming on the front cover, but so too were Posh and Becks. Instead of capturing the delight of the happy couple alone, the photo featured all four of them.

Returning to the subject of Fergie's up-and-down relationship with David Beckham, another aspect of the latter's career that Fergie was unable to control, and which seemed to cause the manager much grief, was the appointment of Tony Stephens as David's agent. I first heard his name when Ted Beckham mentioned to me that Fergie wasn't too happy that David had appointed Stephens without consulting him first.

My first encounter with Stephens was in December 1999, when David was due to appear at Stockport magistrates court for a speeding offence. I arrived at David's flat to collect him for the hearing, and was met by his lawyer, Nick Freeman, and his new personal security man, Mark Niblett. We set off for court and David told me that Stephens was already there, 'dealing' with the press. On arrival at the court I was introduced to the agent and Nick Freeman left to attend to his legal work.

David and I sat and watched as Stephens gave Posh a running commentary via his mobile phone, assuring her that David had arrived at court safely. Once he had finished his call, Stephens regaled me with his full history in the business, speaking for a good ten minutes, virtually without drawing breath. David and I just sat there. I was bored witless and poor David had obviously heard it all before. The player was finally called to court and pleaded 'not guilty'. After hearing the evidence, the magistrates went off to consider their verdict. We went back to the ante-room to await their findings. Stephens went into sycophantic overdrive, telling David he was 'wonderful in there'. In my view he had just hanged himself, but Stephens was now back on the phone to Posh, telling her, 'David was magnificent. We're all sure he'll be found not guilty.'

I did not want to be the voice of doom, but 'we' were not all as confident. After a few minutes, I thought I would try to cheer up a glum-looking Beckham, so I turned his thoughts to football matters. 'You must be in with a shout for the European Footballer of the Year award, David?' I suggested.

While David was thinking of an answer, Stephens took brown-nosing to a whole new level, answering on David's behalf: 'Oh no. That's not the one we want. That'll be the FIFA World Player of the Year. That's what we want.'

I didn't even give the agent the courtesy of a look, but said to the footballer, 'That was clever, David. You answered me without moving your lips!'

The court was recalled and David was found guilty as charged. He was banned from driving for eight months and fined £800, but Nick Freeman immediately appealed against the conviction and at the subsequent appeal hearing the following week, the ban was overturned.

When I dropped them off later on in the day, I called Fergie and let him know what had happened at court. I told him that I had met up with Tony Stephens, and that I was less than impressed with him. Much later, over coffee, Fergie said to me that he had told Stephens that when it came to renegotiating David Beckham's new contract, if the player had any plans to live in the London area he needn't bother coming to the negotiating table. Fergie knew that no one player should ever be considered bigger than the club, and told me later that if anyone came in with a bid of £40 million for David, Manchester United should sell him. (He was eventually sold to Spanish club Real Madrid for £25 million in summer 2003.)

David took great delight in telling me that he had secured the services of an ex-SAS man, Mark Niblett, to guard Posh and his baby, Brooklyn. I was glad another former soldier had found a good job in civvy street, and after meeting Mark at Old Trafford for the first time, I found him to be a nice guy.

Mark seemed to serve the Beckhams well, and with the demands that were doubtless made of him, I was sure that he would have deserved every penny he earned. I enjoyed a drink with him at the 1999 New Year's Eve party that the players had organized at a private club in Manchester.

It was a party and a half, and no expense was spared to ensure that everyone had a night to remember. I watched as Victoria Beckham went round the guests showing them her baby boy. The women were cooing and aahing in delight at the little bundle of joy.

In a quiet moment, I decided to ask Mark an honest question in the hope that I would get an honest answer: 'Tell me, Mark. What really happened outside Harrods regarding the kidnap attempt?'

'Fuck all happened, Ned. Fuck all,' was all he replied.

The Beckhams had received front-page coverage earlier that month after they claimed that somebody had tried to kidnap Brooklyn in broad daylight outside the huge London store. Many thought the story implausible, bearing in mind that the incident was neither captured on film by the Harrods CCTV cameras, or by the waiting photographers who had been within a few feet of their car, and it was considered most unusual that the police had not been the first to be informed of the incident. My only observation was that if I had been guarding them and someone had tried to assault them while I was there, the assailant would be either have been hospitalized or arrested.

Curiously enough, another, more recent, kidnap attempt on the Beckham family led to five people being charged by the Metropolitan Police. In November 2002, a gang of Eastern Europeans allegedly planned to kidnap Victoria and her children, and hold them hostage for a £5 million ransom. Seven months later, however, the trial of the five men collapsed at Middlesex Guildhall Crown Court in June 2003 after it was revealed that the prosecution's key witness had been declared unreliable by the Crown Prosecution Service.

Arising from Victoria's love affair with the Italian city of Milan, the fashion capital of Europe, press speculation has always been rife surrounding the likelihood that David might leave Manchester for a Continental club. After Fergie's spat with David in February 2003, when the manager kicked a discarded football boot in the player's direction, accidently hitting him in the face and causing a cut above his left eye, rumours of David's imminent departure to Italy or Spain grew ever louder. Eventually, by June, his future was decided. Together with his wife and two sons, he would be relocating to the Spanish capital. For £25 million, David had signed for Spanish champions Real Madrid, where he would be playing alongside such footballing greats as Ronaldo, Luis Figo, Zinedine Zidane, Raul and Roberto Carlos.

Taking such a major step, as well as a huge risk, in severing his ties with Manchester United, David Beckham's star is nevertheless still in the ascendant, and I believe it will continue to remain this way until he takes the decision to retire from first-class football.

It seems unlikely that anyone could eclipse the fame and fortune David Beckham has achieved by kicking a ball around a pitch. He is a football icon, a gay icon, a fashion icon and, most bizarrely of all according to a Channel 4 documentary, he is also a black icon. In a poll for the TV company who made the programme, British blacks voted David their number-one icon.

Japan has unveiled a statue in his honour cast in chocolate, and a Buddhist temple in Bangkok has a one-foot high statue of him alongside one hundred other deities. An artist painted his likeness on a crucifixion portrait now hanging in a West London art gallery. It has also been threatened that Victoria and David are to team up with opera singer Russell Watson to record a Christmas single. His superstar status was ultimately confirmed after he appeared in a television advertisement for Pepsi. The director of the commercial, Tarsem Singh, suggested that David had 'it' and could certainly succeed in films, but David has confirmed that he has no ambitions to be another Vinny Jones, which is doubtless a blessed relief to patrons of the arts.

CHAPTER 15

The End of an Era

IN THE SUMMER OF 2001, while Ruud van Nistelrooy was finding his feet in the United camp, another Dutchman was preparing to pack his bags and leave.

Jaap Stam was a brilliant defender with an uncompromising character. A happily married man who never once showed any interest in other women in and around the various club functions or on the trips abroad, he often told me that he absolutely adored Manchester United and it was his greatest wish that he would end his playing career there.

Jaap was a brooding type of man who did not need to shout and bawl to impress. One look from him let you know there was trouble ahead. This dark, silent power exploded one day at Highbury in a highly charged game against Arsenal in October 2000. Roy Keane and Patrick Vieira were at each other like Punch and Judy, but eventually they had a clash of heads. In an instant, rushing to protect his injured colleague, Jaap had Vieira by the throat and almost lifted him off his feet. The 'quiet man' was no more, and Vieira spent most of the rest of the game apologizing to Roy, Jaap and virtually anyone else who was passing. The incident confirmed what I had long thought about Jaap. He was like a volcano waiting to erupt – I recognized the breed from my Army days. I used to joke with Jaap that I wouldn't kick him if he was six foot under.

One of the funniest confrontations I witnessed during my time at Old Trafford was when Jaap Stam kept insisting on calling Jordi Cruyff a 'fucking Catalonian', suggesting that Jordi had forsaken his Dutch origins and was no longer a proud Dutchman like Stam. Jordi just blushed, unable to stand his ground before his hard-nosed countryman.

Many felt it was his literary aspirations, more than his footballing ability, that helped bring Jaap's time at Old Trafford to an abrupt end.

It was, for example, in his autobiography, *Head to Head*, that he claimed that the Neville brothers constantly moaned about every little thing in and around the club, although he had nothing but praise for them in all matters concerning football. Jaap actually phoned Gary to apologize in advance of the book's release, and I always felt that it was a book he regretted writing, especially with regard to his observations about Fergie. The Dutchman had been critical of the manager, and in response Fergie had told the defender that he could not guarantee him a first-team place, and suggested that perhaps he should move on.

I really did not want to see Jaap leave Old Trafford, and asked Ruud van Nistelrooy to have a word with him when they were together on international duty with the Dutch national team. I told Ruud to remind Jaap that Fergie would be leaving Old Trafford sooner or later and then he would almost certainly be playing the first-team football he so rightfully deserved. Unfortunately Jaap refused even to consider this proposition, and told Ruud he would not stay where he was not wanted. I had to resign myself to the fact that his departure from Old Trafford was both inevitable and imminent.

I heard the news on the eve of a League game against Aston Villa in August 2001, when I received a call from a cub reporter by the name of Justin, who used to hang around Old Trafford hoping to get a scoop. He told me that Jaap had been sold to Lazio for £16 million.

Though I was of the opinion that this bloke could not write out a lottery ticket, far less a newspaper article, I knew that he did pick up the odd piece of information, and I was anxious not to be quoted in a Sunday tabloid. I told him I would call him back, before hanging up and immediately telephoning the Manchester United team hotel to try to speak to Ken Ramsden. The hotel called Ken to the front desk, as he was not in his room, and I relayed this latest piece of news to him. Ken went silent then said, 'Hold on, Ned. Alex is just walking past. I'll ask him.'

I heard Ken ask Fergie, and had to laugh at his reply: 'Tell that Ned Kelly he's a nosy bastard.'

'Did you hear that?' chuckled Ken.

I had, and I was also certain that the story was true – Jaap had finally decided that a change of scene was the best course of action.

Jaap Stam's replacement at Old Trafford was to be Frenchman Laurent Blanc, although in my opinion he was a replacement in name only. For his August arrival I found myself in the executive hangar at Manchester airport with a visibly nervous Peter Kenyon and Fergie. Blanc's arrival from Milan was about to end years of frustration for Fergie where this player was concerned, as he had tried on numerous occasions to bring him to Old Trafford, only to have this ambition thwarted by the chairman's reluctance to spend the money required.

As Laurent bounded down the steps just before midnight, he greeted me with a cheery 'Hi, how are you?'

'Hello Laurent,' I replied, as we shook hands and embraced French-style.

Fergie and Kenyon looked on in surprise. I'd forgotten to mention to them that I had met Laurent on numerous occasions in the company of Eric Cantona, and so naturally he recognized me. After the introductions, we went inside to a private room where the serious discussions got under way. I guarded the door and kept an eye out for any press who may have heard a whisper but, as always, Fergie's almost Masonic-like secrecy worked again. The meeting broke up after forty-five minutes and I sped Laurent to the Mottram Hall Hotel in the early hours, and made arrangements to pick him up later that morning to take him to Old Trafford for the medical procedures.

Fergie told me this was the way he preferred to do business without, as he saw it, the interference of greedy agents. I thought this was a strange attitude to adopt, bearing in mind that his son Jason was actively involved in the world of football agenting, having been employed by L'Attitude before joining forces with Dave Gardner at Elite.

Jason and his twin brother, Darren, were both put through the youth programme at Old Trafford but Jason never made the grade as a footballer and never played professionally. Darren, however, did play twenty games for Manchester United and was on the subs bench for another seven, but he couldn't command a regular first-team place. I thought he looked a good passer of a ball but did not seem to possess a lot of pace. In my opinion he believed himself to be a better player than he actually was. I remember when he approached Martin Edwards to negotiate a new contract, with Fergie by his side. News soon filtered through the ranks about his wage demands. Not too long afterwards he was on his way out of Old Trafford; he signed for Wolves for £250,000, his contract negotiated by his father. I always found Darren a nice guy but the two boys were like chalk and cheese, not least because Darren was a big Rangers fan like his dad, whereas Jason supported Celtic.

Laurent Blanc's transfer formalities sailed through without trouble as the agent-less Frenchman was as experienced in the commercial ways of football as he was on the field. He would only sign one- or, at most, two-year contracts with clubs and, after meeting the medical criteria of Doc Stone, became a Red on a one-year contract.

On a social level, I liked Laurent Blanc very much, but as far as his footballing skills were concerned, I found him to be past his best. There was little doubt that Laurent saw his move to Manchester United as possibly his last chance to win a European Champions League medal, the only major honour missing from his collection of awards.

I travelled a great deal with Laurent. On one trip to Paris he looked very troubled, and my questioning nod seemed to be the opening he was looking for.

'Why do people hate Manchester United so much?' he asked, having obviously felt the venom of the legions of non-fans.

'Jealousy, mate. Pure and simple,' I replied. 'It's an English thing. Hate anyone or anything that is successful, especially if they are successful outside England, as we are in Europe.'

'But surely all England would be proud if Manchester United did well abroad?' he asked naively.

'No chance,' I answered, but as it would take a lifetime to explain this most curious of English attitudes, I changed the subject.

The Jaap Stam/Laurent Blanc in/out scenario, to me, as a fan, was not in the best interests of the club. There was no doubt that Jaap had upset Fergie by some of the opinions he voiced in his book, but when Fergie declared to Jaap that he needed someone with more experience, most fans would never have dreamed he'd have chosen the thirty-seven-year-old Laurent Blanc. There were a lot of defensive errors that cost Manchester United their League and European Cup chances in the 2001–2 season, and although the mistakes could not all be laid at Laurent's door, it seemed to me that he had at least his share of them.

In July 2001, Fergie phoned me and asked me whether I would mind collecting Juan Sebastián Verón from the airport the following day as he was flying in from Rome on a private jet. I was glad to be of assistance, and was waiting on the tarmac as his plane taxied to the VIP stand.

Verón was Fergie's second choice to Patrick Vieira and, for a time, it looked as though the latter would be the one coming to Old Trafford. Vieira's agent had spoken to Fergie and indeed, by all accounts, Vieira was interested in joining a club like Manchester United. Arrangements were made for Fergie to fly out to South Beach in Miami and meet up with Vieira, who was holidaying there. However, Fergie realized this could be a potentially troublesome enterprise if the press got to hear of it so it was decided that Peter Kenyon would make the trip. The meeting and the transfer subsequently never took place, however, and instead it was Verón who was on his way to Old Trafford.

I drove Juan, his girlfriend and their children to the Mottram Hall Hotel, and once Juan was happy that his family had settled in, I drove him to the nearby BUPA hospital where we rendezvoused with Doc Stone, who was supervising the Manchester United club medical. After Juan had passed every medical test he was required to take, I drove him to Carrington, the training centre, where Doc Stone carried out eleven more fitness and endurance tests. All went well once again as Juan was fitter than a racehorse and considerably more valuable than most. Once all the checks had been completed, I drove him to Old Trafford where the complex transfer and personal-terms negotiations were to be discussed between him, his agent, his representatives from Lazio, Fergie and the Manchester United board.

As I waited in the corridor, keeping an eye on the boardroom door, I received an unexpected call telling me that Peter Schmeichel had returned to English football after a spell at Sporting Lisbon, and had just signed for Aston Villa. A bigger surprise awaited me, however, when Martin Edwards breezed along the corridor with a man I recognized instantly as the FA chief executive, Adam Crozier. Martin made the introductions and after some idle chit-chat, the two men left the building. I presumed that Crozier was at Old Trafford for discussions concerning the use of Old Trafford, as the stadium was being mooted as an alternative ground in which to hold international games while a decision was being made about the future of Wembley.

Eventually, all was signed and sealed, and Juan Sebastián Verón joined the Reds for a record British transfer fee of £28.1 million. When he left the meeting I mentioned Peter Schmeichel's move to Villa to Fergie, and he laughingly told me that 'Big' Peter had phoned him earlier in the morning with the news, and Fergie had wished him well.

I really liked Juan and as I drove him back to the Mottram Hall Hotel to rejoin his family, he told me to call him Seba – an abbreviation of his middle name. I learned later that this was something of an honour, as few people were privileged enough to call him by his nickname. I spent the weekend driving him around the more affluent areas of Manchester and Cheshire, and Seba seemed to like what he saw. On the second day, he introduced me to his good friend and interpreter, Matias Aldao, whom everyone called Mattie, and I hit it off immediately with this funny and articulate man.

We began house-hunting for Seba and he eventually purchased a beautiful house from Fabien Barthez. Whenever we met over the next few months, Mattie would insist on asking me about my SAS days during the Falklands War. The subject seemed to hold a weird fascination for him. Naturally, I could not discuss any part of my involvement in that or any other conflict, but Mattie would never take no for an answer. I finally found the cure for his inquisitiveness by putting a suggestion to him: 'Right, Mattie. I'll tell you about the SAS and the Falklands War if you tell me about the Italian passport difficulties Seba had.'

He went red and never mentioned the Falklands War to me again. I felt that Mattie was a little shocked that I had been aware of the controversy surrounding Verón's nationality claims. In June 2000, he was alleged to have acquired an Italian passport using false documents. Some other foreign players in possession of Italian passports had also been charged with acquiring them fraudulently. The court case threatened Verón's career, and even his liberty, but there was a positive ending as he was eventually acquitted of all charges in June 2001.

Seba had fabulous taste in women and during his Lazio days in Rome, his affair with topless model Laura Franco became headline news, for she would jet in from Buenos Aires once a week just to see him. True love fizzled out, however, when Laura refused to relocate from Argentina to Italy and the affair came to an end. Seba consoled himself with the affections of another model, Julieta Prandi, but soon his roving eye settled on yet another beauty, Maria Florencia, now the mother of their two children, daughter Iara and son Deaian. Seba calls Maria 'Felicia', and she turned her back on a successful modelling career to be with him full time. In 1999, shortly before their first child was born, Seba was being photographed by the paparazzi in Buenos

Aires as he flirted with a gorgeous model. His temper spilt over into madness and he lashed out at the photographer, breaking his jaw.

He and I would socialize and I would escort him to the games and the training ground and various club functions. I found Seba great company. I know he found it hard to settle in Britain, but he tried his very best to adjust to both the English game and English culture.

The first game in the 2001–2 Premier League saw us defeat newly promoted Fulham 3–2, but it was a far from convincing victory. The Champions League draw was made and we were in a group with Lille of France, Spanish club Deportivo La Coruña, and Olympiakos of Greece.

The day after I discovered that Jaap Stam was leaving for Lazio at the end of August, I travelled up to the Midlands for the game against Aston Villa and joined the team at the hotel. Fergie invited me to join them for lunch, which suggested that he wasn't in the least bit bothered by my 'nosy' enquiry about Stam the previous day.

Once at the ground, I started to collect the players' and officials' complimentary tickets and left them, as instructed, at the ticket pick-up point for their friends and guests. When I returned to the dressing room, Fergie beckoned to me and gave me an envelope containing tickets. 'Find my lad, Jason, and give him these tickets, Ned,' he asked.

I found Jason Ferguson, and duly gave him the tickets. We passed the time of day talking about football and then Jason stopped me in my tracks with a surprising remark: 'We got some price for Jaap Stam, eh, Ned? We couldn't refuse it.'

I wondered who the 'we' were. A few days later, the press were reporting that Jason's Elite agency was involved in the Jaap Stam deal and rumours abounded that £1 million had been earned by the enterprising Jason for his company, after working closely with the Monaco-based agent Mike Morris in arranging the Dutchman's transfer to Lazio. As a consequence there was much speculation that nepotism had raised its fatherly head.

It amused me that in spite of Fergie's barely disguised dislike of footballers' agents, a consequence of his desire to be in control of the players at all times, it was ironic that his son had forged a successful career working for one of the country's biggest agencies.

Our Premier League challenge was heading in the right direction, while in Europe we were triumphant as the Greeks suffered a tragedy: Olympiakos 0, Manchester United 1. However, a series of Fabien

Barthez blunders helped Spanish club Deportivo La Coruña greatly on their Manchester visit, going home 3–2 winners. More tragedy for the Greeks awaited them at Old Trafford as we thrashed them 3–0. Our form was excellent and we progressed to the European Champions League finals. Meanwhile, despite being dismissed from the League Cup by Arsenal, our Premier League hopes were still riding high.

Liverpool games were always a little bit special to me, but I will always remember their visit to Old Trafford in late January 2002 as being the most special of the many football matches I have attended, for the simple reason that it was the last time I would be in charge of security at a Manchester United match, and the last time I ever set foot inside my beloved Old Trafford.

On Friday 18 January 2002, I received a call from a young lady who introduced herself as 'Sinita'. She explained that she handled PR for some very wealthy foreign businessmen. Sinita arranged to meet me in a Manchester hotel where she described in great detail exactly what she would like me and my company to provide for her clients' forthcoming visit.

Close bodyguarding was to be the order of the day and Sinita conveyed the mystery visitors' desire to visit Old Trafford, watch a match or two, and added that the use of an executive box would be nice. I admit that while exchanging pleasantries with her, I was less than discreet as I tried to impress her with my inside knowledge of the stars. I made a few phone calls from my car in her presence and managed to furnish her with costings for the hiring of the box for her clients. We parted company with me hoping to meet up again in the next week or two to get on with the business. A few days later, Sinita phoned me to announce that she wasn't a PR assistant for wealthy businessmen, but in fact was an undercover reporter for a Sunday newspaper. I asked her if that meant I would now have to cancel the Old Trafford treat and she confirmed that that was indeed the case. She elaborated further, however, by implying that I was nothing more than a ticket tout, but I was baffled as to how she could have come to this conclusion on the basis of our earlier conversations. I didn't understand which tickets I was supposed to have been 'touting', and so as far as I was concerned the matter was a complete mystery. Needless to say, her Sunday paper ran a major article about me, one that the Manchester United board could not ignore.

On the Monday morning I was called in to see Arthur Roberts and George Johnson, the stadium manager. They informed me that a police investigation would have to be conducted as a matter of course, and that because of the likely media interest, it would be better for all concerned if I stayed away from Old Trafford, and laid low until the situation had been resolved and it had all blown over. At the mention of 'ticket tout', the good officers of the Greater Manchester Police did indeed swing into action, and confirmed that the 'Great Manchester United Ticket Swindle' was now the subject of a criminal inquiry. In the interests of what I believed was best for the great name of Manchester United, therefore, I elected to maintain a low profile in Florida until investigations were completed by both club and police; I would then take matters from there.

After several months in exile, Manchester police finally confirmed to David Middleweek, my Manchester solicitor, that no ticket touting or other criminal activity had taken place or indeed had even been discussed. Yet despite my further exoneration following the club's extensive internal inquiry into the affair, the Manchester United board chose to adopt the 'no-smoke-without-fire' attitude, and collectively agreed that it would be appropriate if I stood down from my post as Head of Security at Manchester United, as well as Managing Director of SPS, which would enable them to keep using SPS until the end of its existing contract in 2003. The agreement I had come to with David Gill in December 2001, that guaranteed SPS's involvement at Old Trafford for another three years, until 2006, turned out to be worth very little, and I knew that there was no way of saving the situation.

Not unreasonably, I had hoped that the many favours that I had done for so many of the important people around Old Trafford might now be repaid, as it was crucial that I could rely on a group of strong, powerful people in my corner. My spirits were lifted immeasurably in summer 2002, when I received a telephone call from Fergie who assured me that he had spoken at length to David Gill and that I was 'going to be all right'. 'Don't talk to the press, Ned,' he added. 'You know they are all paranoid at Old Trafford.'

'I never speak to the press, Boss, you know that,' I replied. 'She told me that she was in PR, for Christ's sake, but I didn't tell her anything that isn't the talk of any wine bar in Manchester.'

'All right, son. Just stay calm,' Fergie reassured me. 'David Gill is going to rap your knuckles, nothing more. But keep your nose clean from now on, Ned. You'll be OK. Trust me.'

I felt heartened by my conversation with Fergie, and put the phone down believing that the Sword of Damocles had been lifted from over me. I thought that if he told the board that I was to stay, nothing or nobody could remove me. I started to feel that it would not be long before I was totally vindicated. At a meeting with Arthur Roberts and David Gill on 18 June, I was even congratulated on being found not guilty of the ticket-touting charge.

However, the hopes that had begun to lift were soon to be cruelly dashed when, four days after Fergie's call, I received news from David Gill by telephone, informing me that my presence at Old Trafford was neither required nor welcome anymore.

I called Fergie and told him my news, but I could tell from the tone of his voice that he already knew. After an embarrassing silence he mumbled nervously, 'Keep in touch, Ned,' and then he hung up. That was the last time I ever spoke to Sir Alex Ferguson.

Despite being exonerated at every level, and the fact that many good friends and advisers strongly suggested that I should return to Manchester United, I felt that I had enjoyed a great career with the club, and that it was time to move on to pastures new.

My advisers all tried to convince me to sue the Sunday tabloid for damages, but I felt that there was no point. The enormous cost of fighting a legal battle against a powerful newspaper group was more than I could afford, but more importantly, I didn't want to draw out what had already been, for me, a particularly painful ending to my employment with the club. Even if I had launched a successful libel action, it wouldn't have changed the fact that I had lost the valued trust and belief of the board members, whose respect I had earned during my time at the club. The damage was irreparable, and I certainly didn't feel that a prolonged court battle was going to help me get over the huge blow I had suffered. In my view the best course of action for me was to close the book on the whole affair and move on.

It was with a heavy heart that I sold Special Projects Services to my fellow directors, but it was comforting to know that the business I had built up from nothing would remain in safe hands, as they were all men of integrity and expertise, more than experienced in providing top-rate security for fans and players alike.

The End of an Era

★ ★ ★

Living in my new home in Florida, it is with great affection that I often look back at my photographs and videos chronicling almost twelve fantastic years with so many wonderful people at Old Trafford. Working for the club gave me a real chance to make something of myself when I left the Army, virtually penniless, and as the business grew it made me very successful. For that I will be eternally grateful, but, more importantly, my work gave me an opportunity to play a significant role in the smooth running of the club, and allowed me to become part of the amazing Manchester United family.

Sometimes I can hardly believe the things I've seen and done, the far-flung places I've visited, and the fantastic memories I will cherish of each and every player with whom I had the pleasure of working. When I left the Army, I could never have imagined working so hard, while having so much fun at the same time. Without a doubt, I have been a truly lucky man.

From my base in Florida I have become an avid armchair viewer, following the Reds' progress via satellite TV from the comfort of my living room or the local bar. Though it's not the same as being pitchside, or watching from the stands, it's the next best thing, and I can't help but be just as excited watching United on TV as when I used to see the games live.

Even though I have ceased playing an active role in the Manchester United set-up, my passion for the club is as strong as ever. I may have left Old Trafford behind, but my association with Manchester United will never be forgotten, and with pint glass in hand, I'll always be ready to drink to the best football team in the world.

Index

Index

Index

Index

Index

Index